Media, Migrants, and the Pandemic in India

The national lockdown to contain the COVID-19 pandemic in India resulted in the loss of work and displacement of thousands of urban migrant workers. This book records the arduous journey home for many of these workers and analyses the grave effects the pandemic has had on jobs, livelihoods, and the health of urban migrant workers.

A rich compilation of deep analytical articles by journalists, academics, lawyers, and social activists, this book explores various facets of the crisis as it unfolded. It examines the welfare policies of state and central governments and discusses the role of the judiciary and the public policy response to the unemployment, health risks, and mass migration of workers. It also offers readers a better understanding of the complexities of the migrant crisis, how it unfolded, and how it was addressed by the media.

This timely and prescient book will be of great interest to the general reader as well as researchers and students of media studies, journalism, sociology, law, public policy, labour and economics, welfare economics, gender studies, and development studies.

Bharat Bhushan is a journalist and editor based in Delhi. He was the founder-editor of *Mail Today*, Executive Editor of *The Hindustan Times*, Editor (Delhi) of *The Telegraph*, Editor of *Catchnews.com*, and Editor (Express News Service) and Washington Correspondent for *The Indian Express*. He writes on foreign policy and national politics. His other assignments include working as Assistant Editor for *Business India* and *The Times of India* and as Senior Academic Consultant for the Indian Council for Social Science Research.

Media, Migrants, and the Pandemic in India

A Reader

Edited by Bharat Bhushan

Routledge
Taylor & Francis Group
LONDON AND NEW YORK

First published 2023
by Routledge
4 Park Square, Milton Park, Abingdon, Oxon OX14 4RN

and by Routledge
605 Third Avenue, New York, NY 10158

Routledge is an imprint of the Taylor & Francis Group, an informa business

British Library Cataloguing-in-Publication Data
A catalogue record for this book is available from the British Library

Library of Congress Cataloging-in-Publication Data
Names: Bhushan, Bharat, editor.
Title: Media, migrants and the pandemic in India : a reader / edited by Bharat Bhushan.
Description: Abingdon, Oxon ; New York, NY : Routledge, 2022. |
Includes bibliographical references and index.
Identifiers: LCCN 2022011072 (print) | LCCN 2022011073 (ebook) |
ISBN 9781032160863 (hardback) | ISBN 9781032271378 (paperback) |
ISBN 9781003291527 (ebook)
Subjects: LCSH: Migrant labor--India--Social conditions--21st century. |
Migrant labor in mass media | COVID-19 Pandemic, 2020---Social aspects--India. | COVID-19 Pandemic, 2020- , in mass media. | Mass media--Social aspects--India. | Labor policy--India. | Medical policy--India. | India--Social conditions--21st century.
Classification: LCC HD5856.I4 M49 2022 (print) | LCC HD5856.I4 (ebook) |
DDC 331.5/440954--dc23/eng/20220405
LC record available at https://lccn.loc.gov/2022011072
LC ebook record available at https://lccn.loc.gov/2022011073

ISBN: 978-1-032-16086-3 (hbk)
ISBN: 978-1-032-27137-8 (pbk)
ISBN: 978-1-003-29152-7 (ebk)

DOI: 10.4324/9781003291527

Typeset in Sabon
by Deanta Global Publishing Services, Chennai, India

Contents

Figures

Tables

Contributors

Aman Abhishek is a doctoral candidate in the School of Journalism and Mass Communication, at the University of Wisconsin-Madison, USA, with minors in gender and women's studies, history, and political science. He also has a Master's in Physics from the same university, and a BSc-MSc in physics from IIT, Roorkee. During his Master's, he worked at CERN, contributing to the understanding of the properties of the then newly discovered Higgs boson. He believes that his work should have social relevance – hence his choice to redirect himself.

Rosa Abraham is a Research Fellow at Azim Premji University. Rosa completed her PhD from the Institute for Social and Economic Change, Bangalore. Her research focused on forms of informal labour in India, examining the rise of informalisation in the formal/organised sector and the consequent impacts on productivity and inequality. Prior to her PhD, she worked at Ashoka Trust for Research in Ecology and Environment and taught at Madras School of Economics. Her research interests include understanding workers' preferences for alternative work arrangements, the changing nature of informal work, and implications for job polarisation in the Indian context.

Shivani Agarwal is a research analyst at the Centre for New Economics Studies, O.P. Jindal Global University. She is involved with research projects in the field of economics, culture, and philosophy, including primary and secondary research, academic writing, and editing. Some of the research studies undertaken include a study on women engaged in informal sectors of the economy, a report on trade between India and South East Asian countries, studying the concept of "embeddedness" within the economy of the Tibetan community in India, ethnographic analysis of the Indo-Bhutan border trade, and more. She is also engaged with a UNESCO and Bournemouth University project called Media Action Against Rape (MAAR), by primarily managing work with Indian stakeholders. The project covers Indian media reports on cases of sexual violence in India.

Parul Agrawal is an independent journalist and author. She has worked with the BBC, *The Quint*, CNN-IBN, and ANI for 11 years. She is a recipient of the Thomson Reuters Fellowship to study journalism at Oxford. Her research on the advent of citizen journalism in India and its role in making government accountable was published in 2013. Her areas of interest are media research, gender, human rights, and health.

Debashis Aich is a well-known media activist. He works with Video Volunteers, a news-based NGO, to produce audio-visual news of and by the marginalised and human rights organisations. He is also associated with Ground Zero, a web news portal in both English and Bengali. He was awarded The Statesman Rural Reporting award in 2012. He has been associated with the human rights movement and was the General Secretary of PUCL West Bengal unit. His research interests are human rights, citizenship rights, labour studies, etc.

Amit Basole is an Associate Professor of Economics at Azim Premji University. He has been with Azim Premji University since 2017. He taught at Bucknell University and the University of Massachusetts prior to coming to APU. His research has been published in various edited volumes and in journals such as *Economic and Political Weekly*, *World Development*, *Development and Change*, *Rethinking Marxism*, *International Journal of Hindu Studies*, and *International Review of Applied Economics*. He has recently edited a book called *Lokavidya Perspectives: A Philosophy of Political Imagination for the Knowledge Age*. His areas of interest include non-neoclassical traditions in economics and the development of a pluralist undergraduate economics curriculum.

Gaurav Vivek Bhatnagar is the Deputy Editor of *The Wire*. He has 20 years of experience in editing and reporting. He received his education from the University of Delhi. He is passionate about writing on labour and human rights issues.

Bharat Bhushan is a journalist and editor based in Delhi. He was the founder-editor of *Mail Today*, Executive Editor of the *Hindustan Times*, Editor (Delhi) of *The Telegraph*, Editor of *Catchnews.com*, and Editor (Express News Service) and Washington Correspondent of the *Indian Express*. He writes on foreign policy and national politics. His other assignments include working as Assistant Editor, *Business India*, Assistant Editor, *The Times of India*, and Senior Academic Consultant, Indian Council for Social Science Research.

Akriti Chaubey is a practising lawyer and has about four years of experience in litigation and investment treaty arbitration and has been instrumental in assisting us with our legal issues and media releases. Presently, she is an associate at the Maqbool & Co law firm and practising at the Supreme

Court of India. She is also a teaching volunteer for "Adhiyagya", a non-governmental organisation working to provide education for underprivileged children.

Jane Cox is an advocate at the Bombay High Court, Maharashtra. She graduated in law from Wadham College, Oxford. She is registered with the Bar Council of Maharashtra and Goa. Specialising in labour law, she has been representing trade unions and workers before the Bombay High Court for the last 30 years. She has written several articles on labour rights in popular English newspapers and periodicals.

Chhandita Das is an Institute Fellow at the Department of Humanities and Social Sciences, Indian Institute of Technology, Patna. Her hometown is West Bengal, India. She has published important works in association with Dr Tripathi, such as "Social Distancing and Sex Workers in India", "Reconstructing the Changing Urban Landscape beyond Spatio-Temporal Dimensions: Post-Colonial 'Allahabad' in Neelum Saran Gour's Invisible Ink", and "Silhouetting the Self and Society: An Interview with Neelum Saran Gour".

Priya Deshingar is a Professor of Migration and Development, University of Sussex; she is an internationally recognised authority on South-South migration research and policy analysis. She is currently advising the Indian Ministry of Urban Affairs on migration-related issues in the wake of COVID-19. She also works with the University of Addis Ababa on Protracted Displacement Economies. Her most recent book is *Circular Migration and Multilocational Livelihood Strategies in India* (co-edited with John Farrington, 2009) which is a key reference text for scholars working on internal migration. Until 2009, Prof Deshingkar was Research Fellow at the Overseas Development Institute.

Rakhi Ghosh is a freelance journalist based in Bhubaneswar, Odisha. She is a former full-time print and television journalist, and focuses on health, education, migration, and climate change.

Ramapriya Gopalakrishnan is a lawyer practising in the Madras High Court. She is an expert on labour law and legal issues related to the environment. She did her Masters of Law (LLM) at New York University and bachelor's degree at the National Law School, Bangalore. She is a noted columnist and regularly writes for several web magazines like *The Wire*, *Scroll*, etc.

Chahak Gupta is the copy editor of, and a reporter at *NewsLaundry*. Chahak Gupta has contributed over 600 articles to this news agency. She is a former President of the Literary Society of Hindu College, Delhi. She offers clear-cut insights into minute issues often overlooked by others, making her special. She has an innate ability to analyse people and scenarios, and base her commentaries on them.

Mohammad Isa Hakim is an Associate Lawyer at Maqbool & Co practising at the Supreme Court. He did his LLM in Human Rights, Conflict and Justice with the prestigious Felix Scholarship from the School of Oriental and African Studies (SOAS), University of London. Some of his publications include "[Coronavirus] The Nizamuddin Tablighi Jamaat Fiasco: A Collective Failure" (*Bar and Bench*, April 5, 2020) and "How the Supreme Court and the High Courts Have Dealt with Worst Migrant Crisis Faced by the Nation" (*Bar and Bench*, May 28, 2020).

Nandita Haksar is an eminent human rights lawyer, teacher, campaigner, and writer. Her engagement with the people of Northeast India began while studying at Jawaharlal Nehru University in the 1970s. She has represented the victims of army atrocities in the Supreme Court and the High Court and campaigned nationally and internationally against the Armed Forces (Special Powers) Act, 1958. In her capacity as a human rights lawyer, Haksar has helped to organise migrant workers to fight for their rights and voice their grievances. In 1983, she became the first person to challenge the infamous Armed Forces (Special Powers) Act (AFSPA) in the Supreme Court. Her most recent book is *The Flavours of Nationalism* (2018).

Madhunika Iyer is an Analyst in the research team of PRS Legislative Research; she holds a bachelor's degree in Economics from NMIMS, Mumbai, and a master's degree in Economics from Columbia University, New York. Madhunika has interned with Columbia Business School as a research assistant and with the National Stock Exchange of India in the Economics and Policy Research Department.

Nivedita Jayaram works with Aajeevika Bureau, a non-profit organisation that provides services to migrant and informal workers, and conducts research, policy advocacy, and grassroots mobilisation for improving the lives and livelihoods of labour-dependent communities. She is a regular contributor to several journals and digital news portals on labour issues like *Economic and Political Weekly*, *Frontline*, *India Today*, etc. Her research interest lies in the field of labour and gender studies.

Vedika Kakar is a BBA-LLB student at Jindal Global Law School. She has previously worked with Amnesty International and other human rights organisations.

Kensiya Kennedy is a senior research assistant at the Centre for New Economics Studies, Jindal School of Liberal Arts and Humanities. In the past, she has worked with the International Justice Mission, Delhi, as a Communications Intern and with the Center for Human Security Studies, Hyderabad, as a Research Intern. Kensiya's main interests lie in learning about context-based approaches of governance and management, political economy, and conflict management.

Surbhi Kesar is Assistant Professor of Economics at the School of Arts and Sciences at Azim Premji University, Bengaluru. Her research areas include political economy, development economics, and labour economics, particularly informality, exclusion, and structural transformation in labour surplus economies. She received her PhD in Economics from South Asian University, New Delhi, and has been a Fulbright Fellow at the University of Massachusetts, Amherst. She is a coordinator for the Economic Development Working Group of the Young Scholars Initiative of the Institute for New Economic Thinking and is a Steering Group member for the Diversifying and Decolonising Economics initiative.

Smruti Koppikar is an independent journalist and editor based in Mumbai. She has reported on politics, gender, and development for nearly three decades for national publications. She is also the Former Editor – Special Projects at *Hindustan Times*. Boasting over two decades of experience in print and electronic media, she has engaged with multiple social issues. She is a recipient of the Sanskrit Award for Excellence in Journalism. She has held positions such as Associate Editor (West) and Bureau Chief, *Outlook*, City Editor for *Indian Express*, and Principal Correspondent for *India Today*. She was also the Western Region Head for Star News. She has authored chapters on the city and its transformations in books on Mumbai. She is also a teacher of journalism at the Social Communications Media Department of Sophia Manorama Devi Somani College, Mumbai.

Rahul Lahoti is a visiting Faculty at Azim Premji University. His research focuses mostly on issues of poverty, inequality, labour, gender, and political economy. He is interested in understanding women's participation and experiences in labour markets in India. He holds a PhD from the University of Göttingen, Germany, and a Masters in Public Administration from Columbia University, New York. He is also a contributor to Ideas for India, which regularly publishes articles based on evidence-based policy.

Rajiv Khandelwal is co-founder and Executive Director of Aajeevika Bureau. In this role he oversees the organisation's strategies, programmes, liaison, fundraising, and capacity-building functions. Over the course of his 30-year career, Rajiv has held leadership roles in a range of non-profit organisations, implementing programmes, conducting research, and providing advice and guidance to NGOs, donors, and government in Rajasthan. Rajiv worked for many years with the tribal communities of Southern Rajasthan, implementing large-scale agricultural change programmes. He holds a degree in rural management from the Institute of Rural Management, Anand.

Madan B. Lokur is an Indian jurist. He is a former Judge of the Supreme Court of India. He is also former Chief Justice of Andhra Pradesh High

Court and Gauhati High Court and Judge of Delhi High Court. He is also a Judge of the Supreme Court of Fiji.

Nomaan Majid is a Senior Employment Specialist with the ILO's Decent Work Team for South Asia. His research interests are in the subjects of employment, labour markets, income distribution, and growth in developing countries. He holds a doctorate in Economics from the University of Oxford, UK. He is a regular contributor to several academic journals and newspapers like the *World Economic Journal*, *The Indian Express*, etc.

Kunal Majumder is the India correspondent of the Committee to Protect Journalists. He has worked for outlets including the *Indian Express*, *Rajasthan Patrika*, *Tehelka*, and *Vice*. He is a winner of the Statesman Award for Rural Reporting and the UNDP-Laadli Award for Gender Sensitivity. He is on the steering committee of the Impulse NGO Network Press Lab, which supports reporters who cover human trafficking. He is based in New Delhi. His areas of interest include press freedom, politics, democracy, and media capture.

Harsh Mander is a social activist, columnist, researcher, and teacher who works with survivors of mass violence and hunger, as well as homeless persons and street children. He is the Director of the Centre for Equity Studies, a research organisation based in New Delhi. He has served as Special Commissioner to the Supreme Court of India in the Right to Food Campaign and was a member of the National Advisory Council of the Government of India.

Ejaz Maqbool is a Senior Advocate of the Supreme Court and member of Maqbool & Co law firm. He has fought several important cases like Ram Mandir in Ayodhya, and the Triple Talaq Case at the Supreme Court of India. He is a regular contributor to several well-known newspapers like *The Times of India*, *Dailyhunt*, etc. He writes on legal rights and minority rights issues.

Indrani Mazumdar is a Senior Fellow at the Centre for Women's Development Studies, Delhi, an autonomous research institute supported by the Indian Council of Social Science Research. Trained as a historian, her research interests are in labour employment development, women's studies, gender studies, and migration.

Deepanshu Mohan is an Associate Professor of Economics and Director, Centre for New Economics Studies at Jindal School of International Affairs, O. P. Jindal Global. He is also a Visiting Professor at the Department of Economics at Carleton University, Ottawa, Canada, where he teaches courses in Comparative Economic History and Development Economics over the summer term. He holds a bachelor's in Economics from Fergusson College, Pune, and an MSc in Economic History from the London School of Economics. His research work intersects areas of law and economics, political economy, and development economics. During his academic tenure, he has been a Visiting Fellow at research organisations and universities in Brazil, Colombia, Australia, and Cambodia.

Paaritosh Nath is a Postdoctoral fellow at the Centre for Sustainable Employment, Azim Premji University, Bengaluru. Paaritosh has a PhD from the Centre for the Study of Regional Development, Jawaharlal Nehru University, Delhi. His research looked at the dynamics of work, technology, and skills as they play out in the automobile industry of the National Capital Region (NCR). Prior to joining CSE, he was working as a research fellow with the Karwan-e-Mohabbat. His areas of interest include the trajectory of growth of industrial labour markets in India, the impact of labour laws on employment, and processes of skill acquisition and upgradation.

Neetha N. Pillai is a Professor at the Centre for Women's Development Studies, Delhi. She was Associate Fellow and Coordinator, Centre for Gender and Labour at the V. V. Giri National Labour Institute, NOIDA, 1998–2006. Her research interests are labour and employment issues of women, domestic workers, labour migration, and gender statistics and data gaps.

Bhanupriya Rao is an independent researcher and writer. She is one of the founders of Behanbox, a web platform for gender issues. She has also worked with several international organisations like ActionAid, Oxfam, and World Wide Web Foundation as a public policy specialist. Currently, she is working on the political participation of women, agrarian distress, migration, and several other issues. She is one of the regular contributors to several digital platforms like *Scroll*, IndiaSpend, etc.

Ranabir Samaddar is the Distinguished Chair Professor on Migration and Forced Migration Studies at the Calcutta Research Group. He belongs to the critical school of thinking and is considered one of the foremost theorists in the field of migration and forced migration studies. He has worked extensively on issues of forced migration, the theory and practices of dialogue, nationalism, and postcolonial statehood in South Asia, and new regimes of technological restructuring and labour control. The much-acclaimed *The Politics of Dialogue* was a culmination of his long work on justice, rights, and peace. His recent political writings, published in the form of a two-volume account, *The Materiality of Politics* (2007) and *The Emergence of the Political Subject* (2009), have challenged some of the prevailing accounts of the birth of nationalism and the nation-state, and have signalled a new turn in critical postcolonial thinking. His co-authored work on new towns and new forms of accumulation

Beyond Kolkata: Rajarhat and the Dystopia of Urban Imagination (Routledge, 2013) takes urban studies forward in the context of postcolonial capitalism.

Ellina Samantroy is a fellow at VV Giri National Labour Institute. She is associated with the Research Centre for Gender and Labour at the institute. She did her PhD in Sociology at the Centre for Study of Social Systems, School of Social Sciences, Jawaharlal Nehru University, New Delhi. Her research interests include gender and labour issues particularly, in the area of gender statistics, unpaid work, time use studies, work and family life balance, gender and social protection, child labour, labour regulation, and international labour standards.

Ayan Sharma is a correspondent at *NewsLaundry*. He previously worked with several news agencies like DNA, The Hindu, etc. He was also associated with ActionAid for a couple of years. Sharma did a masters in history at the Ambedkar University, Delhi. He has covered many sensitive subjects for them, including the plight of railway workers during COVID-19, Assam floods, and #rammandirbhoomipujan. His writings on North-East India are a reflection of his connection with his hometown, Guwahati, Assam.

Supriya Sharma is the Executive Editor of *Scroll.in*. She was earlier a Special Correspondent with *The Times of India* and a reporter with NDTV. She is a recipient of the Thomson Reuters Fellowship.

Bhupen Singh has been a noted journalist and media academic for more than 15 years. He has been a professor of journalism and communication at the Indian Institute of Mass Communication, Delhi University; and Amity University in Noida. His areas of interest include journalism and media studies, communication, culture, theatre, cinema, critical theory, political communication, public sphere, and social movements. He has also been party to several radio conversations titled "Mulaqat".

Juhie Singh is a politician representing the Samajwadi Party, with a Master's in Public Policy and Management from London University. Ms. Singh is also a pioneer in the field of floriculture. She is also renowned as the Ex-Chairperson of the Uttar Pradesh State Commission for Protection of Child Rights. Ms. Singh has contributed to structuring floriculture policies for several state governments. She is a woman of multifarious talents, and has been a journalist with *Outlook* magazine. Her report on the 1998 national elections was, in particular, a nuanced view of the local problems faced by the people of Lucknow. She is possessed of a keen sense of social consciousness, and the floriculture enterprise set up by her in 1995 has constantly endeavoured towards rural development, geared particularly towards women and children.

Mansi Singh is a Research Fellow and academic tutor at O.P. Jindal Global University. She is also a senior research assistant, Centre for New Economics Studies, Jindal School of Liberal Arts and Humanities. She has a Master's in Diplomacy Law and Business, O.P. Jindal Global University, Jindal School of International Affairs. In the past, she has interned for the Global Counter Terrorism Council, National Maritime Foundation, and Madhya Pradesh Human Rights Commission.

Atul Sood is Professor, Centre for the Study of Regional Development, Jawaharlal Nehru University. He has also worked at the National Council of Applied Economic Research and University of Ottawa, Canada. His current research interests are globalisation and its implications for regional development; Centre State fiscal relations; economic reform, public funding for health and its implications for health sector reforms; and institutional and regulatory issues that strengthen equity and the rights of the marginalised and deprived social groups.

V. Sridhar is a senior journalist and currently an Associate Editor with *Frontline*. He has been a journalist since 1987 and with The Hindu Group since 1991. He specialises in economic journalism.

Jenny Sulfath is Senior Researcher at the Centre for Equity Studies, New Delhi. She was a Research Scholar at the Advanced Centre for Women's Studies, Tata Institute of Social Sciences, Mumbai. She is a prolific writer on labour rights and other rights-based issues. She has an interest in food sociology. She writes regularly on labour and rights-based issues in several web magazines.

Balu Sunilraj is a Senior Researcher at the Centre for Equity Studies, New Delhi. He did his PhD at the Centre for Political Studies, Jawaharlal Nehru University. His current research interests are party politics, political economy, and public policy. He is a regular contributor to several newspapers and web magazines.

Cenny Thomas works with Aajeevika Bureau, a non-profit organisation that provides services to migrant and informal workers, and conducts research, policy advocacy, and grassroots mobilisation for improving the lives and livelihoods of labour-dependent communities.

Priyanka Tripathi teaches at the Department of Humanities and Social Sciences, Indian Institute of Technology, Patna. Her areas of interest include gender studies, Indian writing in English, short fiction, censorship studies, and diaspora studies. She has claimed many prestigious honours such as the Jawaharlal Nehru Memorial Fellowship for Doctoral Studies, 2010–2011, and the National Merit Scholarship, 1995–1999, and is also a member of professional bodies such as the Indian Association of

Commonwealth Literature and Language Studies, All Indian Women's Conference, Indian Society for Commonwealth Studies, and more to the hilt.

Satvik Varma is an advocate based in New Delhi. A graduate of Harvard Law School, he's licensed to practice both in India and New York. He is a Litigation Counsel and Corporate Attorney. Prior to setting up his private practice, he was a partner at India's premier law firm, (undivided) Amarchand Mangaldas and also served as the Vice-President and Counsel in the corporate law group at Lehman Brothers (2003–2005) headquarters in New York.

Acknowledgements

This compendium of articles is essentially the result of the collective desire of the members of the Mahanirban Calcutta Research Group, with tremendous expertise in migration studies, to embark on such a project. The idea began as the need to prepare a media reader on migrants in a meeting in January 2020. However, after the outbreak of the COVID-19 pandemic it metamorphosed into one of the migrant crisis caused by it. The collection was shaped under the guidance and help of my colleagues at the MCRG, especially Rajat Roy who coordinated this project, Ranabir Samaddar, Samir Das, and Piya Srinivasan. I am grateful to Harsh Kapoor (who runs the excellent South Asia Citizens' Web), Rammanohar Reddy (Editor-in-Chief of *India Forum*), and Monobina Gupta (senior journalist and author) who helped in identifying authors and articles that could be included in this collection as well nudging me in the right direction. I am thankful to all of them, but ultimately the choice of articles for inclusion was mine alone.

Introduction

Bharat Bhushan

Even if the media was unaware of the difficult role it would be called upon to perform in the unfolding coronavirus pandemic, the government certainly was not. On March 24, 2020 before announcing the national lockdown, Prime Minister Narendra Modi invited 20 owners and editors of media houses for a virtual consultation on the pandemic. He requested them to "act as a link between the government and the people and provide continuous feedback" on the government's handling of the COVID-19 crisis.

It was reported that the prime minister personally took notes on the suggestions made in the meeting which lasted for an hour and half. It included owners and editors working in 11 different languages as well as senior representatives of national media houses. The prime minister apparently impressed upon them that "it was important to tackle the spread of pessimism, negativity and rumour" and that it was imperative that citizens be "assured the government is committed to countering the impact of Covid-19".

Six hours later he went on national television to announce a three-week lockdown across the nation.

According to the prime minister's official website, the media representatives agreed to "work on the suggestions of the prime minister to publish inspiring and positive stories" about the pandemic. Indeed, media leaders who met the prime minister were full of praise for him and played up the meeting on Twitter and in their respective media platforms the next day. Their egos primed, they seemed to revel in a role that went counter to the basic principles of journalism in a democracy.

The attempt to make the media complicit with the government's handling of the pandemic seemed to succeed initially. There was hardly any public debate over why despite the WHO's early warnings there was no stockpiling of personal protection equipment (PPE) for healthcare workers or of testing kits. While there was a shortage in the country, domestically manufactured PPE kits were being exported to Italy and Spain, with suppliers making money hand over fist. The government woke up to this fact only on March 19, 2020, banning PPE exports. The export of ventilators was banned only on March 24, 2020.

DOI: 10.4324/9781003291527-1

There were other areas where the media failed to take the government to task early on. Its failure for example to provide a safety net for those identified as the most vulnerable section of the population likely to be affected by an economic lockdown. It also refrained from questioning the government's use of pandemic restrictions to disband the peaceful protests against amendments to citizenship laws and to label them as a danger to the public. The real test of the media, however, came after the nationwide 21-day lockdown was announced.

Contextualising reporting on migrants

No one was prepared for the scale of the desperate defiance of the lockdown order by the urban migrant workers. The sight of thousands of people walking back to the villages could not be ignored. However, when the media began reporting the phenomenon, the government accused it of peddling "fake news" and triggering panic. The media was blamed for the fallout of its own poor planning.

Young reporters had some difficulty in finding an adequate language to report on this phenomenon. Why for example were the returning workers described as "migrants" in their own country? What legal protection could they ask for and which civic institutions could they make demands on?

In recent political discourse "migrants" were equated with refugees, illegal immigrants, infiltrators, asylum seekers, or "termites" that Union Home Minister Amit Shah said were "eating the grain that should go to the poor and taking our jobs". But clearly the returning workers were none of these.

As Indian citizens they had a legal right to live both at the place of work and their places of origin. Yet using the term migrants suggested that somehow they were outsiders to normal life in the city and could be "returned" or repatriated to their "proper place" in this moment of crisis.

Media reportage of the unprecedented walk back of the migrants in the mainstream media seldom went beyond voyeuristic footage/reports of the difficulties of finding the way home. The constant reference to the term "return migration" to describe their march back to their villages did not capture the unprecedented defiance of the lockdown and the government's order to the migrant workers to stay put. It was therefore not a voluntary act in normal times of returning home from a job in the city but an unprecedented expression of lack of faith in the state. The use of the term "return migration" by the media therefore neutralised this singular expression of defiance by the migrant workers. Not only the media but several other institutions of the state were caught on the wrong foot in uncritically adopting the descriptor "return migration" for the unusual phenomenon India witnessed.

There was no discussion in the media on the crucial economic role of the migrant worker or analysis of the administration's ineptitude in cushioning their sudden loss of livelihood. Despite having created a National Disaster

Management Agency no simulation exercises to deal with a pandemic had ever been conducted which might have prepared the administration to deal with the crisis. Nor did the Union government consult widely with those outside the government, scientists, economists, opposition leaders, civil society leaders, to build a collective understanding of the social consequences of the pandemic and a common approach to control its spread and minimise its impact.

Digital and social media

Unlike the failure of most of the legacy print media, however, digital media and its associated social media platforms came into their own during the COVID-19-induced migration crisis. It produced complex news reports – old-style academic articles full of scholarship on migrant workers and human interest spot reports by bright young reporters with amazing response time. Social media platforms like Facebook, Twitter, Instagram, and WhatsApp became both sources of news about the migrant phenomenon as well as its efficient disseminators.

The print media with some minor exceptions has painted itself into a formulaic packaging of news – publishing short reports which barely skim the surface, routine photographs, and only occasionally, analytic pieces which went deeper. Factors that shape this kind of dull news packaging are the shortage of space, limitation of formats in which the report can be presented or enhanced (i.e. text, pictures, maps, and illustration/cartoons), the editorial habit of following the market leaders, and adherence to the dominant narrative (mostly determined by the state). Television news channels are not very different. They also tend to follow each other in terms of choosing topics to cover and trying to make up for shallowness of reportage by screaming anchors and sensational headlines.

By contrast digital media is less inhibited by these constraints as it does not use costly newsprint or pay for up-linking to a satellite. There are no limitations on the length of reports or the number of accompanying photographs. Editors are free to innovate with new forms/formats of presenting news – a mix of text, video, audio, and pictures. The readers are free to access news in the format they want. There are no limits on distribution as there is no physical distribution required through hawkers or through satellite up-linking facilities. What's more, news can also be broadcast and promoted through social media to specific target audiences, including policymakers and influencers. There can be cross-references to related reports or video content, allowing the interested reader to dive deeper into the subject.

In addition to innovation in the format and distribution of news, digital media also expanded reportage of the migrant crisis in other significant ways. First, it brought experts and scholarship to the issue in addition to spot reports and vivid photo-essays.

Second, since unlike in newspapers there is no limit on the frequency of updating news, digital media was able to provide a continuous stream of news updates on the migrant crisis.

Third, specialist digital platforms covering legal and policy issues brought in subject expertise to expand the understanding of the migrant crisis and its handling by the government. For example, one witnessed labour experts writing on the gap between laws governing the migrant workers and their implementation, labour economists assessed the size of the workforce that had walked back to their distant homes, and yet other experts wrote on women migrants and labour laws, and the impact of the lockdown and social distancing on sex workers and on domestic workers.

And lastly, by its extensive use of vivid and heart-rending pictures of the long march of the migrants the digital media elicited a quick political and societal response. These pictures (and short videos) by both professional photojournalists as well as reporters using smartphones shook the conscience of the nation. Who can forget the picture of a young boy sleeping on a suitcase being wheeled by his mother in Jhansi on her 800-km journey home on foot or the few dry *rotis* scattered on the railway tracks in Aurangabad after 16 migrant workers had been run over by a train? The picture of the boy sleeping on the suitcase was compared by many on social media with the seminal photograph of the refugee child Aylan (aka Alan) Kurdi whose dead body washed up ashore in Turkey during the Syrian migrant crisis.

Whether it was the pictures of men, women, and children walking hundreds of kilometres with their feet wrapped in cloth or plastic bags, of mothers with their belongings perched on their head and their children in their arms, or of desperate workers who had travelled in the tanks of cement mixers because of lack of transport – iconic images of the misery unleashed on the poor – pictures managed to move the nation in a way no words or textual descriptions could have. The pictures and videos of the suffering of the migrant workers kept pouring in on social media throughout their march back home as well as the apathy towards them – recall the picture of the worker who had to build a makeshift tree house at the edge of his village to quarantine himself as his extended family refused to keep him at home.

Traditional media – whether newspapers or television – could not have captured such a vast spectrum of the migrant crisis and in this manner by using short vidoes and a large number of pictures. Television could have done much more but somehow failed to rise to the occasion, losing the battle to social media and digital news platforms.

Social media played yet another crucial role during the migrant crisis. Studies of migration have noted how social media opens up new channels of communication which strengthen migrant networks and help ameliorate the suffering of migrants. The smartphone revolution in India meant that migrant workers were able to network with their kin and friends and update them about their return home through social media apps, directly broadcast messages about their suffering, link themselves to individuals and organisations who could assist them in returning home by either providing food and shelter or transport, and create a pool of knowledge outside the official structures of the state on their condition amongst concerned citizens' groups, non-governmental organisations (NGOs), charities, and religious organisations who then stepped forward to help them.

The direct results of social media engagement with the migrant workers were there for everyone to see. Who can forget the iconic role played by Bollywood actor Sonu Sood who was only a social media message away to help stranded and hungry migrants or the "Mazdoor Kitchens" and community kitchens that sprung up on major migration routes run by volunteers and the donation of food and monetary contributions by individuals and organisations? This also helped build public pressure on the government to address the issue of returning migrants through public interest litigation and by opposition political parties.

At an individual level, social media mitigated to an extent the misery of migrants returning home by connecting them to their kin and community. At the larger societal level, it provided invaluable information which directly or indirectly influenced public perception and public policy.

There was of course a downside to the ease of social media use as well. Notably in Mumbai 30 social media accounts and a TV channel were identified by the cyber wing of the Mumbai Police for spreading a false rumour about special trains for migrants starting from Bandra Railway Station in mid-April. In Maharashtra alone, by mid-April more than 200 cases had been registered by the police for spreading fake news and rumours about COVID-19 and spreading hate messages aimed at creating enmity between two religious communities. The social media platforms used for this ranged from WhatsApp messages, Facebook and YouTube posts to TikTok videos.

Social media posts were also used selectively against members of the Tablighi Jamaat who attended a convention at its headquarters between March 13 and 15 at Delhi's Nizamuddin Basti. This, coupled with the government's own public statements linking the spread of COVID-19 to the Tablighi convention, led to the religious profiling of COVID-19 victims. Social media in this case was used to abuse Muslims in general, boycott individuals and their businesses, suspect Muslim health workers, and even to incite attacks on the minority community.

Lack of awareness about migrant workers

This compendium of representative writing on migrant labour is both for journalists and lay readers. The extreme upheaval caused by the COVID-19-induced sudden lockdown presented an opportunity not only to see how media practitioners reacted to the mass exodus but also to examine different facets of the crisis. This is useful not only for journalists but also lay readers because there is no one truth about the migrant crisis which captures its entirety.

This collection of articles has been divided into six parts, each examining one facet of the migrant crisis. It does not, however, examine the return of the migrant workers to the cities once again in search of their old jobs or new employment. It thus limits itself to the brief time period which began with the sudden lockdown, the tragic march of the migrant workers back home to their places of residence, and how government policy, the legal system, and the media addressed the crisis.

What began as lack of knowledge about migrant workers when their exodus began ended up as a considerable body of knowledge in the public and popular sphere about their condition. For the first time the popular imagination had to grapple with questions of who and how many the migrant workers were. It came as a surprise that the government itself had no tally of their number; not even the Ministry of Labour and Employment had bothered to collect such data which must necessarily be the starting point of formulating policy for them.

The only government estimates available were outdated and from the 2011 census. The scale of the forced return migration compelled journalists as well as scholars to re-examine the data on migrant labour and estimate how many of them might have decided to return home. The articles in this section range from discussing the number and nature of migration within India to the differing estimates of the number of migrants who left their jobs to return home. This helped put the massive upheaval in context (Part 1: Lost in Counting).

One would have expected that once such a mass migration began, the state would act or laws and the judiciary would kick in to help them. Here the media and legal experts writing for popular digital platforms helped to expose the shortcomings of the legal safeguards. The articles in this section deal with the inadequacy of laws governing migrant workers, why they need to be reconfigured, and the manner in which the High Courts and the Supreme Court dealt with the crisis (Part 2: Abandoned by Law).

The third part recounts the horrors of the long march home by the migrants. Reporters, not bothering about their health, went out into the field to produce reports describing the heart-rending journeys home undertaken by the migrant workers by walking with them and telling their stories. Their stories will remain a testimony to how democratic India treated its most vulnerable workers during the pandemic (Part 3: The Long March Home).

The media also played a stellar role in showing the gap between government policy and the denial of wages, lack of food, and growth of hunger. Although the government mandated that lockdown period wages were to be paid in full, as time progressed it backtracked from its own order. The migrants were often disappointed on returning to their villages where they were ostracised as possible carriers of COVID-19. The media also learnt to disaggregate the category of migrant workers to write about intra-state migrants, differently abled workers, and women migrant workers who worked from home (Part 4: No Wages, No Jobs, No Food).

In Part 5, the perfidy of some state governments has been exposed by labour lawyers, NGO activists, and reporters to weaken even the existing labour laws using the pandemic as an opportunity to push through their agenda. They tried to systematically dilute the existing labour laws to extend the working day and the working week. Several states used the ordinance route to change these laws as state legislatures were unable to meet due to the pandemic. They did this in the name of "ease of doing business" and some to apparently attract multinational corporations trying to relocate from China (Part 5: Pandemic as Opportunity: Changing Labour Laws).

In the concluding part, this compendium tries to present a cross-section of writing on how the media addressed the migrant issues before and during the crisis. Before the crisis, there was no "news" to report as the migrant workers were not "visible" to the public. After the lockdown induced by the pandemic, the attempt by the government to get the media to present only "positive stories" met with limited success. The government even got the Supreme Court to direct the media to present the official point of view as it probably suspected that the reportage on COVID-19 and on migrant workers both was spinning out of control. It is difficult to say whether in the end these attempts at controlling or moulding media were very successful. However, the media was not without blame when it bought into the dominant propaganda about the Tablighi Jamaat members as COVID-spreaders which was then used to target the Muslim minority of the country (Part 6: Media and Migrant Workers: Invisible Become Visible).

This collection of articles is primarily designed to encourage the reader to think about how the migrant crisis was addressed in terms of media craft, journalistic and specialist skills, and the analytical tools used. It does not claim to have included the "best" writing on each of the issues chosen. What it has attempted, however, is to pick representative writings to highlight different facets of the upheaval that India witnessed and link it to social, political, and policy failures. Not all the articles are written by reporters in a popular journalistic style – some are interactions of reporters with migrants and their telling of the migrants' stories, while others are scholarly analyses of the crisis or legal experts writing on the subject. The effort is to showcase how the migrant exodus was understood initially and how it could have been thought about with greater appreciation of its various dimensions.

However, given the format of this collection and limited resources, a wider cross-section of excellent reports on the migrant crisis could not be included. Nothing of the media content that television news channels showed could be included for obvious reasons. Two additional shortcomings of the collection are that it is based only on English-language sources and does not include photo-essays on migrants, once again because of resource constraints.

Part 1

Lost in counting

1.1 Faceless and dispossessed

India's circular migrants in the times of COVID-19[1]

Priya Deshingkar

The 2011 Census said India has 454 million migrants, 54 million of whom are interstate workers. But the data accounts for a fraction of workers in circulation.

India's model of capitalism and social reproduction among the elite has depended heavily on a precarious workforce that circulates between underdeveloped regions and the urban informal sector, industrial zones, and middle-class homes.

A significant chunk of workers are interstate migrants. They come from poor, historically disadvantaged castes and classes and work outside suffocating agrarian relations of serfdom and indebtedness, patriarchal norms, and stagnant wages in the countryside.

But these migrant men and women are adversely incorporated into urban and industrial economies – they work low-paying jobs, do not have formal contracts, and are outside the reach of the law.

They provide critical labour that sustains India's economy, but remain on the margins. In their already precarious existence, the abrupt lockdown prompted by the novel coronavirus disease (COVID-19) pandemic and loss of livelihood resulted in a migrant exodus, which has been compared to the great migration during Partition.

So how many circular migrants are we talking about?

This seems to be the burning question, especially since state governments, labour departments, and other agencies have been scrambling to find representative data. According to the 2011 Census, India has 454 million migrants, out of whom only 54 million are interstate migrants.

But we have known for some time that these numbers are gross underestimates and account for only a fraction of workers in circulation. In order to address the imbalance, I estimated the extent of circular migration in India at 100 million just over a decade ago, based on industry estimates by subsector. The data is backed by rigorous empirical studies.

According to my calculations, migrant workers contributed to about 10 per cent of the national gross domestic product.

DOI: 10.4324/9781003291527-3

Given the galloping pace of development in export industries such as textiles and other domestic industries over the last decade, it is time to revisit these numbers. Let us examine the key sectors that provide employment to migrants with few formal qualifications. My calculations, based on estimates from reliable and established industrial development agencies, international organisations, and non-profits, are as follows.

The textile and garment industry employed 119 million workers in 2015 at a time when its market value was $108.5 billion. Given that the industry is on a growth trajectory with a projected market share of $223 billion by 2021 and the trends point towards outsourcing, piece rate, and informalisation, it is likely that the numbers of workers would have doubled and most of them would be in the informal sector.

Studies of Tirupur and the National Capital Region clusters show that 70–100 per cent workers are interstate migrants from Bihar, Uttar Pradesh, and other poor states, while the Bengaluru cluster employs mainly intrastate migrants. Thus, one can conservatively assume that at least 100 million migrants work in this sector.

Another giant is the construction industry which employs around 60 million workers, mainly migrants working as carpenters, masons, and plumbers. Add to this the growing number of migrant female domestic workers coming from impoverished parts of Jharkhand, West Bengal, and Chhattisgarh to work in middle-class homes in Delhi, Mumbai, Hyderabad, and other cities.

According to International Labour Organization estimates, there are 20–90 million domestic workers in India. If we take an average of the two and assume that at least half are migrants, the estimate is roughly 27.2 million.

Other significant employers of circular migrants are brick kilns, which have 23 million workers, according to Anti-Slavery International, an international non-profit. This is followed by small-scale mines (12 million), street vendors (10 million), rickshaw pullers (10 million), and gem polishers and cutters (1.5 million).

These numbers add up to 243 million and would be higher if we were to include other significant sub-sectors, including fisheries and seafood processing, footwear, ceramics, and leatherwork.

My informed guess is that the overall number is close to 250 million. But let us not get obsessed with precise numbers – it is the overall scale that I want to draw attention to – and the fact that the lockdown was imposed without a thought to workers who lost their livelihoods and accommodation overnight.

I believe this was due to the interconnected problem of inaccurate data and because a majority of disenfranchised migrants were lower caste and poor. It was only after their plight became visible and there was public outcry that action was taken.

But even this has been fraught with problems: The relief package of Rs 3,500 crore, to feed stranded migrants and Shramik trains and take them home, has failed to reach a majority of migrants who lack documents such as Aadhaar cards or registration under the Interstate Migrant Workmen Act.

First-hand accounts from the Stranded Workers Action Network and others indicate that only 10–25 per cent of workers have left so far and a second, larger wave of return migration is expected.

Migrants have lost faith in the city, and many have vowed to not return. Even though migrants are extolled for their tenacity in the face of adversity, few will forget the humiliation of being abandoned in their time of need. Many do not even know who their bosses are due to multiple layers of subcontracting.

The arrogance and indifference to the plight of poor, lower caste, and uneducated labouring classes continue and are manifest even in the relief measures provided – there have been reports of Shramik trains not providing food or water to their passengers in a dignified manner.

Till date, only five million workers have been sent home on these trains and many more are waiting to go home. Taking advantage of the gap in services, an industry of *dalals* (middlemen) has sprung up, and it charges Rs 3,000 or more to take them home. Here, too, those without the means are being left behind.

The response of the authorities to this has been to take migrants off unauthorised vehicles and place them in detention centres. Migrants continue to travel on foot, tempos, buses, and other means, often at night to evade detection. They have been criminalised in their own country.

It may not be too late for the government to amend its approach and offer rapid assistance on a humanitarian basis without insisting on documentation. Help could be offered on the basis of community validation – numerous good citizens and civil society organisations who are offering help on the ground could be asked to help the authorities to identify who should be given assistance.

Likewise, the government should move away from a system where its own agencies have a monopoly on generating migration data and involve others who generate statistics of their own. This is critical for understanding the scope of invisible migrant workers who are hard to reach through conventional surveys.

Finally, serious steps must be taken to provide migrant workers with greater security at destination including insurance against loss of pay due to shocks such as the COVID-19 pandemic, regardless of proof of identity and domicile.

More also needs to be done to support vulnerable families whose breadwinners have returned. State governments are starting to set up commissions to provide migrants with jobs and business loans, but they should consult them to better understand their aspirations.

Here, too, the identification of beneficiaries should be done through community involvement rather than government alone to ensure fair distribution.

Note

1 Reproduced with permission from Down to Earth where this article was first published on June 16, 2020.

1.2 How many casual workers in the cities have sought to go home?[1]

Nomaan Majid[2]

There has been no count of the number of workers returning to their home states. An analysis of NSS data tells us that the first wave of returnees is likely to be mainly urban casual workers who lost their livelihoods and lived in insecure accommodation.

The public focus on "migrant labour" emerged almost as soon as the COVID-19 lockdown was announced on March 24, 2020. Many poor workers, who found they were without work and were very short of funds, took it upon themselves to walk to their villages: some with families, many more on their own.

Most of these persons began their journey on foot. Their miserable state was caught on camera, and there has been considerable discussion of their plight. It can be said without doubt that these persons were very poor urban workers who had lost their jobs.

However, how many of them were on the road, whether they represented the bulk of redundancies in urban areas, whether they were all migrants, and, if so, of which kind—these questions began to stick to the images of workers walking out of the cities. The violence that some of these workers met with during their journey emotionally charged the issue further.

That they were going out of urban areas to the perceived safety of their non-urban destinations in itself does not mean that they were all or mostly short-term migrants. Similarly, the fact that most of these workers were very poor and had been dismissed from their jobs, tells us little about how much they represent others who had been made jobless in urban areas.

Loss of jobs

The scale of job losses at the all-India level and indeed in urban India from where these persons have been moving out is difficult to ascertain, as there are not many current surveys. The estimate of job losses is distinct from the estimate of persons who potentially may have incurred damage to livelihoods. This number can be inferred from the baseline data we do have of

DOI: 10.4324/9781003291527-4

workers, as in the Periodic Labour Force Survey (PLFS) of 2017–18. The headcount of the poor or the self-employed and casual workers is an obvious upper limit. Some evidence that is emerging now suggests that very large sections of the working population have indeed lost jobs.

One survey that we must rely on is from CMIE,[3] which estimates that 122 million workers lost their jobs in April. This is more than a quarter of all employed persons. Of these, it identifies 91.3 million as labourers and small traders—the corresponding category in standard employment data being casual workers and the self-employed.

While the scale of estimated job loss is huge according to CMIE, the survey does not give an urban-rural split. Researchers at Azim Premji University have done another, much smaller, purposive survey, which is very useful (the "APU Survey"[4]). This survey gives a breakdown of jobs lost by location and employment type. We are, of course, interested here in the urban job loss.

As far as urban jobs are concerned, the APU survey shows that by mid-May, 81% of casual workers, 84% of self-employed, and 76% of regular salaried workers had lost their jobs.

The PLFS urban shares and employment estimates and shares are given in Table 1.2.1. Therefore, if we apply APU's 81% to the PLFS estimate of 18.96 million casual workers (Usual Principal Status or UPS), we get 15.35 million. This is the large number of casual workers in urban India who may have lost their jobs.

The figure is slightly higher if we take the Usual Principal + Subsidiary Status (UPSS) estimates of workers. The number is, of course, going to get slightly higher if we take the 2020 adjusted population estimate as opposed

Table 1.2.1 Size and distribution of work force (usual principal status, 2017–18). Source: PLFS 2017–18

PLFS 2017-18 Population Adjusted Estimates (in number)	Urban	Total
Self employed	48,888,488	228,533,506
Casual workers	18,963,028	111,832,733
Regular salaried workers	61,513,763	104,287,666
All workers	129,365,279	444,653,905
PLFS 2017-18 shares (%)	**Urban**	**Total**
Self employed	37.8	51.4
Casual workers	14.7	25.2
Regular salaried workers	47.6	23.5
All	100	100

to the estimate for 2017–18. The absolute number clearly depends on the population estimate we take, but the difference is not much.

The identity of urban workers who are leaving

There are many poor people living in urban areas. They include workers of many descriptions. Many self-employed are very poor, and almost all casual workers are poor. There are also poor regularly employed persons without social security, who too are affected by the lockdown. It is our view that in the first round of the lockdown, it is the casual workers who have been affected the most.

The PLFS numbers suggest that in urban areas, casual workers were around 14.6% of total urban employment in 2017–18: the 18.96 million number. This would indeed be the count of the exodus if all casual workers were to leave, all 18.96 million. As we saw, applying the APU survey-based percentage of urban casual labour job loss (81%) to this number would give us an affected casual worker population of 15.35 million.

Many casual workers are persons who either have accommodation arranged for them, for which they pay through contractors, or who live on work premises (as on construction sites), or rent rooms on an informal basis, or make do in temporary spaces for which they pay directly.

In any event, it is safe to assume that a considerable minority of casual labour in urban areas does not live either in premises that have properly written rent leases with emergency clauses, or in owned premises. Moreover, these casual workers who have such adverse accommodation arrangements are likely to be the poorest and must be amongst those who lost their jobs after the lockdown was imposed. After all it is most of the casual workers that we suspect have lost jobs.

The NSS Housing Survey of 2018 allows us to identify urban casual workers, their sectors of occupation, their duration of stay in residence on a premises, and their residential contractual arrangements. The last of these categories also allows us to distinguish between owned, owned-leased, and rented accommodation with written contracts. We term these non-adverse accommodation arrangements.

This is in contrast to less formal arrangements that are based on employer-provided spaces (like construction sites, spaces near factory compounds, or makeshift quarters) and informal rentals without written contracts. We call these adverse accommodation arrangements.

While the bulk of urban casual workers in all sectors live in non-adverse conditions of accommodation, a significant minority—around a quarter—live in adverse accommodation arrangements (Table 1.2.2). We estimate that number to be 25.69% of the 18.96 million casual workers estimated by the PLFS 2017–18. This comes to about 4.87 million living under adverse accommodation arrangements.

The other point to note here is that those who have non-adverse accommodation arrangements and who live in owned and leased abodes are in a majority. Around 74.3% of casual workers in urban areas live in owned and leased accommodation. It is inconceivable that these casual workers, who are long-term occupiers or quasi-owners of their urban abodes, would immediately give up their foothold in urban areas, or immediately move out after they lose their jobs.

We can now look at the duration of stay in premises for casual workers. Tables 1.2.3 –1.2.5 show three things.

First, Table 1.2.3 shows that as the duration of stay increases, there is a decrease in the share of casual labourers living in premises under adverse arrangements. Thus, as expected, shorter period rentals and stays correlate with less secure accommodation arrangements. Adverse accommodation arrangements decline as the period of stay by casual workers lengthens.

Table 1.2.2 Accomodation arrangements of casual workers (2018, percentage distribution). Note: from Housing Survey 2018 (non-adverse = owned and leased or dwelling with contract. Adverse = employer-provided, dwelling without written contract, or no dwelling)

	All (%)	Rural (%)	Urban (%)
Non-adverse accommodation arrangement	74.3	97.13	74.31
Adverse accommodation arrangement	25.7	2.87	25.69

Table 1.2.3 Distribution of accommodation arrangements of casual workers (by period of stay). Source: estimates from Housing Survey 2018

Casual workers' period of stay by accommodation arrangement	Adverse accommodation arrangements (%)	Non-Adverse accommodation arrangements (%)
less than 1 year	78.47	21.53
1 to 2 years	75.46	24.54
2 to 5 years	66.03	33.97
(Up to 5 years)	(71.22)	(28.78)
5 to 10 years	36.94	63.06
10 to 20 years	21.41	78.59
20 to 40 years	9.25	90.75
40 to 60 years	5.21	94.79
60 years or more	4.68	95.32
not known - 10)	34.51	65.49
Total	25.54	74.46

Table 1.2.4 Distribution of adverse accommodation arrangements of casual workers by duration. Source: estimates from Housing Survey 2018

Period of stay	Percentage of all adverse accommodation contracts
Less than 1 year	10.17
1 to 2 years	17.02
2 to 5 years	24.07
(Up to 5 years)	(51.26)
5 to 10 years	19.15
10 to 20 years	14.60
20 to 40 years	9.26
40 to 60 years	3.62
60 years or more	1.29
Not known	0.82
Total	100.00

Table 1.2.5 Size of select casual labour catogeries. Note: author's estimates from PLFS 2017–18 and Housing Survey 2018. PLFS adjusted number is percentage in the second column multiplied by the absolute urban casual worker number (population adjusted)

	As a percentage of all casual workers in the 2018 Housing Survey (%)	PLFS urban casual workers (population adjusted)
1. All urban casual workers with less than one-year stay and living under adverse accommodation contracts	2.60	492,276
2. All urban casual workers with less than one-year stay	3.31	627,363
3. All urban casual workers living under adverse accommodation contracts	25.54	4.84 million

While this is not a guarantee for identifying short-term migrants, it is still plausible to infer that short-term migrants, under the Census definition, will be amongst those who are living in accommodation for less than one year, and especially amongst those who are also living under adverse accommodation contractual arrangements.

The adverse contracts are clearly bunched in accommodation arrangements for stays of less than five years. They are not just located in the less than one-year category but can go up to the five-year group. Table 1.2.4

shows the distribution of adverse accommodation arrangements for casual workers by duration.

Table 1.2.5 shows us the shares of select classifications of casual workers in the 2018 Housing Survey and the inferred absolute numbers from the estimates of the casual labour population as in the 2017–18 PLFS.

The worst-off group are casual labourers with less than one-year accommodation and adverse housing contracts. They number around 492,000, say half a million. According to our reasoning this is the category in which short-term migrants will most likely be.

The next category does not bind the group to adverse accommodation arrangements but retains the restriction of a stay of less than one year. This number is larger, around 627,000.

Finally, we have that category of urban casual workers that has adverse accommodation arrangements but without the restriction of period of stay. This is the 4.8 million number. If we use the estimates for population in 2020, the ball-park figure should be around 5 million.

These casual workers, numbering 4.8 million–5 million, are the ones who are likely to have found themselves without work after the lockdown and who, living on premises with adverse accommodation arrangements, would have been compelled to leave the cities in the first wave of movement home.

This estimate clearly looks conservative in the light of speculation that has been going on. It also suggests that the group of leaving workers is less likely to be of the very short-term workers but comprise a wider range of workers.

One extension to these estimates may be to examine all workers rather than just casual workers. This is tantamount to saying that we are not focussing on one worker type. After all, the APU Survey also says that 84% of self-employed and 76% of regular employed were also made redundant.

Our view in this context is that there is no exclusivity of worker group amongst those returning, but it is likely that casual workers dominate the first wave. The reason for this is that we think self-employed persons may have a slightly longer staying power than casual workers. On average their consumption levels are higher.

Keeping the restriction of short term of stay (less than one year) and those with adverse accommodation contracts, the number of all urban workers (casual, self-employed, and regular salaried) in this category is 3.45 million. The number of urban workers with less than one-year stay and without adverse contracts increases to 5.28 million (Table 1.2.6, Row 2).

Of course, by removing the restriction of time of stay altogether, we get a higher number of 32.5 million workers who have adverse accommodation arrangements (Table 1.2.6, Row 1). It must be noted that because we have removed the time constraint, it would be difficult to argue that short-term migrants dominate the larger number even if it was close to the actual exodus number.

Table 1.2.6 All urban workers with adverse accommodation contracts. Note: author's estimates from PLFS 2017–18 and Housing Survey 2018. PLFS adjusted number is percentage in the second column multiplied by the absolute urban worker number (population adjusted) in Table 1.2.1

All urban workers with adverse accommodation contracts	As a % of all workers in Housing Survey	PLFS 2017-18: All urban workers in population (adjusted, million)
All urban workers with adverse contracts	25.1%	32.48
All urban workers with less than one-year stay	4.08%	5.28
All urban workers with period of stay of less than 1 year and adverse accommodation contracts	2.67%	3.45

In our view, this is a large but plausible number of 32.5 million workers with adverse accommodation arrangements, which includes 3.45 million short-term migrants with adverse contracts. This is because there is rampant urban poverty in India and there are many permanent residents in urban areas who are poor and who do not have secure accommodation arrangements, and yet stay put in urban areas. Needless to say, over time if there is a weak recovery, many amongst them too will be without shelter.

Some remarks

Our considered estimate of workers initially wanting to move out of urban areas is around 5 million. This would tend to include around a half million short-term migrants—the indicator being the interface between casual work, adverse accommodation arrangements, and a short period of stay. A further slowdown and the incapacity of the economy to restart may bring about a second wave with more self-employed and some regular workers (without security), some of whom will no doubt wish to leave urban areas.

Given that these numbers are based on many assumptions it is expected that they are not plausible to some researchers. This is natural in a situation of limited data. New data, especially the Census of 2021, will shed light on this issue when it comes out. There are, however, two distinct sources from which confusion can arise that can be addressed even at present.

The first point we need to make is that one should recall that 81% of casual workers in urban areas have lost their jobs according to the APU Survey. This comes to roughly 15.3 million. If we assume that the proportion of these 15.3 million who are in adverse accommodation arrangements is the same as in the 2018 Housing Survey—25.1%—then the absolute number of workers in adverse accommodation arrangements who have lost their jobs comes to around 3.84 million. So, the number when extrapolated even from the APU survey is on the low side and is close to our estimate. This is despite the fact that the overall job loss percentages from the APU survey, if translated into absolute numbers, would be very high.

So a low estimate of casual workers with adverse accommodation arrangements (the proxy for those who are walking out of urban areas) is not inconsistent with estimates of very high job losses.

Inter-state and intra-state demarcations, in conjunction with alternative classifications and definitions of migrants, and data from independent surveys may well give different numbers. However, these will be different numbers and different categories. Moreover, to assume that those who are moving from urban areas towards rural areas at this present junction necessarily belong to these alternative migrant classifications needs more than just independent estimates of the circulatory and floating migrants.

The issue was to ascertain the scale of persons moving out from urban areas. In the first wave, they are likely to have been casually employed, very poor, and living in adverse accommodation arrangements. Undoubtedly, many of these persons are also likely to be working in the urban areas on a short-term basis. Where would they go? Many must have relatives in other parts of the country. They do not have money. They are desperate, so they are walking. The overall number for this group is likely to be around 5 million in the first wave—persons who find themselves without shelter and have mostly been casually employed.

Depending on the speed of recovery, other affected groups like the self-employed may increasingly join a second wave. There is a possible confusion between the estimated scale of job losses, which are highly plausible, and alternative notions and estimates of migration. The two are not systematically linked.

Notes

1 Reproduced with permission from *The India Forum* where it first appeared on May 29, 2020. https://www.theindiaforum.in/article/how-many-casual-workers-cities-have-sought-go-home

2 The author would like to thank Abhishek Kumar for research assistance and Ajit Ghose and Radhicka Kapoor who discussed some aspects of the topic with him.
The views expressed in the text are the author's and not of the organisation he works for.

3 Please see https://www.cmie.com/kommon/bin/sr.php?kall=warticle&dt=2020-05-05%2008:22:21&msec=776

4 Please see https://cse.azimpremjiuniversity.edu.in/covid19-analysis-of-impact-and-relief-measures/

1.3 Migration in India and the impact of the lockdown on migrants[1]

Madhunika Iyer

What are the patterns of inter-state migration in India, its causes, and the size of the migrant labour force? The problems faced by migrant workers are many including poor implementation of laws meant to protect them, the lack of portability of social security benefits, and the lack of affordable housing and basic amenities in urban areas. After the mass exodus of migrant workers from cities during the pandemic, relief measures were announced by the government and directives issued by the Supreme Court to provide some protection to the migrant population during the lockdown.

India has been in lockdown since March 25, 2020. During this time, activities not contributing to the production and supply of essential goods and services were completely or partially suspended. Passenger trains and flights were halted. The lockdown has severely impacted migrants, many of whom lost their jobs due to the shutting of industries and were stranded outside their native places wanting to get back. Since then, the government has announced relief measures for migrants, and made arrangements for migrants to return to their native place. The Supreme Court of India, recognising the problems faced by migrants stranded in different parts of the country, reviewed transportation and relief arrangements made by the government.

On June 9, the Court directed central and state governments to complete the transportation of remaining stranded migrants and expand the focus of relief measures to facilitate employment for returning migrants. In this chapter, we highlight some facts about migration in India and summarise key relief measures announced by the government and directives issued by the Supreme Court for the migrant population in relation to the lockdown.

Overview of migration

Migration is the movement of people away from their usual place of residence, across either internal (within country) or international (across countries) borders. The latest government data on migration comes from the 2011 Census. As per the Census, India had 45.6 crore migrants in 2011 (38% of

DOI: 10.4324/9781003291527-5

the population) compared to 31.5 crore migrants in 2001 (31% of the population). Between 2001 and 2011, while the population grew by 18%, the number of migrants increased by 45%. In 2011, 99% of total migration was internal and immigrants (international migrants) comprised 1%.[2]

Patterns of migration

Internal migrant flows can be classified on the basis of origin and destination. One kind of classification is: (i) rural-rural, (ii) rural-urban, (iii) urban-rural, and (iv) urban-urban. As per the 2011 Census, there were 21 crore rural-rural migrants which formed 54% of classifiable internal migration (the Census did not classify 5.3 crore people as originating from either rural or urban areas). Rural-urban and urban-urban movement accounted for around 8 crore migrants each. There were around 3 crore urban-rural migrants (7% of classifiable internal migration).

Another way to classify migration is: (i) intra-state, and (ii) inter-state. In 2011, intra-state movement accounted for almost 88% of all internal migration (39.6 crore persons).

There is variation across states in terms of inter-state migration flows. According to the 2011 Census, there were 5.4 crore inter-state migrants. As of 2011, Uttar Pradesh and Bihar were the largest source of inter-state migrants while Maharashtra and Delhi were the largest receiver states. Around 83 lakh residents of Uttar Pradesh and 63 lakh residents of Bihar had moved either temporarily or permanently to other states. Around 60 lakh people from across India had migrated to Maharashtra by 2011.

Reasons for internal migration and size of migrant labour force

As of 2011, the majority (70%) of intra-state migration was due to reasons of marriage and family with variation between male and female

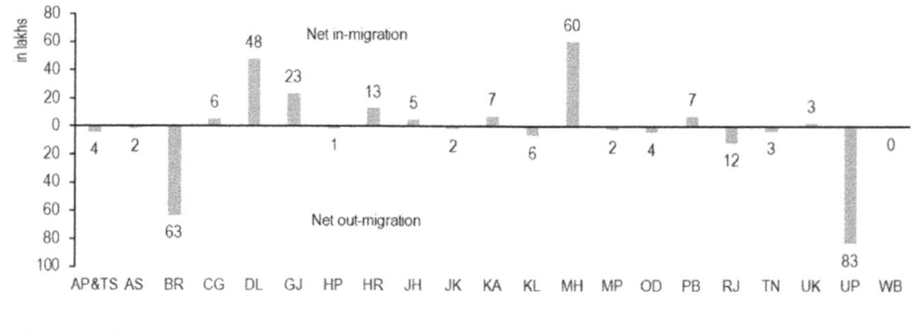

Figure 1.3.1 Inter-state migration (in lakh). Note: A net out-migrant state is one where more people migrate out of the state than migrate into the state. Net in-migration is the excess of incoming migrants over out-going migrants. Sources: Census 2011; PRS.

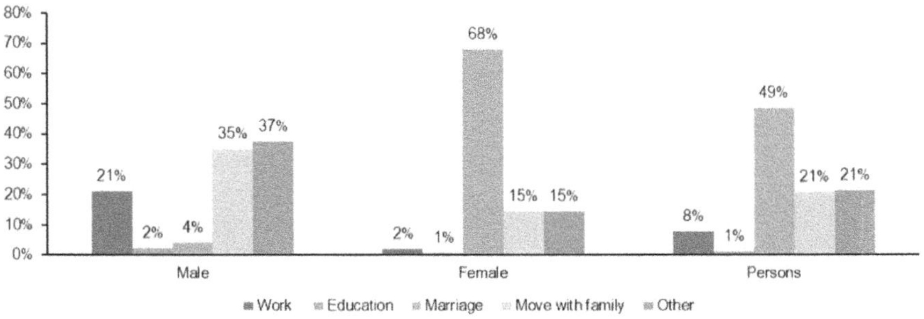

Figure 1.3.2 Reasons for intra-state migration. Sources: Census 2011; PRS.

migrants. While 83% of females moved for marriage and family, the corresponding figure for males was 39%. Overall, 8% of people moved within a state for work (21% of male migrants and 2% of female migrants).

Movement for work was higher among inter-state migrants – 50% of male and 5% of female inter-state migrants. As per the Census, there were 4.5 crore migrant workers in 2011. However, according to the Working Group Report on Migration, the Census underestimates the migrant worker population. Female migration is recorded as movement due to family since that is the primary reason. However, many women take up employment after migrating which is not reflected in the number of women moving for work-related reasons.[3]

According to the Economic Survey, 2016–2017, Census data also underestimates temporary migrant labour movement. In 2007–2008, the NSSO estimated the size of India's migrant labour force at seven crore (29% of the workforce). The Economic Survey, 2016–2017, estimated six crore inter-state labour migrants between 2001 and 2011. The Economic Survey also estimated that in each year between 2011 and 2016, on average, 90 lakh people travelled for work.

Issues faced by migrant labour

Article 19(1)(e) of the Constitution guarantees all Indian citizens the right to reside and settle in any part of the territory of India, subject to reasonable restrictions in the interest of the general public or protection of any scheduled tribe. However, people migrating for work face key challenges including: (i) lack of social security and health benefits and poor implementation of minimum safety standards law, (ii) lack of portability of state-provided benefits especially food provided through the public distribution system (PDS), and (iii) lack of access to affordable housing and basic amenities in urban areas.

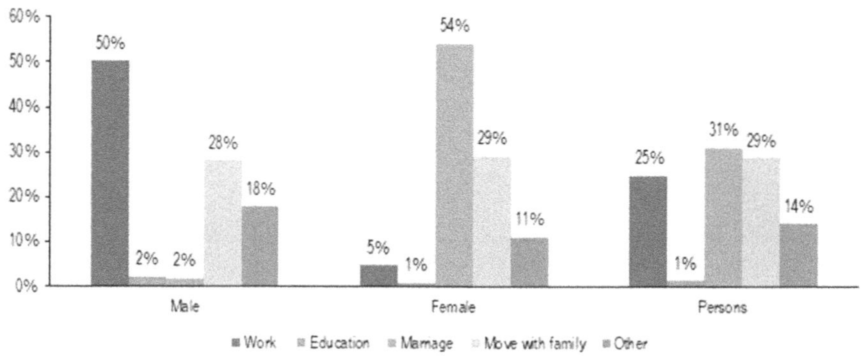

Figure 1.3.3 Reasons for inter-state migration. Sources: Census 2011; PRS.

Poor implementation of protections under the Inter-State Migrant Workmen Act, 1979 (ISMW Act)

The ISMW Act provides certain protections for inter-state migrant workers. Labour contractors recruiting migrants are required to: (i) be licensed, (ii) register migrant workers with the government authorities, and (iii) arrange for the worker to be issued a passbook recording their identity. Guidelines regarding wages and protections (including accommodation, free medical facilities, protective clothing) to be provided by the contractor are also outlined in the law.

In December 2011, a report by the Standing Committee on Labour observed that the registration of workers under the ISMW Act was low and the implementation of protections outlined in the Act was poor. The report concluded that the central government had not made any concrete and fruitful efforts to ensure that contractors and employers mandatorily register the workers employed with them enabling access to benefits under the Act.

Lack of portability of benefits

Migrants registered to claim access to benefits at one location lose access upon migration to a different location. This is especially true of access to entitlements under the PDS. Ration cards required to access benefits under the PDS are issued by state governments and are not portable across states. This system excludes inter-state migrants from the PDS unless they surrender their card from the home state and get a new one from the host state.

Lack of affordable housing and basic amenities in urban areas

The proportion of migrants in the urban population is 47%.[1] In 2015, the Ministry of Housing and Urban Affairs identified migrants in urban areas as the largest population needing housing in cities. There is inadequate supply of low-income ownership and rental housing options. This leads to the spread of informal settlements and slums. The Prime Minister Awaas Yojana (PMAY) is a central government scheme to help the economically weaker section and low-income groups access housing. Assistance under the scheme includes: (i) slum rehabilitation, (ii) subsidised credit for home loans, (iii) subsidies up to Rs. 1.5 lakh to either construct a new house or enhance existing houses on their own, and (iv) increasing availability of affordable housing units in partnership with the private sector. Since housing is a state subject, there is variation in the approach of states towards affordable housing.[2]

Steps taken by the government with regard to migrant labour during the lockdown

During the lockdown, many inter-state migrant workers tried to return to their home states. Due to the suspension of public transport facilities, migrants started walking towards their home states on foot. Subsequently, buses and Shramik Special trains were permitted by the central government subject to coordination between states.[4,5] Between May 1 and June 3, more than 58 lakh migrants were transported through specially operated trains and 41 lakh were transported by road.

Measures taken by the government to aid migrants include

Transport

On March 28, the central government authorised states to use the State Disaster Response Fund to provide accommodation to travelling migrants. States were advised to set up relief camps along highways with medical facilities to ensure people stay in these camps while the lockdown is in place.

In an order issued on April 29, the Ministry of Home Affairs allowed states to coordinate individually to transport migrants using buses. On May 1, the Indian Railways resumed passenger movement (for the first time since March 22) with Shramik Special trains to facilitate the movement of migrants stranded outside their home states. Between May 1 and June 3, Indian Railways operated 4,197 Shramik trains transporting more than 58 lakh migrants. Top states from where Shramik trains originated were Gujarat and Maharashtra and states where the trains terminated were Uttar Pradesh and Bihar.[6] Note that these trends largely correspond to the migration patterns seen in the 2011 Census data.

Food distribution

On April 1, the Ministry of Health and Family Affairs directed state governments to operate relief camps for migrant workers with arrangements for food, sanitation, and medical services. On May 14, under the second tranche of the Aatma Nirbhar Bharat Abhiyaan, the Finance Minister announced that free food grains would be provided to migrant workers who did not have a ration card for two months. The measure is expected to benefit eight crore migrant workers and their families. The Finance Minister also announced that a One Nation One Ration card would be implemented by March 2021, to provide portable benefits under the PDS. This will allow access to rations from any Fair Price Shop in India.

Housing

The Aatma Nirbhar Bharat Abhiyaan also launched a scheme for Affordable Rental Housing Complexes for Migrant Workers and Urban Poor to provide affordable rental housing units under PMAY. The scheme proposes to use existing housing stock under the Jawaharlal Nehru National Urban Housing Mission (JnNURM) as well as incentivise public and private agencies to construct new affordable units for rent. Further, additional funds have been allocated for the credit-linked subsidy scheme under PMAY for the middle-income group.

Financial aid

Some state governments (like Bihar, Rajasthan, and Madhya Pradesh) announced one-time cash transfers for returning migrant workers. The UP government announced the provision of maintenance allowance of Rs. 1,000 for returning migrants who are required to quarantine.

Directions by the Supreme Court

The Supreme Court reviewed the situation of migrant labourers stranded in different parts of the country, noting inadequacies and lapses in the government response to the situation.

- On May 26, the Court issued an order to the central and state governments to submit a response detailing all measures taken by the respective governments for migrant labourers.
- On May 28, the Court provided interim directions to the central and state/UT governments for ensuring relief to the migrant workers: (i) no train or bus fare should be charged to migrant workers, (ii) free food should be provided to stranded migrants by the concerned state/UT government and this information should be publicised, (iii) states should simplify and speed up the process of registration of migrants for transport and those registered should be provided transportation as early as possible, and (iv) the state receiving migrants should provide last-mile transport, health screening, and other facilities free of cost.

- Reiterating their earlier directions, on June 5 (full order issued on June 9), the Supreme Court further directed the central and state/UT governments to ensure: (i) the transportation of all stranded workers wanting to return to their native place is completed within 15 days, (ii) the identification of migrant workers is immediately completed and the process of migrant registration be decentralised to police stations and local authorities, (iii) records of returning migrant labourers are kept including details about place of earlier employment and the nature of their skills, and (iv) counselling centres are set up at the block level to provide information about central and state government schemes and other avenues of employment. The Court also directed the state/UT governments to consider withdrawal of prosecution/complaints under Section 51 of the Disaster Management Act filed against migrant labourers who allegedly violated lockdown orders.

Notes

1 Reproduced with permission from www.prsindia.org. First published on June 10, 2020.
2 Census, 2011, Office of the Registrar General and Census Commissioner, Ministry of Home Affairs.
3 Report of Working Group on Migration, Ministry of Housing and Urban Poverty Alleviation, January 2017, http://mohua.gov.in/upload/uploadfiles/files/1566.pdf.
4 Order No. 40-3/2020-DM-I (A), Ministry of Home Affairs, April 29, 2020, https://prsindia.org/files/covid19/notifications/4233.IND_Movement_of_Persons_April_29.pdf.
5 Order No. 40-3/2020-DM-I (A), Ministry of Home Affairs, May 1, 2020, https://prsindia.org/files/covid19/notifications/IND_Special_Trains_May_1.jpeg.
6 "Indian Railways operationalizes 4197 'Shramik Special' trains till 3rd June, 2020 (0900hrs) across the country and transports more than 58 lacs passengers to their home states through "Shramik Special" trains since May 1", Press Information Bureau, Ministry of Railways, June 3, 2020, https://pib.gov.in/PressReleseDetail.aspx?PRID=1629043.

1.4 Labour Commissioner puts total number of migrant workers at 26 lakh, says 10% in relief camps[1]

Gaurav Vivek Bhatnagar

The information uploaded by the government does not provide several essential details on the background of migrant workers.

At a time when the Railways has stated that it has transported over 57 lakh migrant workers by Shramik Special trains, the office of the Chief Labour Commissioner of the Central government has put out data on its website which claims that there are only around 26 lakh migrant workers across the country.

The release of this data is important because Right to Information applications had been filed with the Ministry of Labour and Employment to learn of the status of migrant workers and how they are spread across India.

The Labour Commissioner has now, on his RTI page, published statewise figures on migrant workers and how around 10% of them have been staying in relief camps or shelters, around 43% were in-situ labour at workplaces, and about 46% were staying in other localities where migrants are clustered.

While the difference between the Railways' figure and that of the Labour Ministry may be attributed to the fact that the former has been counting the family members of the workers too in its tally, the two-page data released by the Labour Ministry points to the scale of the spread of migrant workers across the country.

Overall, it states that there are 2,597,218 migrant workers. An additional 20,000 are mentioned as workers in Maharashtra, taking the tally up to 2,617,218.

Chhattisgarh has over a million migrant workers

Of these workers, data reveals how a big chunk of nearly 10.85 lakh are in Chhattisgarh alone. The other states with a large number of migrant workers are Kerala at 2.86 lakh, Maharashtra at 2.01 lakh (including the additional 20,000), Tamil Nadu at 1.93 lakh, Telangana at 1.84 lakh, and Andhra Pradesh at a little over 1 lakh.

DOI: 10.4324/9781003291527-6

Other states or Union Territories with over 50,000 migrant workers include Odisha, Rajasthan, Karnataka, and Jammu and Kashmir.

The lower numbers of migrant workers in highly populous states like Uttar Pradesh (36,421), Bihar (7,719), Jharkhand (16,616), and Madhya Pradesh (9,621) indicate how they contribute to the presence of workers in other states and themselves lack much opportunity to witness an inflow of workers from other states.

Kerala has most workers staying in relief camps, shelter homes

When it comes to hosting migrant workers in relief camps or shelter homes, data reveals that Kerala provides such facilities to the largest number of 134,384 workers, which constitutes nearly 45% of its migrant work force. In Kerala, more than 1.07 lakh workers also stay at the work sites.

On the other hand, in states like Chhattisgarh, Telangana, Maharashtra, and Andhra Pradesh, the data reveals that very little arrangement has been made for the stay of migrant workers in relief camps and shelter homes. While in Maharashtra and Andhra Pradesh, a vast majority stayed at their workplaces themselves, in Chhattisgarh over 80% stayed in other localities while in Telangana they stayed both at the work sites and other clustered localities.

"Data can't answer all queries"

Appreciating that some data has been put out, RTI activist Venkatesh Nayak, of Commonwealth Human Rights Initiative, said it was nonetheless patchy and did not answer most of the queries that had been raised.

In his petition, filed on May 5 with the Central Information Commission, Nayak stated the Chief Labour Commissioner had issued an order on April 8 to all regional heads regarding the urgent collection of data about migrant workers.

He had thus asked for the state-wise names of districts from which data about the stranded migrant workers had been received, and also the district-wise numbers of male and female migrant workers belonging to categories mentioned in the Chief Labour Commissioner's order.

Nayak also sought the occupation-wise number of male and female migrant workers reported from each state as per the list of occupations and the sector-wise number of male and female migrant workers reported from each state as per the list of sectors.

He said that since only partial information has been uploaded, and that too without any dates on which it was collected, and without gender breakdown, he would be seeking further details.

Note

1 Reproduced with permission from *The Wire* where this article first appeared on June 5, 2020. https://thewire.in/labour/labour-ministry-migrant-workers-relief-camps.

Part 2

Abandoned by law

2.1 Why India's legal and labour system needs to be reconfigured to really help migrant workers[1]

Satvik Varma

Those who argued that migrant workers could take recourse to the many existing Central government schemes for relief need only see the current humanitarian crisis to understand why this logic is flawed.

Until very recently, most Indians were unaware of a statute titled the Inter-State Migrant Workmen (Regulation of Employment and Conditions of Service) Act, 1979.

At the time the Act was introduced, these "*dadan*" (those towards whom charity is done) labourers were recruited by contractors to work on large construction projects with no fixed working hours. Aside from being ill-treated, often, they weren't even paid.

Since existing laws were inadequate, new legislation was promulgated with the object and reasons stating that

> the inter-State migrant workmen are generally illiterate, unorganised, and have normally to work under extremely adverse conditions and in view of these hardships, some administrative and legislative arrangements both in the State from where they are recruited and also in the State where they are engaged for work are necessary to secure effective protection against their exploitation.

It's one thing to have a law, and altogether a different matter for it to be effectively implemented. As witnessed by the recent hardships which the migrant labourers confronted, our law and correspondingly the legal system failed these voiceless citizens. But it's really the collective failure of our society. The government, law enforcement agencies, businesses, and civil society have all let down this section of Indians who have been termed the "builders of our booming economy".

DOI: 10.4324/9781003291527-8

Lure of migration

Before examining the provisions of the Act, which could have come to the rescue of these migrants, let us look at some data which will also detail that they are by no means insignificant. According to the 2011 Census, India has 5.6 crore inter-state migrants, most of whom come from the Hindi-speaking belt of Uttar Pradesh, Bihar, Jharkhand, Rajasthan, and Madhya Pradesh. A majority of such migrants work in the informal/unorganised sector; a large number are daily wagers and very few have any form of a valid identity card, given their transient existence. Notably, while the number of inter-state migrants grew by 55% between the 1991 and 2001 Census, it decreased by 33% between the 2001 and 2011 Census. While most migration is to states like Delhi and Maharashtra, termed "*sapno ki nagri*" (dream cities), owing to them being the hub of commercial activity, between 2001 and 2011, there was a steady increase in the movement of migrants to other destinations within their own states and sometimes even to other locations within the same district. But in recent years, these migrants were once again drawn towards the "*bada shehar*" (big city).

The contractors who lure these migrants, enticing them with the promise of fulfilling their dreams, are required under the Act to obtain a license from an authority both of the state to which the workman belongs (home state), as well as the one in which they are proposed to be employed (host state). Establishments hiring them are also required to obtain a certificate of registration before employing them. The Act stipulates that the license may contain conditions regarding the arrangements under which the inter-state migrant will be recruited, the remuneration payable, hours of work, fixation of wages, and other essential amenities to be provided. There is an explicit provision regarding the wages to be paid to these migrant workmen, the date from which they are due, and their entitlement to a displacement allowance. Suitable residential accommodation, adequate medical facilities, and protective clothing are also amongst what is to be provided.

The Act lays down provisions for the appointment of inspectors by the appropriate government, and inspectors from the home state may visit the establishments where these workmen are employed in the host state to ensure compliance. Punishment for non-compliance is fairly stringent and includes imprisonment. Regrettably, most inter-state migrant workmen aren't even aware of their rights and those who dare raise questions risk losing employment, as well as their wages, as the contractor usually keeps them on a hand-to-mouth existence.

With a view to streamlining existing labour laws, the Occupational Safety, Health And Working Conditions Code, 2019, was introduced in the Lok Sabha in July 2019.[2] This code subsumes and replaces 13 labour laws, including the Act, and, amongst others, attempts to strengthen migrant labour rights. It provides that where any establishment is employing migrant labour through a contractor who is required to obtain a licence, but who has not done so, then the migrant labour so engaged through the contractor shall be deemed to be employed by the principal employer. It reiterates the provisions relating to the entitlement of migrant workers to receive a displacement allowance equal to 50% of the monthly wages payable to them.

The code was referred to a standing committee towards the end of 2019. In February 2020, the committee made its report and on the issue of migrant labour noted the unanimous view of the state governments and the labour ministry that an exclusive chapter on migrant workers be introduced in the Code, notwithstanding the special provisions currently referred to in it. The committee also noted that the Code should have initiatives similar to those adopted by Odisha for migrant workers such as a toll-free Shramik (labour force) Sahayata Helpline, Migrant Labour Help Desk, seasonal hostels for the children of migrant workers, strengthening Anti-Human Trafficking Units, and the setting up of migration support centres.

Laws not enforced

If the law is there, then why was it not implemented? If the migrants are entitled to a dislocation allowance, then why was it not given to them? In fact, why were even the monies due to them not paid? If the contractor who hires them is to be licensed, then how did he disappear, deserting them and leaving them to fend for themselves? Why were health facilities and other basic amenities not provided? If even some of this would have happened, then we may have been able to hold back these workers from embarking on the journey back home. The answer is that the Act is in many ways obsolete and hardly enforced anywhere. One may wonder how that is even possible, but that is the harsh reality.

Aajeevika Bureau, an agency that provides "services, security and solutions for migrant workers", states that

> a serious constraint in framing an effective policy [for migrants] is the lack of credible data on incidence of seasonal migration. Census and NSS that have a significant impact on policy making are unable to capture seasonal and circular migration. Migrants may also be missed out in BPL Surveys. Above all, they are unable to participate in the formal electoral system and are denied a fundamental citizenship right – their right to vote.

So while the data, from the Census noted above, records them as a numerical percentage, their interests are largely ignored. Those who pontificate that no migrant worker was left starving and could take recourse to many of the government schemes need a dose of reality.

Indus Action, a policy implementation organisation that seeks to bridge the gap between law and action, conducted a survey over a month during the lockdown across 15 major states, involving 3400 families, speaking with over 11,000 migrant workers from various districts, and found that 19% of those surveyed didn't have enough food to satisfy their hunger. Their report notes that

> majority of others reported having limited food stock ... Although eligible for free ration, some of them are forced to buy ration, prices being double/triple the normal rates due to a complete shutdown of ration shops and inaccessibility. A part of those who were able to access ration using ration cards has complained about receiving a lesser portion than what they were eligible for. Instances of only rice being distributed have also surfaced; Dal, oil, sugar (other ration items) remain out of reach for many ... Access to vegetables, milk, and kerosene (not included in ration) poses another challenge.

As someone commented, they wanted rations, not Bhashan (speech).[3]

Another survey conducted by Stranded Workers Action Network reported that the rate of hunger and distress exceeded the rate of relief. This network also spoke with over 11,000 migrants and found that a large number were on the brink of starvation, sometimes not having eaten for 4 days and often with just 1 day's worth of rations remaining.[4] Their survey also revealed that with 89% not having received salaries or payments, 78% had less than Rs. 300 on their person. Their kids often didn't have milk, and the migrants had to resort to feeding them sugar water.

Of course, no one is to blame for the pandemic. But can the same be said about the ensuing humanitarian crisis? It brought to the fore the pre-existing vulnerabilities of our labour workforce and the shortcoming of our labour laws. And for the migrant worker, it stole their dignity. Scores of civil society folks doing good work have shared stories that the migrants didn't want charity. They just wanted their due share. Let us just accept that we collectively failed in giving them that.

As regards the various schemes rolled out by the government, Indus Action reported their reach as "questionable". Ninety-four per cent of the surveyed families were eligible for at least one benefit scheme, but the survey notes that nearly 20% of them did not receive any benefit. Indus notes that "this worrying trend can be credited to Aadhar linkage problems and mobile numbers of the stakeholders not registered with banks". So, while we were all worried about the novel coronavirus, the migrant worker, who witnessed near starvation, was also plagued by worries about his future. Rightly so, Indus's survey observed that "48% of the respondents will be unemployed post lockdown". And those employable will be willing to put their dreams on hold for a while, being in no rush to return to the big cities which treated them with disdain.

Course correction needed

From a legal perspective, some course correction can be to share the lessons from the present crises with the standing committee considering the

Code or have the issues taken up in Rajya Sabha before it finally becomes a law. Amongst others, what can be incorporated in the chapter proposed for migrant workers are some suggestions of the Aajeevika Bureau. These include schemes like the universalisation of PDS (as proposed by the government) and the elimination of domicility-based eligibility criteria, providing safe and hygienic shelter facilities. Provision also must be made for the security of single women migrants, and allowing migrant groups to live together with their communities. These circular workers must also have access to urban healthcare systems, and the new legislation must entirely remove the burden of providing documentation from migrant communities.

For now, and understandably, these migrants have no faith in the system and are justified in looking at us with doubt. In due course, and let us manage our expectations on the time-line, when their measly savings, if any, are exhausted, chances are the migrants will eventually be compelled to return to the same cities where their dreams turned to nightmares. They may even be the "bigger person" and forgive us for how we treated them. But let us not forget what happened. It will be a reflection of our moral compass if, going forward, we as a nation and as a society, in our own microcosm, don't treat our labour force with the respect they deserve. Or extend to them the protection which our laws and the legal system must give them. If extending to them fair and equitable treatment sounds like it reeks of concepts from public international law or just too utopian, can we at least be humane. Or is that also expecting too much?

Notes

1 Reproduced with permission from *The Wire* where this article first appeared on May 19, 2020. https://thewire.in/labour/india-labour-legal-system-migrant-workers
2 "Occupational Safety, Health and Working Conditions Code, 2019", *PRS India*. Retrieved from https://prsindia.org/billtrack/the-occupational-safety-health-and-working-conditions-code-2019, last accessed on October 26, 2021.
3 Pranav Bonde, "How are 'THEY' faring amidst the Lockdown?", *Indus Action Blog*, May 16, 2020. Retrieved from https://www.indusaction.org/blog/how-are-they-faring-amidst-the-lockdown, last accessed on October 26, 2021.
4 "Stranded Migrants Hadn't Been Paid Wages During Lockdown Period, Report", *Business Standard*. Retrieved from https://www.business-standard.com/article/economy-policy/89-stranded-migrants-hadn-t-been-paid-wages-during-lockdown-period-report-120041700786_1.html, last accessed on October 26, 2021.

2.2 COVID-19 crisis exposes India's neglect of informal workers[1]

Jenny Sulfath and Balu Sunilraj

It is up to forces aligned with labour to change a system that is geared to exploit workers.

Several post-lockdown incidents have highlighted the plight of workers, who have been left to their own devices, without any state support, and forced to travel hundreds of kilometres to their homes. In the most recent episode, 16 migrants attempting to return home were run over by a train in Aurangabad.

The common thread that connects them is their dependence on the informal economy. However, two other things cannot be overlooked. First, their life before the pandemic was relentlessly back breaking. Second, the post-lockdown distress[2] which workers in the informal economy are facing has to do with structural factors that define the sector—unequal power relations, lack of job security, and absence of regulatory mechanisms. In the face of a crisis, it explodes, destroying the lives of many.

Informal economy: its size, role, and roots

India's informal economy is enormous. It consists of export-driven industrial clusters, manufacturing hubs, enterprises which deal with precious gems, a vast majority of agrarian production, street vendors, and a large part of the black economy. Estimates for 2018 indicate that 80% of India's 461 million workers, or 369 million of them, are in the informal sector.[3] Even in the formal sector, many workers are employed as informal workers, as casual labour.

Despite islands of prosperity such as the diamond-cutters—who live in conditions comparable with workers in the formal economy—for a large number of informal-sector workers, domestic and work spaces converge into one. These workers either eat and live at their place of work or their work is conducted in congested domestic spaces. Unlike the formal sector, there is no regulation of wages, living conditions, working hours,[4] or other social security nets. Due to their paltry wages, occupational multiplicity is the only way many workers can make ends meet.

DOI: 10.4324/9781003291527-9

Scholars have pointed out that the formal-informal duality should not let one lose sight of the continuum between the two: the informal economy plays an active role in the functioning of the formal economy, for it is symbiotically linked to big businesses, which subcontract and outsource cheap informal labour.

Now, how has the informal economy come to occupy such prominence? Scholars have pointed to the development trajectory of the post-colonial Indian state to explain this phenomenon. They find that budget deficits were the norm for the rural underclass, as a direct result of the development trajectory of Indian capitalism. The urban-rural mobility in the industrial West is characterised by "free labour" deciding for itself how and where to sell its labour-power; but this has proven non-applicable to the post-colonial Indian situation. In particular, because of the absence of land reforms, the only option for the Indian rural poor was to migrate (including as bonded and neo-bonded labour) in order to survive.

Second, labour legislations which were passed immediately after Independence were mainly designed to define the industrial procedures and to solve disputes between employers and workers. These legislations exclusively addressed labour and employment in the organised sector. These laws were designed mainly with the hope of expanding into an industrial society, even if the size of this sector was always minuscule compared to the economy as a whole. As a result of diminished attention to a great segment of the urban population and neglect of the social relations of production in agriculture, the process of informalisation was accentuated.

To sum up, informalisation—which ensured a precarious existence for the vast majority of workers left at the mercy of their employers and contractors—should be understood against its background in the post-colonial development trajectory of our country.

Asymmetrical power relations, toothless legal protection, and the impact of the COVID-19 lockdown

The asymmetrical power relations which define the informal economy are also apparent in the legal framework which covers it. On the one hand, laws specifically formulated to deal with labour in the informal economy often overlook certain key questions regarding the target group. Second, even when the text of the law is honestly intended, the implementation is significantly influenced by existing social power relations, which are skewed against informal labour. It is this entrenched powerlessness that has had a decisive impact on the informal labourers during the lockdown.

For instance, only enterprises which have employed 20 or more contract labourers over the previous 12 months come under the ambit of the Contract Labour (Regulation and Abolition) Act, 1970. Micro-enterprises in India regularly employ less than 20 people; therefore, despite its progressive components, a large number of employees of informal enterprises remain outside the purview of this law. Concerning implementation, large-scale corruption due to the collision of the state with contractors and the absence of sufficient state capacity to implement the Act has made it ineffective in many places. Despite flaws in this law, if implemented properly, its provisions could have enabled the government to access data on contract labourers and provide them assistance during the lockdown.

Similarly, the stated objective of the Interstate Migrant Workmen Act, 1979, is to regulate and lay down the conditions of service of inter-state migrant workers. This Act mandates the registration of contractors who employ migrant workers and for employers to maintain a record of their workers. However, by design itself, it excludes a vast majority of self-employed wage labourers and intra-state agrarian and other migrants in the informal economy.

The 2011–12 report of the Standing Committee on Labour records that 11 states do not have a single employer or contractor registered under this Act. The highest numbers of registered contractors and principal employers under the Act were in Bihar, but the figures were as low as 20 and 56 respectively. If reviewed and implemented correctly, this law would have made it much easier for the government to assist migrant workers during the lockdown. Unfortunately, that was not the case.

The rare progressive legislation, such as the Building and Other Construction Workers (Regulation of Employment and Conditions of Service) Act, 1996 (BOCW), acknowledges the seasonality and precarious nature of employment and defines anyone who worked in the construction industry for 90 days in the past year as a construction worker. This law makes registered establishments responsible for providing housing and child care facilities to workers and obliges state construction boards to register workers as beneficiaries of several welfare measures. However, each worker needs the employer or a trade union to certify them as a construction worker to avail of these benefits. The lived reality of a large section of informal workers is overlooked by this legislation—they keep migrating from place to place and are largely non-unionised and undocumented.

Further, a recent study conducted by Jan Sahas finds that only 29% of the 20.37 lakh labourers registered under the BOCW Board in Uttar Pradesh had access to a bank account. Predictably, the study also finds that more than 90% of the construction workers they interviewed were outside the ambit of this Act since they did not have BOCW cards. In this situation, the central government directive to the state governments to use the collected BOCW cess funds to aid workers during the lockdown becomes toothless.

Another Act, the Unorganised Sector Workers Social Security Act, 2008 (USSA), mandates the registration of unorganised workers—including home-based workers—by state social security boards as beneficiaries of several schemes. As many schemes under this Act already exist and overlap with other target populations, there is no database to assess the registration of informal workers.

A PIL filed in 2013 in the Jharkhand High Court by the National Domestic Workers Welfare Trust points out that the entire state of Jharkhand had not registered a single beneficiary under the Master Craft Persons scheme, one of the ten schemes covered by the USSA. So while the Act professes to protect the rights of unorganised workers, its vague directives and the state's lack of will in registering workers result in many exclusions.

During the lockdown, several states started surveying their migrants. Had there been specific schemes for informal workers, coupled with the will to register them as beneficiaries in the states, and clear directions in the Act to fund the state boards, the system would have been better equipped to deal with this crisis.

The existing legal discourse is, at least theoretically, guided by a vision of welfare, but the guiding principle of the ongoing labour "reforms" is simply "Ease of Doing Business". The recently passed code on wages, for example, allows a state government to "fix the number of hours of work which shall constitute a normal working day", without adopting a weekly limit on working hours. The earlier Minimum Wages (Central) Rules, 1950, had specified that a normal working week will comprise 48 hours of work.

The consequence of changing these provisions will strip even the formal-economy workers of the rights they previously enjoyed, while depriving informal workers of the bargaining power to negotiate their working hours and wages. The culmination of such a draconian wage code is that several states are issuing ordinances to extend working hours.

It is in this context that we must place the plight of informal labourers during the lockdown. The government's post-lockdown directives, like many of the aforementioned Acts, have honest intentions, at least on paper: for instance, a Ministry of Home Affairs order dated 29 March categorically states that wages must be paid to all workers. It should be noted that this order was issued five days after the lockdown announcement, true to the history of insensitivity shown towards informal labourers. Several states asked employers to ensure the needs of workers were met.

However, in an environment marked by unequal power relations, widespread governmental apathy, and insufficient infrastructure, miracles cannot be expected. In many states, even if they had wanted to carry out this task, there was almost no data to rely upon due to loopholes in different Acts and their incapacitated implementation thus far.

The way forward

From workers walking for days to reach home to the long queues for a single meal, the COVID-19 crisis has reiterated the perilous situation of informal workers. Neither their rights as labourers nor their rights to state welfare are adequately addressed by the existing approach. Only a radically altered development model, which addresses the conditions that foment informalisation, can ameliorate these conditions. These would include significant investment in agriculture, ensuring stable livelihoods in the villages to prevent the hunt for precarious jobs by the rural masses; formulating new state policies that address the increased dependence on metropolises; and increasing state capacity to implement existing laws covering the informal sector.

But all these measures would require the principle of equity as a guiding force of state policy. Unfortunately, the opposite has been the case. Several states have issued ordinances to weaken existing labour laws, thereby deepening the precarious existence of informal labourers. The task at hand, therefore, is a political one. As this crisis continues and the state turns a blind eye to the suffering of workers, forces aligned with labour have no option but to take up this task.

Notes

1 Reproduced with permission from *Newsclick.in* where this article first appeared on May 12, 2020. 1. https://www.newsclick.in/Covid-19-Crisis-Exposes-India-Neglect-Informal-Workers.

2 See, Death of Migrant Workers, COVID-19 Update and More, *NewsClick,* May 8, 2020. Retrieved from https://www.newsclick.in/death-migrant-workers-covid-19-update-and-more, last accessed on October 27, 2021.

3 National Statistical Office (2019) "Annual Report: Periodic Labour Survey 2017–18," Ministry of Statistics and Programme Implementation, Government of India, New Delhi.

4 Rabindra Nath Sinha, "Migrant, Unorganised Workers Acts Worst Examples of Disregard: Labour Unions Told NewsClick That They Are Considering Going to Court over the Extension in Working Hours", May 8, 2020. Retrieved from https://www.newsclick.in/Migrant-Unorganised-Workers-Acts-Worst-Examples-Disregard, last accessed on October 27, 2021.

2.3 National Commission for Women

Advisory to address needs of internal women migrants in India during COVID-19 lockdown

Editor's note: The National Commission for Women (NCW) issued comprehensive guidelines on the protection of the rights of migrant women during the pandemic. However, it is not known if the NCW itself monitored whether these guidelines were followed by the states or the states took the advisory seriously.

The COVID-19 epidemic has affected many countries and the World Health Organization has declared it a "pandemic". The Government of India (GOI) has been taking several proactive preventive and mitigating measures to contain the spread of this virus early on. The announcement of a 21-day lockdown by the Honourable Prime Minister came in the wake of this outbreak to enable "social distancing", an effective non-pharmaceutical prevention and control intervention. The far-sighted and unprecedented step of lockdown, however, saw a large-scale movement of migrant workers across the country due to a lack of livelihood, food, and shelter.

The National Commission for Women is aware that the Government of India has been relentlessly working for the welfare of these migrants and checking of any exodus during this lockdown. The Commission, being the apex statutory body working for women's empowerment in the country, deems itself duty-bound to propose certain interventions in light of its mandate.

In these testing times, it is extremely pertinent to respect the dignity and fundamental rights of all migrant women and girls by ensuring food, safety, shelter, and health care. India is established as a welfare state by the Constitution and is responsible for the social security of its citizens through the Directive Principle of State Policy. Articles 39, 42, and 47 of the Constitution are dedicated to ensuring social security including appropriate health care, food, shelter, and safety to its citizens, especially workers.

Since women are the most adversely affected in situations of crisis, it becomes extremely pivotal that the safety and security of women migrants

DOI: 10.4324/9781003291527-10

are ensured. In view of this, the Commission issues this advisory on April 7, 2020 to address the following needs of "Internal Women Migrants in India During COVID-19 Lockdown".

1. Food
2. Shelter/accommodation
3. Safety and security (from gender-based violence)
4. Health
5. Mental health
6. Hygiene

Food

a. Ensure migrant women and girls have access to nutritious food prepared in hygienic conditions and safe drinking water. The free provision of essential food and medicines to be ensured for migrant women irrespective of their entitlement or registration status.
b. Ensure provisions like cooking oil, other essential food items, and cooking fuel to all migrant women and girls.
c. The government should work towards identifying marginalised migrant workers and provide an uninterrupted supply of essential commodities to them, in particular, door-to-door ration delivery should be arranged keeping in view the WHO and Ministry of Health and Family Welfare (MoH&FW) guidelines on sanitisation and hygiene in place.

Shelter/accommodation

a. Family separation should be avoided as much as possible when reallocating accommodation due to crisis, and children should not be left unaccompanied.
b. Ensure that migrant women and girls do not live in congested arrangements that heighten their vulnerability to COVID-19 infection.
c. Inspect accommodation facilities provided by industrial units to women and girls regularly or as needed. For those migrant workers living in employer-provided accommodation, ensure the provision of information and promote practices to prevent infection including physical distancing and [protection] from being forcibly evicted.
d. Any temporary shelter home arranged by the Government must ensure that women migrants can live there with dignity and that it maintains their adequate privacy by ensuring access to appropriate and safe sanitation facilities.
e. Ensure the distribution of sanitary napkins and special provision for lactating women in temporary shelters.

Safety and security (protection from gender-based violence and harassment)

a. Ensure that mechanisms are in place and human resources are ready at the central, state, district, and local levels to respond to incidences of violence and harassment at central, state, district and local levels.
b. Helplines to be set up or publicised widely with an adequate number of counsellors to help women in distress.
c. State Legal Services Authority (SLSA) and District Legal Services Authority (DLSA) may provide legal aid to women by phone and mail. They may also work towards providing a list of lawyers working at home under their legal aid programme.
d. Ensure the availability of shelters for those escaping from violence and harassment.
e. Any such incident should be immediately reported and addressed preferably by women police officers.
f. Strict action against any form of police excess on women and children to be taken by the appropriate government.
g. Ensure availability of local grievance redressal mechanisms for migrants especially women migrants that are accessible and inclusive in terms of language and distance.

Health care

a. Ensure women migrants' access to medical care including mental health care, medicines, and other health care services depending on their health situation, including health care for children.
b. Mobile COVID screening units may be deployed in major residential pockets/shelters of migrants, for regular screening services for symptoms and also providing health care.
c. Ensure women's reproductive health including access to maternal care and other pre-natal and post-natal emergencies that may arise.
d. Urban Health Centres should reach out to migrant clusters for medical care and other health care facilities.
e. Supply of contraceptives and sanitary napkins should be flagged as essential services that ought to be available to every woman. They should be provided from door to door, in vulnerable communities and as part of ration supplies.

Mental health

a. Address specific trauma (including violence and harassment, managing unwanted pregnancies, abortions, miscarriages, and deliveries) through mental health interventions and psycho-social services where possible through helplines and physical help desks.

b. Ensure that women migrants have access to means of communication to communicate with their families and relative, places of origin, etc.

Hygiene (water and sanitation facilities)

a. Ensure that the sanitation facility is made safe and accessible for 24 hours while ensuring privacy and access to menstrual hygiene.
b. Ensure free provision of sanitary napkins and toiletries (soaps and sanitisers) to maintain hygiene. Handmade masks may also be provided.
c. Ensure availability of running water.

Quarantine measures

a. A gender-responsive and child-sensitive protocol should be designed, adopted, and implemented with regards to the separation of children from mothers who are infected and in the absence of other family members.

Role of government authorities (central, state, and local authorities)

a. Sensitise, train, and inform government officials at all levels who have to specifically provide services to migrant women and girls for their specific needs. The [training] topic should cover but not be limited to human rights, non-discrimination, violence, and harassment prevention and response.
b. Ensure that migrant women and girls have access to or are supported through all procedures such as registration with local authorities.
c. Government authorities should ensure the availability and decent working conditions of officials, volunteers, and health care workers who speak the language of the migrants to provide assurance and informed support and guidance to migrant women and girls.
d. Governments should carry out a quick survey/identification of migrants to assess the number of women and adolescent workers (with family and without family) for planning and ensuring benefits to the women and girls in an adequate and timely manner. Civil Society Organisations (CSOs) can be actively involved in this exercise for maximum outreach.
e. Ensure coordination between Government authorities at all levels within State Government, amongst states and between State and Central Governments on all aspects of the protection of women migrant workers including providing them with adequate access to basic relief measures and decent quarantine conditions as per the Government's Advisories and orders.

f. Governments at all levels should collaborate with each other and with workers' organisations, employers' organisations, civil society organisations, medical health providers, media, recruitment agencies, and other relevant stakeholders to ensure the safety of migrant women and girls
g. A special task force may be set up to document hardships faced by women migrant workers and to ensure that they receive benefits during and after the lockdown period.

Specific advisory for certain groups of women migrants

a. Women migrants from the north-east working in several states and cities outside the north-east region have been reported to face harassment due to their physical features identifying the contagion/COVID crisis to their community. Law for the prevention of atrocities should therefore be widely publicised and immediate action be taken against offender(s). Any such racist violence has to be discouraged with positive messaging by the Government.
b. State Governments must ensure nutritious meals for pregnant and lactating women, health checks for pregnant women, supply of medicines and health care for pregnant women, and provisions for safe deliveries. Health care for new-born babies and provisions for their nutrition must be provided.
c. Keeping in view the urgency and significance of the matter, the Commission requests support from all concerned ministries and State Government/authorities copied herein for effective implementation of this advisory.

2.4 How the Supreme Court and the High Courts have dealt with the worst migrant crisis faced by the nation[1]

Ejaz Maqbool, Akriti Chaubey, and Mohammad Isa Hakim

The High Courts have been comparatively more sensitive than the apex court to the humanitarian crisis caused by the sudden lockdown imposed by the coronavirus. Several High Courts tried to hold the states to account on the migrant crisis and the measures taken to mitigate their suffering. However, they are handicapped because they cannot coordinate with the state government. This is a task that the Supreme Court is capable of as it has all-India jurisdiction.

In our country's efforts to contain the COVID-19 pandemic, the migrant labourer has paid a huge, painful price. While on one hand, the government has managed the pandemic commendably and has even come forward to support businesses, the migrant worker, who is the very essence of these institutions, has remained largely ignored.

It is ironic that for a virus which was brought into the country by the rich and the privileged, it is the poor worker who is walking hundreds of miles on foot in scorching heat, dying of starvation, and getting killed in accidents.

It is deeply unfortunate that despite having a glorious tradition of commitment to social justice, we have failed the poorest of our society. The government should have considered deployment of the Army to contain the migrant crisis since the present situation is akin to a war and is reminiscent of the 1947 Partition.

The Supreme Court has never shirked from resolving the common man's problems, be it pollution issues or human rights issues. However, migrants have thus far faced only disappointment, as the apex court dismissed plea after plea, maintaining a policy of non-interference.

The question at the moment is whether the *suo motu* cognisance taken by the Court on May 26, two months after the migrant crisis came to the fore, is delayed. Did the Supreme Court grant too much leeway to the government? The answer to these questions is not possible without examining the manner in which the Supreme Court has treated the various petitions that were filed before it.

DOI: 10.4324/9781003291527-11

Mahua Moitra v. Union of India [dismissed on April 13]

When the Supreme Court took *suo motu* cognisance of a letter written by Lok Sabha MP Mahua Moitra, it seemed like a ray of hope. The letter highlighted the plight of migrant workers and appealed that unless a serious and immediate intervention was made by Executive agencies, thousands would perish from starvation and lakhs more will face the risk of contracting and spreading the COVID-19 virus.

She urged the Supreme Court to take notice of this grave humanitarian crisis and sought directions to the Executive agencies to make arrangements for these workers and ensure that their employers provide them full wages, food rations, and shelter till the crisis abates.

However, the hope was short lived, as the Court dismissed the petition on April 13, without giving any reasons.

Harsh Mander & Anr. v. Union of India & Anr. [disposed of on April 21]

This petition sought directions to the Central and state governments to ensure payments of wages/minimum wages to all the migrant workers. On April 3, when the matter was taken up, the Supreme Court directed the Union to respond to the petition. On April 7, the matter was again taken up and it was directed that it would be listed on April 13 and the Union would meanwhile provide a copy of the status report to the petitioners. According to several news reports, it was on this date that a rather strange question was put to Prashant Bhushan, counsel for the petitioners. CJI SA Bobde reportedly asked:

> *"If they are being provided meals, then why do they need money for meals?"*

Thereafter, on April 21, when the matter was finally heard, Bhushan intimated to the Court that despite governmental measures, thousands of labourers still lacked access to basic amenities. Solicitor General Tushar Mehta responded by saying that various measures were already in place to address the issue of migrant workers including a helpline number where people could report issues concerning the implementation at the ground level. Relying on the government's statement at face value, the Court disposed of the writ petition by observing as follows:

> Taking into consideration the material placed before us, we call upon the respondent-Union of India to look into such material and take such steps as it finds fit to resolve the issues raised in the petition.

Swami Agnivesh & Anr. v. Union of India & Ors. [disposed of on April 21]

Swami Agnivesh filed a plea seeking immediate relief to the poor, informal sector workers, slum dwellers, homeless, and economically weaker sections living in hunger during the COVID-19 lockdown. It was alleged in the petition that the government hardly made any provision for providing basic humanitarian aid and emergency services for the poor for the period of lockdown.

It was also mentioned in the petition that the Central and state governments took the initiative for providing relief packages, but the feedback from the ground was that this relief mainly remained on paper. It was further mentioned that thousands of workers had begun walking from different parts of Delhi towards the Uttar Pradesh border and that there were no feeding centres, drinking water facilities, etc. It was also mentioned that in the existing shelter homes, thousands of people had gathered in the hope of finding food and water.

Again, on April 21, the Supreme Court disposed of the matter after recording the statement of the Solicitor General that the aspects highlighted in the petition would be looked into and if necessary, the government would issue requisite directions.

Aruna Roy & Anr. v. Union of India & Anr. [matter directed to be listed two weeks after the lockdown]

This Public Interest Litigation (PIL) was filed seeking directions for the payment of wages to workers under the Mahatma Gandhi National Rural Employment Guarantee Act (MNREGA) during the lockdown and issuance of temporary cards to all migrants who had been able to return to their villages. It is relevant to note that this is one of the few petitions which is still pending and has not been disposed of by the Supreme Court yet.

However, the order which has been passed effectively disposes of the petition. On April 8, the Court simply recorded the submission of the Solicitor General that an amount of Rs. 6,800 has been paid towards arrears of wages and directed that the matter be listed two weeks after the lockdown.

Alakh Alok Srivastava v. Union of India [disposed of on April 3]

On March 31, the Supreme Court heard two more writ petitions filed for redressal of grievances of migrant labourers in different parts of the country. In these petitions, the petitioners highlighted the plight of migrant workers who were walking hundreds of kilometres from their work places to their villages/towns. On March 30, the Union was directed to submit its response. Subsequently, when the matter was taken up on March 31, the Union had filed a status report.

The Centre claimed that the mass migration had stopped and that all the migrant workers who were on the road had been shifted to relief camps/shelter homes set up at various points in each state/union territory.

The Court lamented the proliferation of fake news as the reason for the panic which caused migration and directed the media to publish the official version of developments, made available by the government in the form of a daily bulletin. Here also, the statement of the Solicitor General was simply recorded where he ensured that trained counsellors and/or community group leaders of all faiths would visit the relief camps/shelter to deal with the issues faced by migrants.

The matter was ultimately disposed of on April 27, and the guidelines contained in the order dated March 31 were to continue.

Jagdeep S Chhokar & Anr. v. Union of India [disposed of on May 5]

This plea was filed for a direction to the Union to allow migrant workers across the country to return to their hometowns after conducting necessary testing for COVID-19 and to arrange for their safe travel. On April 27, the Court directed the Solicitor General to place on record the proposed protocol, if any, for the movement of migrant workers between states. Ultimately, the matter was disposed of on May 5, since the government had permitted the movement of migrant workers and was also starting Shramik Special Trains for them.

It was observed that the substantial part of the prayer was taken care of and though the government had directed the migrant workers to pay 15% of the train fare, it was not for the Supreme Court to issue any directions in that regard under Article 32.

Sagheer Ahmed Khan v. Union of India [notice issued on May 15]

This petition was filed by a migrant lawyer who is currently practising before the Bombay High Court. In this petition, it was highlighted that the nationwide lockdown had caused a large exodus of migrant workers. The petitioner himself, being a migrant from Sant Kabir Nagar in Uttar Pradesh, sought urgent directions for the provision of suitable arrangements to repatriate the migrants belonging to his district by arranging train(s) or any other mode of transportation from Mumbai.

He expressed willingness to personally deposit a sum of Rs. 25 lakh with the Supreme Court for the safe repatriation of these migrants, who belonged to his hometown.

On May 15, the Supreme Court issued notice in the said matter, returnable in two weeks' time.

It is concerning to read such orders, where matters have been casually disposed of, placing over-reliance on the assurance of the learned Solicitor General. In one of the petitions, the Court has even recorded that there are no migrants on the roads merely based on a statement by the government. The most basic right to life of the poor migrants is being crushed on a daily basis, while petitions are disposed of in a routine manner.

It bears clarification that the Executive must be given some additional elbow room while it is dealing with a global pandemic of the present nature. However, when the failure of the State is so apparent, the Court could have played a major role in verifying its claims, monitoring the process, and holding the government accountable for its failures.

Response of High Courts

In comparison to the Supreme Court, the High Courts till now have been much more sensitive and forthcoming in dealing with the humanitarian crisis. Some of the recent orders are summarised below.

Karnataka, Gujarat, and Tamil Nadu

Mohammed Arif Jameel v. Union of India [orders dated May 12, 18, and 21]

A remarkable order which has received praise from eminent jurists like Fali Nariman, the order of the Karnataka High Court dated May 12 deserves to be discussed. In the controversy surrounding fares of the special trains arranged by the government to repatriate migrant workers, the High Court made strong observations against the state government's refusal to bear the cost. The High Court directed the state government to immediately take a decision on the issue, while observing,

> Prima facie, it appears to us that considering the constitutional rights of the migrant workers, no one should be deprived of an opportunity to go back to his own State only for the reason that he has no capacity to pay for the transport. The reason is that inability to pay is due to loss of livelihood.
>
> (Karnataka HC)

A day after the Karnataka High Court directed it to clarify its stand on whether it will bear the cost of travel for outgoing migrants amid the COVID-19 lockdown, the state government decided to do so.

Suo Motu *v. State of Gujarat [orders dated May 11 and 14]*

The High Court of Gujarat had registered a *suo motu* petition in the wake of COVID-19 on March 13. On May 11, the High Court issued fresh notice to the state, after taking cognisance of certain news reports which showed the extreme suffering of migrant workers in the state on account of the lockdown. The Court sought a reply from the state with the following observation:

> We would not like to interfere with the day-to-day functioning of the State Government in this regard, but, at the same time, we should ensure that the situation does not go from very bad to worst. In such circumstances, the judiciary will have to intervene.

On May 14, the Court took note of various measures taken by the state, but also sought a reply on the steps taken to ensure the repatriation of migrant workers without charging money, or providing them with food and necessary facilities if they chose to stay.

AP Suryaprakasam v. Superintendent of Police [order dated May 15]

While hearing Habeas Corpus petitions of 400 migrant workers from Tamil Nadu who were detained in Maharashtra, the High Court of Madras expressed its anguish at the lack of coordination and cooperation between the Central and the state governments to provide necessary aid to the migrant workers. The Court strongly criticised the near-complete abdication of responsibility by the governments in dealing with the sufferings of the migrant workers:

> It is not only the duty of the native State of the migrant workers but also the duty of the States where they were working to care for their safety and well-being. India is a welfare State and Article 21 of the Constitution of India is paramount and safety and security and supply of food are important. This Court is well aware that Covid-19 is not only a national crisis but also an international crisis. But, it is a pity to see the migrant labourers walking for days together to reach their native places and in the process, some of them had lost their lives due to accidents. The Government authorities of all the States should have extended their human services to those migrant labourers.

Since the passing of these orders, the High Courts of Bombay, Allahabad, Telangana, and Andhra Pradesh have all passed similar orders seeking the respective governments' response on the measures taken by them to mitigate the suffering of migrant workers.

The Supreme Court of India is considered to be the most powerful apex court in the world because of the wide powers of judicial review which have been conferred on it by the Constitution, and the powers it has assumed for itself by way of public interest litigation (PIL) jurisdiction.

In fact, the very invention of PIL was specifically made to address glaring violations of fundamental rights like we have seen during the present migrant labour crisis.

The decisions of the High Courts, inspiring as they are, are handicapped for the reason that they cannot coordinate with other state governments. It is, therefore, clear that the Supreme Court, which has jurisdiction over all authorities in the country, can play a huge role in helping the migrants by issuing orders to different state governments/authorities.

In such circumstances, as the crisis is still ongoing, the Supreme Court has again taken *suo motu* cognisance of the matter. This has reignited the hopes of millions of people and perhaps the Supreme Court will now rise to the occasion by discharging its constitutional responsibility to the lowest sections of our society.

Note

1 Reproduced with permission from *Bar and Bench* where this article first appeared on May 28, 2020. https://www.barandbench.com/columns/homecoming-the-worst-migrant-crisis-of-the-nation

2.5 Migrant workers, the lockdown, and the judiciary[1]

Harsh Mander[2]

The millions of migrants who have lost their livelihoods have a fundamental right to a life of dignity. The refusal of the Government of India to provide comprehensive support and the Supreme Court's ruling on a petition seeking relief have left them adrift.

From midnight on 24 March 2020, India went into what has been rated[3] as the most stringent lockdown[4] of physical movement and economic activity in the world in response to the COVID-19 pandemic.

SWAN Report I and II: Conditions of migrant workers

Three weeks later, a survey[5] of 11,159 migrant workers by the Stranded Workers Action Network (SWAN), reported on 20 April by *The Hindu*,[6] opened a troubling window to the intense distress of migrant workers stranded by the lockdown.

The first SWAN survey revealed an urgent hunger crisis. Fifty per cent of the workers had rations left for less than one day; 72% of the people the team spoke to said that their rations would be finished in two days. Because they had little or no cash in hand and were continuously beset by uncertainty about the next meal, many had been eating frugally. Ninety-six per cent had not received rations from the government, and 70% had not received any cooked food from any source.

Along with food, cash had almost run out for most of the workers: 78% of people had less than Rs. 300 left with them. About 70% were left with less than Rs. 200 (less than half a single day's wage) for the rest of the lockdown period. Around 98% had not received any cash relief from the government.

During the second phase of the lockdown, half of the workers had rations left for less than one day; 46% reported being with no food or money.

Eighty-nine per cent had not been paid by their employers at all during the lockdown; about 9% had been partially paid. Some who had been given rations by the employers were told that the money for the rations

DOI: 10.4324/9781003291527-12

would be deducted. Some workers have also been threatened and told not to complain.

Into the second phase of the lockdown (15 April–3 May), a second report from SWAN covered the period until 26 April and was titled "32 Days and Counting".[7] The report showed that precarity remained high. During the second phase of the lockdown, half of the workers had rations left for less than a day; 46% reported being with no food or money. More than four out of five persons had still not received rations in the second phase. Sixty-four per cent had less than Rs. 100 of cash with them, while 74% had less than half their daily wages with them to see them through for the rest of the lockdown. Only 6% had been fully paid and 16% partially paid.

Seventy-eight per cent had not been paid by their employers at all during the second phase of the lockdown; 89% had not been paid at all in the first phase. Ninety-nine per cent of the self-employed have had no income during the lockdown period.

Among the migrants surveyed, 41% said they would stay in the city because they were anxious about unpaid rent, loans and had no cash to travel or survive even at home. One-third planned to continue in the same line of work or with the same employer; another one-third were unsure about what to do. Roughly 16% planned to leave and then return after some time, and about 13% planned to find work back in their hometown, and about 5% wanted to earn some money and leave.

Distressed by the indignity meted out to the migrant workers, a particularly anguished migrant labourer from Jharkhand working in Mumbai said (SWAN, "21 Days and Counting", page 9): "*Modi ki nazron mein hum keedein hi hain na, waisi maut marenge*" ("We are after all insects in the eyes of Modi so we will have to die that kind of death").

Petition for relief

A week into the lockdown, lawyers Prashant Bhushan and Cheryl D'Souza filed a public interest petition in the Supreme Court, seeking the upholding of the right to life with dignity under Article 21 of the Constitution for the migrants who were badly hit by the sudden and severe lockdown. The petitioners were Anjali Bhardwaj and this writer.[8]

The petition pointed to the humanitarian crisis created by the lockdown. Its central demand was that the central and state governments must "jointly and severally" ensure payment of minimum wages to all migrant workers within a week, for the entire period of the lockdown. This should be agnostic to whether they were employed in an establishment, engaged by contractors, or self-employed. The petition also demanded that this must be done by self-attestation and self-identification, because the state has no comprehensive record of employed workers, let alone casual and self-employed workers.

The petition detailed first what it felt were grave inadequacies and gaps in the financial package of Rs. 1.70 lakh crore under the Pradhan Mantri Garib Kalyan Yojana. The Union government maintained to the Supreme Court that this package would ensure that citizens were not deprived of the basic amenities of food, drinking water, medication, etc.

We replied that Rs. 1.70 lakh crore constitutes just over 1% of the GDP of India. Further, many elements of the scheme merely front-load instalments of existing schemes, or provide for the disbursement of cess funds already earmarked for welfare of particular sectors, or programmes. For instance, the scheme includes a daily wage increase of Rs. 20 under MGNREGA, which is a regular adjustment against inflation made every year and, therefore, in no way, can be reasonably considered an additional resource to deal with the lockdown distress. Similarly, the announcement that emergency support will be granted through the Building and Other Construction Workers' Cess funds is not an additional resource. The funds (accumulated to Rs. 52,000 crore) are specifically earmarked for the welfare of construction workers, and in fact the non-utilisation of these funds has even been raised in the Supreme Court.

The Union government announced that PDS card holders would be given 5 kg of food grains and 1 kg of pulses free of cost every month for three months. We replied that a large section of migrant workers is excluded from the PDS because the system is a domicile-based entitlement that requires proof of permanent address. There is no scheme or law for inter-state portability of ration cards. We maintained that the only way to ensure a modicum of food security to migrants would be universalised access to food grains, pulses, cooking oil, and soap, and provide them to everyone who seeks them, irrespective of whether they have a ration card or not.

We also pointed out that the ex-gratia of Rs. 500 to 20.4 crore women who have Jan Dhan accounts is extremely inadequate, both in terms of the amount and its inclusion only of those with functional accounts. Once again universal cash transfers equivalent to minimum wages would alone assist households to hold hunger at bay.

The Union government claimed that construction workers (most of whom, according to the government, are migrant workers) would receive financial assistance through the "Welfare Fund for Building and Other Construction Workers" which would cover 3.5 crore registered workers. However, the petitioners pointed out that the vast majority of construction workers are not actually registered under the Building and Other Constructions Workers (Regulation of Employment and Conditions of Service) Act, 1996, and therefore only a very small percentage of construction workers would benefit. A rapid survey[9] conducted by Jansahas in March–April of 3,196 migrant construction workers from north and central India found that 94% of its respondents did not have cards registered under the 1996 Act.

The Union government claimed overall that its financial package took care of the daily needs of every poor person, including migrant workers and their families, so there was no imperative for migrant workers to rush to their villages. Their daily needs were being taken care of wherever they were working, and the needs of their families were being taken care of in the villages. It added that the central government had directed states to provide food, shelter, and medical facilities to migrant workers who have been quarantined en route to their places of origin.

The petitioners contested this last claim as well, stating that the figures for the number of active relief camps and shelters for migrant workers submitted by the government itself laid bare the complete inadequacy of the official provisions made for migrants. The government informed the Supreme Court in its first reply to the petition that there are a total of 26,476 active relief camps and shelters in which 1,037,027 persons are housed. From the government's own data, it was apparent that Kerala alone accounts for 59% of the relief camps and shelters even though the state's population constitutes only 2.6% of India's population. Of the number of persons housed in relief camps, Kerala and Maharashtra together account for 72% of the total. Large states like Uttar Pradesh, Bihar, and Jharkhand, which saw huge numbers of people moving back because of the hardships caused by the lockdown, together accounted for only 12% of the active relief camps and shelters and persons housed.

Of around the 15 lakh persons who had been given food, two states – Haryana and Delhi – accounted for 51% of the total, showing the wide regional variation and the overall complete inadequacy of such facilities.

Limited support for migrant workers

The Union government, under the Disaster Management Act, 2005, directed all public and private employers to continue to pay workers their wages through the period of the lockdown. It also prescribed that landlords should not seek rent from workers during the lockdown. It observed adversely that "the movement of a large number of migrants have taken place in some part of the country so as to reach their home towns. This is in violation of the lockdown measures on maintaining social distance".[10]

As petitioners, we argued that the two main protections for migrant workers during the lockdown as contained in the 29 March order in effect shifted the entire burden of protecting the earnings of migrant workers and preventing their eviction from rented homes, to the employers and landlords. The order instituted no mechanism to secure the implementation of this order, nor for redress when it was flouted.

Moreover, many migrant workers are employed in micro, small, and medium enterprises (MSMEs). The petition argued that the small employers of modest means would not be in a position to pay workers their salaries because their businesses and establishments had been abruptly closed by the lockdown. The government also does not have any accurate or comprehensive record of workers employed in the informal sector, and therefore, would also not have the necessary information to enforce the order. The same would apply also to their landlords for rent waivers. As most migrant workers live in slum settlements, in jhuggis, or at worksites such as construction sites and small restaurants, there would be no formal rent agreement to prove that they were staying there; and once more, the government would also have no record of this, making enforcement again untenable.

There was also no reason why employers and landlords – many of whom would incidentally be of limited means – had to bear the economic costs of a lockdown which they did not order or a pandemic which they did not create or spread.

Further, this order of 29 March, as the petition points out, makes no provision for the financial security of the large proportion of migrant workers who are self-employed and are therefore not paid any salaries, such as street vendors, rickshaw pullers, dhobis, petty service providers, ragpickers, and sex workers. It also ignores completely one of the most vulnerable segments of the labour market, namely casual daily wage workers. Studies show that only 17% of workers in the informal sector have identifiable employers.[11] The earnings of the remaining 83% would not be protected even if every employer obeyed the 29th March order.

It is noteworthy that in all its responses to the petition, the Union government at no stage gave any information about the numbers of migrant workers who had been paid wages by their employers, or the numbers who had not been evicted by their landlords, or any action that had been taken against those who violated its 29 March instructions.

The Government of India, while issuing this directive, also did not provide any funds for wage support to the employers, especially small employers, nor did it provide any income support for self-employed workers. Contrasting responses and measures by governments worldwide show the way forward.[12] The Denmark government announced it would cover 75% of the wage bills, Canada introduced a wage subsidy scheme, England provided for 80% of average earnings subsidised, and Australia framed a "job keeper" wage subsidy plan.

Judiciary's response

In the course of the hearing on the 7 April, the Chief Justice asked why, since the workers were being provided meals, they would need money.

The bench stated that in times of such crisis, it did not want to interfere with government decisions. On complaints raised by the lawyer Prashant Bhushan about inedible food in crowded shelters or the lack of access to food at the feeding centres opened by the government, the Court dismissed this stating that it would ask the government to put in place a helpline for complaints.

In this and subsequent hearings, the Court did not pay heed to the additional affidavits by the petitioners about starving families; police brutality towards workers who attempted to leave their homes to access food in the feeding centres; employers' associations writing to the Court about their inability to pay wages; and ABOUT landlords evicting their worker tenants because of their inability to pay rent.

The abysmal conditions of shelters for migrants in Delhi was confirmed from an unlikely official source: the Delhi police. The *Indian Express* quoted[13] the key observations of ten Delhi Police Station House Officers (SHOs) who were tasked to prepare a report on these shelters:

> Fans not working and no power back-up; sanitisation of toilets rarely done; most of the migrants want to leave as their families cannot survive. Rude behaviour of civil defence staff; food quality not good; no hand wash and sanitizers; foul smell in toilets; water supply in toilets only between 7 am and 11 am; one soap for bathing and no detergent for washing clothes; mosquito bites.

Despite many pleas for urgent redressal, the Supreme Court adjourned the two next hearings on 7 and 13 April (all held by video-conferencing) without passing any order.

In the final hearing, a newly constituted bench (therefore not fully versed in the petitioners' submissions in the previous hearings) very briefly heard the case. In this hearing, the petitioners additionally placed on the record of the Supreme Court the SWAN study. The Court, however, was still not persuaded by the grim picture of distress, destitution, and hunger which, the lawyer stated, was mounting dangerously with every day of the hearings.

The bench said it could not rely on studies by private bodies when the government portrayed a completely different picture. They accepted instead the assurance from the Solicitor General that a "helpline number has been provided" and that "whenever any complaint is received, the authorities are attempting to address the same immediately".

With this, they chose to finally close the case, without giving any relief to the migrants during the lockdown. The final order simply read: "we call upon the respondent – Union of India – to look into such material and take such steps as it finds fit to resolve the issues raised in the petition".

Whither a life with dignity?

In past decades, the Supreme Court of India on many occasions has ruled[14] that the fundamental right to life guaranteed by Article 21 is the fundamental right of every citizen to a life more than "mere animal survival", but to a life with dignity.

For millions of migrant workers stranded in cities without work and food in the lockdown, confined to overcrowded and underserved shelters, standing in long lines for every meal, walking hundreds of miles with the single aspiration in this uncertain time of suffering and crisis to be with their families, uncertain about how they will ensure food and medicine for their children and parents, the prospect of a life with dignity has become even more remote.

Notes

1 Reproduced with permission from *The India Forum* where this article first appeared on May 11, 2020. https://www.theindiaforum.in/article/migrants-workers-lockdown-and-judiciary

2 *I am grateful for generous research support from Cheryl D Souza and Misbah Rashid. A shorter version of this article titled "For India's Migrant Workers, the Prospect of a Life with Dignity Has Become More Remote" has been published on Scroll.in*

3 Shoaib Daniyal, "Not China, not Italy: India's Coronavirus Lockdown Is the Harshest in the World", March 29, 2020, *Scroll.in*. Retrieved from https://scroll.in/article/957564/not-china-not-italy-indias-coronavirus-lockdown-is-the-harshest-in-the-world, last accessed on October 26, 2021.

4 "World's Biggest Lockdown May Have Cost Rs 7–8 Lakh Crore to Indian Economy", *Economic Times,* April 13, 2020. Retrieved from https://economictimes.indiatimes.com/news/economy/finance/worlds-biggest-lockdown-may-have-cost-rs-7-8-lakh-crore-to-indian-economy/articleshow/75123004.cms?utm_source=contentofinterest&utm_medium=text&utm_campaign=cppst, last accessed on October 26, 2021.

5 "Lockdown-and-Distress_Report-by-Stranded-Workers-Action-Network", *The Hindu*. Retrieved from https://www.thehindu.com/news/resources/article31442220.ece/binary/Lockdown-and-Distress_Report-by-Stranded-Workers-Action-Network.pdf, last accessed on October 26, 2021.

6 The Hindu Data Team, "96% Migrant Workers Did Not Get Rations from the Government, 90% Did Not Receive Wages During Lockdown: Survey", *The Hindu,* April 20, 2020. Retrieved from https://www.thehindu.com/data/data-96-migrant-workers-did-not-get-rations-from-the-government-90-did-not-receive-wages-during-lockdown-survey/article31384413.ece, last accessed on October 26, 2021.

7 "'32 Days and Counting: COVID-19 Lockdown, Migrant Workers, and the Inadequacy of Welfare Measures in India", *SWAN*. Retrieved from https://covid19socialsecurity.files.wordpress.com/2020/05/32-days-and-counting_swan.pdf, last accessed on October 26, 2021.

8 "Covid-19: Supreme Court to Hear Plea for Payment of Wages by Government to Migrant Workers", LiveLaw, https://www.livelaw.in/top-stories/covid-19-sc-to-hear-plea-for-payment-of-wages-by-government-to-migrant-workers-read-petition-154634. And the petition *Harsh Mander and Anjali Bhardwaj vs. Union of India*, at https://www.livelaw.in/pdf_upload/pdf_upload-372004.pdf

9 "Voices of the Invisible Citizens: A Rapid Assessment on the Impact of Covid-19 Pandemic on Internal Migrant Workers", *Jan Sahas*, April 2020. Retrieved from https://freedomfund.org/wp-content/uploads/Voices-of-Invisible-Citizens.pdf, last accessed on October 26, 2021.

10 Ministry of Home Affairs order of 29 March. Retrieved from https://www.mha.gov.in/sites/default/files/MHA%20Order%20restricting%20movement%20of%20migrants%20and%20strict%20enforement%20of%20lockdown%20measures%20-%2029.03.2020.pdf, last accessed on October 26, 2021.

11 S. Irudaya Rajan (ed.), *Social Security for the Elderly: Experiences from South Asia* (New Delhi: Routledge, 2008), p. 92.

12 Anand Gopalan, "What Are the Legal Obligations to Pay Wages During a Lockdown?", April 8, 2020. Retrieved from https://www.thehindubusinessline.com/opinion/what-are-the-legal-obligations-to-pay-wages-during-a-lockdown/article31262286.ece, last accessed on October 26, 2021.

13 Sourav Roy Barman, "Delhi Police Report on Migrant Camps: Fans Not Working, Bad Food", April 28, 2020. Retrieved from https://indianexpress.com/article/india/delhi-police-report-on-migrant-camps-fans-not-working-bad-food-6382213/, last accessed on October 26, 2021.

14 P Bhagwati, Francis Coralie Mullin vs The Administrator, 13 January, 1981. Retrieved from https://indiankanoon.org/doc/78536/, last accessed on October 26, 2021.

2.6 Justice Madan Lokur

Supreme Court deserves an "F" grade for its handling of migrants[1]

Madan B. Lokur

After humanitarian law died a million deaths, the Supreme Court finally took suo motu cognisance of the plight of the workers forced to set out for distant rural homes because of the lockdown.

News has come in that on May 26, 2020, the Supreme Court took suo motu cognisance of the problems and miseries of migrant labourers stranded in different parts of the country.

While taking cognisance, reference was made to newspaper and media reports of the

> unfortunate and miserable conditions of migrant labourers walking on-foot and cycles from long distances. They have also been complaining of not being provided food and water by the administration at places where they were stranded or in the way i.e. highways from which they proceeded on-foot, cycles, or other modes of transport.

Will some good come out of this? Better late than never? Is it a face-saving attempt to atone for past follies? Is it an indictment of the state that has dealt (or not dealt) with the tragedy? You be the judge.

The first among many petitions pertaining to the migrants was filed by Alakh Alok Srivastava, a practising lawyer. The petition was in the public interest, and the Supreme Court recorded in its order of March 31, 2020,[2] that it "highlighted the plight of thousands of migrant labourers who, along with their families, were walking hundreds of kilometres from their work-place to their villages/towns".

By way of an example, the averment in the petition was noted to the effect that thousands of migrant labourers left Delhi to reach their homes in the states of Uttar Pradesh and Bihar, by walking on the highways. The petitioner's concern pertained to their welfare, and a direction was sought to the authorities "to shift the migrant labourers to government shelter homes/accommodations and provide them with basic amenities like food, clean drinking water, medicines, etc".

DOI: 10.4324/9781003291527-13

On the request of the solicitor general, the court took on record a status report of March 31 and noted that it dealt with steps taken to prevent the spread of coronavirus, measures taken by the Central government in providing basic amenities like food, clean drinking water, medicines, etc., to the "lower strata" of society. A reference is also made to a relief package under the Pradhan Mantri Garib Kalyan Yojana and other schemes to ensure that persons in need are taken care of.

The report recorded that the initial reaction of the state governments and Union territories to the thousands of migrant labourers leaving Delhi was to transport them from their borders to their villages. But, on March 29, the Ministry of Home Affairs issued a circular

> prohibiting movement as transportation of migrant labourers in overcrowded buses would cause more damage than help to the migrant labourers. The very idea of lock down was to ensure that the virus would not spread. It was felt that transportation of migrant labourers would aggravate the problem of spread of the virus.[3]

The circular worked like a magic wand and abracadabra, the solicitor general stated that as per information received by the control room more than 21,000 relief camps had been set up in which more than 6.5 lakh persons (migrant labour) had been provided shelter and more than 22.8 lakh persons had been provided food and other basic amenities like medicines, drinking water, etc. He further stated on instructions that as of 11.00 am "there is no person walking on the roads in an attempt to reach his/her home towns/villages".[4]

State blames "fake news" for migration

What triggered the migration? According to the status report, panic was caused by fake news that the lockdown would last for more than three months. So, the migrant labourers chose to believe fake news rather than the hon'ble prime minister who had announced, a few days earlier, only a three-week lockdown. Fake news had circulated despite an advisory by the Government of India on March 24 to the authorities to effectively deal with rumour mongering. Obviously, the authorities failed in the discharge of their duty. Therefore, the court expected all concerned to "faithfully comply with the directives, advisories and orders issued by the Union of India in letter and spirit in the interest of public safety". As far as the media was concerned, the court expected the print, electronic, and social media to "maintain a strong sense of responsibility and ensure that unverified news capable of causing panic is not disseminated".[5] Scapegoating had started.

Additionally, the court recorded the statement of the solicitor general that

> within 24 hours the Central government will ensure that trained counsellors and/or community group leaders belonging to all faiths will visit the relief camps/shelter homes and deal with any consternation that the migrants might be going through. This shall be done in all the relief camps/shelter homes wherever they are located in the country.

Two features clearly stand out. First, the Supreme Court accepted what it was told – hook, line, and sinker. True, there was nothing on March 31 to doubt the correctness of the statement that no person was walking on the roads at 11.00 am, but is the court so naïve as to seriously believe such a statement? Is the court also naïve enough to believe that a circular issued by the Central government could work wonders and ensure that a few lakh persons (not thousands) actually stayed off the roads? If a statutory order issued by the National Disaster Management Authority and the Ministry of Home Affairs acting in exercise of powers conferred by the Disaster Management Act could not ensure the implementation of a complete lockdown, could a mere circular prevent migrants from hitting the road? Really?

Subsequent hearings in the case on April 3 and 7 confirmed that as on March 31, the Supreme Court did not even bother to question the statement made or hold the Central government to account, despite more than enough evidence available everywhere. Newspaper and media reports were ignored.

Second, did the Central government fulfil its commitment that "trained counsellors" would visit the camps and deal with the "consternation of the migrants"? Even this was not questioned by the court during the hearings on April 3 and 7. This is very important since the court was aware that "panic can severely affect mental health. We are informed that the Union of India is conscious of the importance of mental health and the need to calm down those who are in a state of panic".

Constitutional obligation of the Supreme Court

Given the circumstances, was it not the constitutional obligation, not duty, of the Supreme Court – a court for the people of India and not a court of the people of India – to ascertain that a few lakhs (not thousands) of migrants were well taken care of, physically and emotionally? It is not that the court was expected to disbelieve or distrust the establishment represented by no less than the solicitor general, the court was only required to ensure through the principle of continuing mandamus that the solemn assurances given to it are faithfully carried out. Sorry, the court completely failed in this – forgot what public interest litigation is all about. If a grading is to be given, it deserves an F.

True, the events were unprecedented as far as the government is concerned, but the events were also unprecedented as far as the migrants are concerned. Unfortunately, the lack of interest and compassion shown by the court was also unprecedented. Here was an opportunity handed over on a platter to the court to be more proactive and assertive, keeping the interest and constitutional rights of the hapless people in mind.

The initial failure of March 31 and in two subsequent hearings was compounded in the final hearing on April 27, when the Court passed a rather tepid order to the effect that the solicitor general had agreed that the interim directions passed on March 31 would be continued (actually no interim directions had been passed) and the suggestions made would be examined and appropriate action taken. On this basis, the petition was disposed of. On that day, humanitarian law died a million deaths.

Surely, but surely, the court could not have been oblivious to the continuing migration to rural areas during this period in April. If the court was aware of the migrant crisis (as it should and must have been) why did it not act? Did the court feel helpless and if so, why? Leaving the migrants – men, women, children, and infants – to their uncertain fate was certainly not a policy decision that necessitated a hands-off attitude from the court; and if it was a policy decision, it was a perverse policy decision that should have been set aside in less than a minute.

The Supreme Court and public interest

What could the court have done? Public interest litigation is all about public interest. Well-meaning persons approach the Supreme Court for the enforcement of the constitutional and statutory rights of those who have no access to justice. This is precisely what the petitioner (and others) did. The Supreme Court was approached on behalf of migrant labourers on the road for a do-something direction. Sadly, the court let them down, badly. The court could have asked pointed questions of the state. It could have asked if the Central government had a plan of action for the "unforeseen development" (an expression used in the status report); it could have asked for the steps taken and proposed to be taken to mitigate the hardships that the migrants faced; it could have asked if the state governments were geared up for the massive influx of migrants whose presence "would aggravate the problem of spread of the virus". Issues of socio-economic justice and constitutional rights are vital and raise a whole host of questions, but not one was asked in a public interest litigation, and the issue was buried ten fathoms deep. If any event ever shook the collective conscience of the nation, the travails of the migrant labourers did.

Why do I say that the court could not have been unaware of the migrant labourers issue? A second petition filed by Harsh Mander and Anjali Bhardwaj[6] came up before the Supreme Court on April 3. They had asked for a direction to the Central government and state governments to ensure payment of wages/minimum wages to all migrant workers within a week. It was contended that despite governmental measures, thousands of labourers still lacked access to basic facilities, and that studies conducted by NGOs indicated that there were several areas where the aid was not reaching the migrant workers.

On April 7, a status report was presented to the court on behalf of the state. Annexure B to this report gave some startling figures. The status report of March 31 stated that there were 21,604 relief camps and 666,291 persons had been provided shelter while 2,288,279 persons had been provided food. As per the report of April 7, the number of relief camps and shelters (including those of NGOs) had gone up to 26,476; shelter had been provided to 1,037,027 persons and food provided to 8,426,509. In addition, 1,505,107 workers were said to have been given shelter and food by employers/industry where they were working. Given this massive increase in numbers within a week, how could the court be unaware of the problem facing the country and how could the court not do anything about it? It seems to me that after the migrant workers, empathy and compassion were the next casualties.

The status report goes on to debunk newspaper reports by stating: "The petition as well as further Affidavit filed is bereft of any facts and is based on some newspaper reports". The newspaper reports that the Supreme Court has now referred to are also not worthy of credence? The status report trashes the studies relied on by the petitioners by not even bothering to refer to them. Unfortunately, neither does the Supreme Court.

And then what happened? The petition filed by these two social activists was adjourned to April 21, and the following order passed: "Taking into consideration the material placed before us, we call upon the respondent – Union of India – to look into such material and take such steps as it finds fit to resolve the issues raised in the petition". Excuse me? What about payment of wages? Executivisation of constitutional justice?

The status report points out, interestingly, that

> when the country is facing such unprecedented crisis, filing of such petitions and attempting to sit in appeal over all actions taken by the respective governments by few individual needs to be discouraged as it diverts energy and attention of the statutory functionaries which ought to have been utilised to its optimum in discharging their duties on ground.

The Supreme Court can very well be similarly told at the next hearing in the suo motu proceedings – don't interfere since you are diverting our energy and attention and effectively preventing us from utilising them in discharging our duties on the ground.

A third opportunity came the way of the Supreme Court when Jagdeep Chhokar filed a petition for a direction to the Government of India to allow migrant workers across the country to return to their hometowns and villages after conducting necessary testing for COVID-19 and to arrange for their safe travel by providing necessary transportation to this effect.[7]

Justice disregarded

It was noted by the court on May 5 that an order of the government issued on April 29 allowed the movement of migrant workers, pilgrims, tourists, and students stranded at different places. All state and Union territory governments were required to designate nodal authorities and develop standard protocols for receiving and sending such stranded persons. "The main relief which was sought in the writ petition, thus, stood substantially satisfied by the aforesaid order". QED. Shouldn't questions of this nature have been asked on March 31? Any follow-up steps?

The court also noted that on May 1,[8] an order was issued by the Ministry of Railways to run "Shramik Special" trains to move migrant workers, tourists, students, and other persons stranded at different places due to lockdown. A grievance was made by Prashant Bhushan appearing for the petitioner that the migrants were required to pay 15% of the fare, which they could not afford. Remember, the court had earlier declined to pass any order for the payment of wages to the migrant labour. What was the answer now?

> Insofar as charging of 15% of Railway tickets' amount from workers, it is not for this court to issue any order under Article 32 regarding the same, it is the concerned State/Railways to take necessary steps under the relevant guidelines.

The petition stands disposed of.

One thing is clear – the migrant workers, women (some of them pregnant), children, and infants will remember these dark days till the very end. Images that have haunted us for two months and the horrific struggles of millions will remain etched in our psyche, and many will long remember that, when it came to the crunch, the Supreme Court did not see those images or read those stories. Over the past few months, constitutional rights and remedies were overlooked and socio-economic justice, a cornerstone in the preamble of our constitution, was disregarded. Some eminent members of the legal fraternity have already expressed dissatisfaction[9] with the present-day functioning of the Supreme Court. Isn't that tragic or is it farcical?

The facts speak for themselves. Can the court redeem itself and reimage its brand as a court for the people of India and not of the people of India? By addressing the plight of the migrant workers suo motu, as the court has now done, will the situation on the ground change? Will the Supreme Court change? You be the judge.

Notes

1 Reproduced with permission from *The Wire* where this article first appeared on May 28, 2020. https://thewire.in/law/after-humanitarian-law-died-a-million-deaths-the-supreme-court-has-finally-stirred-itself

2 See "Alakh Alok Srivastava vs Union Of India on 31 March, 2020". Retrieved from https://indiankanoon.org/doc/129422211/, last accessed on November 10, 2021.

3 See Order no 40-3/2020-DM-I(A), Government of India, Ministry of Home Affrairs. Retrieved from https://www.mha.gov.in/sites/default/files/MHA%20Order%20restricting%20movement%20of%20migrants%20and%20strict%20enforement%20of%20lockdown%20measures%20-%2029.03.2020_0.pdf, last Accessed on November 11, 2021.

4 Jagdeep S. Chhokar, "Migrant Worker Crisis: The Supreme Court Has Abdicated All Responsibility". *The Wire*. May 19, 2020. Retrieved from https://thewire.in/law/supreme-court-migrant-workers-crisis-abdicate-responsibility, last Accessed on November 11, 2021.

5 "Coronavirus v. Free Speech: Modi Government Opens New Battlefront in Supreme Court". *The Wire*. April 1, 2020. Retrieved from https://thewire.in/law/coronavirus-v-free-speech-modi-government-opens-new-battlefront-in-supreme-court, last accessed on November 11, 2021.

6 Prashant Bhushan, "The Supreme Court Is Locked Down and Justice Is in 'Emergency' Care". *The Wire*. April 28, 2020. Retrieved from https://thewire.in/law/lockdown-supreme-court-justice, last accessed on November 11, 2021.

7 Jagdeep S. Chhokar, "Migrant Worker Crisis". *The Wire*.

8 "SC: Centre Refuses to Disclose Details of Train Fares Charged from Migrant Workers". *The Wire*. May 8, 2020. Retrieved from https://thewire.in/law/suprem-court-petition-migrant-workers-train-travel, last accessed on November 11, 2021.

9 "Read: What Senior Lawyers Told the Supreme Court Before It Spoke on Migrants". *The Wire*. May 27, 2020. Retrieved from https://thewire.in/law/supreme-court-migrant-workers-lawyers-letter, last accessed on November 11, 2021.

2.7 Women workers in labour codes[1]

Indrani Mazumdar and Neetha N. Pillai

The absence of a gender perspective in the labour laws is detrimental to the interests of migrant women workers in India. The new labour codes have not addressed the absence of gender sensitivity in the labour laws. There is wide gap between the lip service to gender equality and the actual ground-level experience of the women workers.

"Labour reforms" has been the buzzword of India's labour policy since the dominance of neo-liberalism in its economic policy framework since 1991. While the centrepiece of the arguments for such reforms is that labour laws in India are too many, and too protective, creating restrictive rigidities in the operation of the market, there is also another line of argument that finds labour laws only protecting the organised sector workers at the cost of the vast majority of unorganised and informal workers. Three decades of a policy discourse that sanctions the dismantling of the protective structures of labour laws in the name of "majority" of the workers has shifted the balance towards the "ease of doing business" over workers' rights.

Currently, the focus of such change is on the four labour codes that are to repeal and replace some 30 labour laws. And among these codes, the one on wages has already become a law. We examine some implications of these labour codes for women workers.

Code on wages (CoW)

It defines an employee or a worker only in relation to the establishment or industry, thus precluding private households. It makes no mention of out-workers/home workers, among whom home-based beedi workers, at least, were earlier covered by the minimum wages and other regulations.[2] In its present form, the CoW thus disentitles the increasingly feminised domestic workers, who, over the past decade or so, had successfully fought for inclusion in the minimum wage schedules under MWA in most states. Home-based beedi workers, mostly women, are similarly disentitled to minimum

DOI: 10.4324/9781003291527-14

wages, equal remuneration, mechanisms to ensure payment of wages, and entitlement to bonuses.

The CoW's specific exclusion of apprentices has adverse implications for any entitlement to minimum wage for "sum-angali" workers, who are designated apprentices.[3] Since the apprenticeship law—as amended in 2014—has (i) set the minimum age of 14 for apprenticeship in "non-hazardous" industries (including apparel and textiles), (ii) permitted employers to engage apprentices from other states and determine the hours of work, and (iii) removed imprisonment as a punishment for employer violations, its effects will be felt particularly by the extremely young interstate migrant women workers.

While the CoW retains the provisions of the ERA against discrimination on the grounds of gender in pay for the same or similar work, it amalgamates the advisory board for minimum wages and the ERA committee for increasing employment opportunities for women into one single board. Its stipulation that one-third of the board representatives are to be women may be an advancement in relation to minimum wages, but reduces the 50% stipulated earlier by the ERA.

Further, the (draft) central rules of the code propose to extend the normal working hours for all workers from the eight-hour norm (as in the Factories Act) to nine hours. Equally significant is that there is no national minimum wage, and the criterion for the calculation of minimum wages, as laid down by the Indian Labour Conference (ILC) and Supreme Court, is not included.[4] Even the central government's floor wage does not provide a national floor, since the floor itself is to be different across different geographical areas.[5]

This code also gives the sanction of law to administrative restraints imposed on autonomous inspections. The replacement of surprise inspections by web-based pre-determined schedules and the reliance on self-certification of compliance by the employers have given a pro-employer tilt to the labour administration, expressed in the changed designation of the labour inspectors to inspector-cum-facilitator.[6]

As such, the CoW adds neither universality, nor clarity, let alone any additional benefit, in comparison to earlier laws, whereas it nullifies some of the entitlements that had been acquired by women workers.[7]

Occupational safety, health and working conditions code (OSHWCC)

Currently, this code, pending before the parliament, amalgamates 13 labour laws, of which 11 are for particular sectors/types of establishment (including for the beedi workers), the other two being the Inter-state Migrant Workmen (Regulation of Employment and Conditions of Service) Act (ISMWA) and the Contract Labour (Regulation and Abolition) Act (CLRAA).[8]

This bill perhaps best illustrates the lack of wisdom in amalgamating a range of laws that address industry- or sector-specific characteristics. In the range of enterprises from factories, to mines, plantations, motor transport undertakings, newspapers, beedi establishments, etc., with respect to which it defines an employee, it again excludes private households. Hence, none of its regulations regarding safety, health, or working conditions (weekly and daily working hours, leave, overtime, night shifts, etc.) are applicable to domestic workers or home-based workers as among the beedi workers. In fact, for the latter, the removal of "home worker" as the appropriate term to mean home-based work leaves it open to interpretation as to what is meant by workers working "outside" a beedi establishment/premises. Like the CoW, new provisions regarding electronic modes and systems have been specifically included, and so has a special category of audiovisual workers, but women workers from the poorer classes continue to be excluded.

OSHWCC has chapters that summarise the industry-based labour laws that are being repealed. In the process, some important health stipulations in relation to crèches under the Factories Act have been dropped. Plantation managements have been given the option to transfer liabilities and the responsibility for the provision of medical facilities, housing, and food supplies to the government and panchayats. Under the Plantation Labour Act, 1951, employers had these responsibilities. Strangely, while protection against rain and cold is provided for transport workers, a similar provision that existed for the plantation workers, the majority of whom are women, has been dropped. The CLRAA and ISMWA are summarised together in such a way that the provision of paying migrant workers no less than the local wage rates is left out, the liability of the principal employers is reduced, and there is continued silence regarding the denial of independent wages to migrant women working in family units at piece rates.

"Special Provision Relating to Employment of Women" is the briefest chapter, which essentially sanctifies night work for women workers (after 7 pm and before 6 am), "with her consent", and without any obligation on the part of employers to provide safe transport. Such obligations were earlier necessary for exemptions to the prohibition of night work for women under various acts, and specified for working journalists.[9]

Significantly, prevention of and protection from sexual harassment finds no mention in the OSHWCC bill, and the Sexual Harassment of Women at Workplace (Prevention, Prohibition and Redressal) Act, 2013 (POSH Act) has been kept out of the amalgamation process. While this raises a question as to why sexual harassment in the workplace is not considered a part of either occupational safety or working conditions for women workers, it draws attention to the fact that the POSH Act has also been kept out of the framework of the labour laws.

The enforcement authority under the POSH Act is the (additional) district magistrate or deputy collector; it is monitored by the ministry/department of women and child development, and no provision was made for the inclusion of any labour officer in any of its committees, let alone a female labour officer, which could have helped increase the presence of women in the labour law enforcement systems. Despite much debate on the applicability of the POSH Act for unorganised women workers, its role in labour laws was never clarified. Such a subliminal tendency to segregate key workplace issues of women from the labour law framework, and/or to maintain the constituency of women workers as outside the working classes, has added to both the continued absence of gender perspectives in labour laws, and the denial of workers' entitlements to a large contingent of women workers. A corollary to such segregation is that the labour law enforcement machinery remains gender insensitive to the detriment of the equality agenda in the labour laws.

Finally, the repetitive motif of leaving basic issues, such as limits to hours of work, to "as may be notified by the appropriate government" in contrast to the strictly defined eight hours under the Factories Act, moves core rights under labour laws away from legislative certainty to the discretion of the government (the opposite being the case when it comes to removing some rights of workers). Double wage rates for overtime in the OSHWCC mean little if the normal hours of work are enhanced.

Code on social security (COSS)

This code specifically includes home-based workers and domestic workers in its definition of "wage worker" as well as "unorganised worker".[10] Although no actual social security schemes are specified in COSS, it lists the types of benefits for "social security organisations", of which are the Employees' Provident Fund Organisation (EPFO), the Employees' State Insurance Corporation (ESIC), the National Social Security Board (NSSB) for unorganised workers, and the state-level Building and Construction Workers' Welfare Boards (BCWWBs), whose administrative structures and modes of funding are delineated in the code. All schemes, under these social security organisations, have been left to "as may be framed" at the government's discretion, thereby creating uncertainty regarding the well-functioning existing schemes.

Considering the accumulated experience of a variety of existing schemes, some of which have been implemented centrally for more than 60 years by the EPFO and ESIC, their lack of delineation generates more uncertainties, rather than security.[11] Schemes with a shorter life, such as CESS funded by the BCWWB, which are still evolving, or the NSSB, which in the absence of any other fund source, had largely declared pre-existing central social assistance schemes for the below poverty line (BPL) category citizens as schemes for the unorganised workers.[12] While the above social security organisations remain operative under the code, welfare funds for beedi workers that were earlier cess based are not mentioned. Instead beedi workers are to be covered by the NSSB for unorganised workers, despite the schemes being of a lesser order than what was available under the Beedi Workers' Welfare Fund. COSS is silent about other sectoral cess-based welfare funds and organisations.[13] While the thresholds for the applicability of the Employees' Provident Fund (EPF) (establishments with 20 or more employees) and the Employees' State Insurance (ESI) (10 or more employees) schemes have been retained, for the cess-funded welfare schemes under the BCWWF, COSS is silent on whether the brick kiln workers would be included.[14]

The chapter on maternity benefits in COSS reiterates the provision for 26 weeks' paid maternity leave by employers, and the discriminatory provision for a maximum of 12 weeks' leave for any pregnancy beyond two children, as introduced by the 2017 amendment to the Maternity Benefit Act. It also reiterates the provision of crèches with 4 visits a day for establishments with 50 or more workers, and all other health protective provisions from the original 1961 Act. The chapter remains applicable only to the organised sector—factories (minimum 10 workers with power, and 20 without), mines, plantations (minimum 10 workers), government institutions, and shops or establishments with 10 or more workers. For unorganised workers and construction workers, maternity benefits as provided by their respective boards (not employers) are in the form of cash assistance. These range from transfers conditional upon institutional delivery under the public health programme of Janani Suraksha Yojana (JSY)—`700 for high-performing and `1,400 for low-performing states—to `6,000 under the 2018 Model Welfare Scheme for Construction Workers of the central government.

Considering that even the top end of these schemes (as also other public health schemes for maternity assistance such as the Pradhan Mantri Matru Vandana Yojana) is equivalent to just 22 days at wage rates under the Mahatma Gandhi National Rural Employment Guarantee Scheme (MGNREGS) in Haryana and 35 days for Bihar (MGNREGS wage rates taken as a proxy for a national floor), the absence of any criteria for the calculation of maternity assistance for construction and other unorganised sector workers that could be equal to 26 or even 12 weeks of paid maternity leave is particularly glaring.

Industrial relations code (IRC)

This bill assumes a special importance for women workers.[15] A dynamic and increased role being assumed by women in the trade unions is evident not only in their increased visibility, but also their share in membership. Women's membership reached 32% of total trade union membership in 2014, which is far greater than women's share in the country's workforce, hovering between 22% and 23% between 2011–12 and 2017–18.[16]

All trade unions, without exception, have opposed the IRC for imposing restrictions on strikes by universalising and adding to prohibitions that were earlier only applicable to public utility services.[17] The IRC stipulates (i) 60 days' notice and prohibits any strike within 14 days of such notice; and (ii) no strike during the pendency of proceedings before a conciliation officer or tribunal, and within 7 days after the conclusion of conciliation, and within 60 days after the conclusion of proceedings before a tribunal. It additionally allows anyone to initiate direct proceedings (without requiring a reference from the conciliation machinery as earlier), so an individual can just go to a tribunal and render strikes illegal. It also redefines strikes to include mass casual leaves. In all, under such conditions, almost no strike can be legal. The IRC thus denies workers a basic right and/or mode of protest against the employer or state exploitation.

It also gives legislative sanction to fixed-term employment (FTE) that had been introduced by a backdoor amendment to the rules under the Industrial Employment (Standing Orders) Act in 2018, thereby removing restrictions on easy hire and fire. FTE has particularly adverse implications for the "sumangali" workers, who have been fighting for regularisation after their peculiar fixed-term contracts come to an end.

In relation to the trade unions, all of the 2001 amendments to the Trade Union Act, 1926, which were introduced as part of the neo-liberal reform's restrictive agenda for unionisation, have been incorporated in the IRC. These include: (i) the stipulation that union registration would require at least 10% of the workers in an establishment/industry or 100 members (as opposed to the original requirement of just 7 workers to begin with), and (ii) restriction on the number of office bearers to half for the unions of unorganised workers and one-third for other unions. While restricting the number of whole-timers that a union may need by fiat, apart from interfering with the workers' right to elect their leaders as they see fit, these stipulations have made it increasingly difficult to register unions, particularly for the unorganised segments such as domestic workers or home-based workers.

The IRC retains provisions that provide unions with immunity against certain forms of civil action on the grounds of breaking a contract of employment or for interfering with the trade, business, or the right of any person to dispose of his capital or labour, as well as immunity against criminal action on the grounds of criminal conspiracy, which were part of the Act of 1926. But given the restriction on strikes, and sweeping powers conferred on the government to exempt any industry from the application of this code, it again means little for labour welfare.

In all, the thrust of the IRC seemingly aims at subverting a basic framework of labour laws of allowing the countervailing collective force of actions of workers against the inequality that inheres in their employment relationships. From our perspective, it seems that the labour codes, on the whole, have failed to address the absence of gender sensitivity in the labour laws, and/or the gap between the lip service to gender equality and the actual ground-level experience of women workers.

Notes

1 Excerpted with permission from *Economic and Political Weekly* (Volume 55, Issue number 20) where this article appeared in full on May 16, 2020. https://www.epw.in/journal/2020/20/review-womens-studies/crossroads-and-boundaries.html

2 The CoW repeals (i) the Payment of Wages Act, 1936, (ii) the Minimum Wages Act, 1948, (iii) the Payment of Bonus Act, 1965, and (iv) the Equal Remuneration Act, 1976.

3 Although the Madras High Court dismissed a petition by the Tamil Nadu Spinning Mills Association challenging the sumangali workers' entitlement to minimum wages on the grounds that they were apprentices, it remains an open question as to whether that will stand now. Importantly, the apprenticeship law is not being repealed by any of the codes.

4 The ILC, 1957, had set out the norms for the calculation of a need-based minimum wage as (i) three consumption units for one wage earner; (ii) a minimum food requirement of 2,700 calories per adult person per day; (iii) clothing requirements at 72 yards per annum for an average working family of four; (iv) a house rent corresponding to the minimum area provided for under the Government's Industrial Housing Scheme; and (v) 20% of the total minimum wage for fuel, lighting, and other miscellaneous items. To this, the Supreme Court had added children's education, medical requirements, minimum recreation, including festivals/ceremonies, and contingencies such as old age and marriage as 25% of the total minimum wage.

5 A commitment to a below-subsistence minimum for workers became evident when the Labour Minister announced a floor-level minimum daily wage of `178 (`4,628 monthly) just two weeks before introducing the CoW. This was after the government-appointed committee had suggested that the national minimum wage should be `375 per day (`9,750 per month), which suggests that the advisory committees for minimum wages included in CoW may also meet the same fate.

6 In the first bill, it was only facilitator, abolishing the inspector role completely. This would have been in violation of ILO Convention No 81, ratified by India in 1949.

7 It may be recalled that ahead of the 2019 elections, ten central trade unions—INTUC, AITUC, CITU, AICCTU, HMS, UTUC, TUCC, SEWA, AICCTU, and LPF—had collectively demanded a national minimum wage. Only BMS did not support this demand.

8 The OSHWCC repeals the (i) Factories Act, 1948, (ii) Mines Act, 1952, (iii) Dock Workers (Safety, Health and Welfare) Act, 1986, (iv) Building and Other Construction Workers (Regulation of Employment and Conditions of Service) Act, 1996, (v) Plantations Labour Act, 1951, (vi) Contract Labour (Regulation and Abolition) Act, 1970, (vii) Inter-state Migrant Workmen (Regulation of Employment and Conditions of Service) Act, 1979, (viii) Working Journalist and Other News Paper Employees (Conditions of Service and Miscellaneous Provision) Act, 1955, (ix) Working Journalist (Fixation of Rates of Wages) Act, 1958, (x) Motor Transport Workers Act, 1961, (xi) Sales Promotion Employees (Conditions of Service) Act, 1976, (xii) Beedi and Cigar Workers (Conditions of Employment) Act, 1966, and (xiii) Cine Workers and Cinema Theatre Workers Act, 1981.

9 Although the safety provision for night work by women is mentioned in the Statement of Objects and Reasons for the OSHWCC, employer liability is not mentioned.

10 The COSS repeals the (i) Employees' Compensation Act, 1923, (ii) Employees' State Insurance Act, 1948, (iii) Employees' Provident Funds and Miscellaneous Provisions Act, 1952, (iv) Employment Exchanges (Compulsory Notification of Vacancies) Act, 1959, (v) Maternity Benefit Act, 1961, (vi) Payment of Gratuity Act, 1972, (vii) Cine-Workers Welfare Fund Act, 1981, (viii) Building and Other Construction Workers' Welfare Cess Act, 1996, and (ix) Unorganised Workers Social Security Act, 2008.

11 Despite problems related to narrow coverage of workers, and paltry pension schemes, EPFO and ESIC have provided a model of social security that has worked well for the social security needs of the workers they cater to.
12 The COSS has added two new categories of workers (gig and platform workers) to the category of unorganised workers. Gig workers in India are known to be mostly male, with women still accounting for less than 5% of the workers. For platform workers, in India women's share is less than 25%. See Berg et al (2018).
13 The cess laws for beedi workers' welfare, for iron ore mines, manganese ore mines, and chrome ore mines labour welfare, for cine workers' welfare, for the Mica Mines Labour Welfare Fund, and for limestone and dolomite mines labour, were all repealed earlier to pave the way for GST.
14 Backed by the ILO, many state welfare boards for construction workers had begun to include brick kiln workers in their schemes.
15 The IRC repeals the (i) Trade Unions Act, 1926, (ii) Industrial Employment (Standing Orders) Act, 1946, and (iii) Industrial Disputes Act, 1947. Opposition to the IRC, 2019, has come even from the BMS, which has supported the other codes.
16 Government of India, Labour Bureau statistics for women's membership in trade unions in India, 2014 (latest).
17 It may be recalled that strikes were rendered illegal in export zones by giving them public utility service status under the ID Act.

Bibliography

Agnihotri, I and I Mazumdar (2009): "Dusty Trails and Unsettled Lives: Women's Labour Migration in Rural India," *Indian Journal of Gender Studies*, 16(3): 375–399. doi:10.1177/097152150901600304

Berg, J, M Furrer, E Harmon, U Rani and M Six Silberman (2018): "Digital Labour Platforms and the Future of Work: Towards Decent Work in the Online World," ILO, Geneva, https://www.ilo.org/wcmsp5/groups/public/---dgreports/---dcomm/---publ/d....

Brand, MC (2010): "International Cooperation and the Anti-trafficking Regime," Working Paper 71, Refugee Studies Centre, Oxford Department of International Development, University of Oxford.

Chakravarty, L (1978): "Emergence of an Industrial Labour Force in a Dual Economy: British India, 1880–1920," *IESHR*, Vol 15(3): 249–327. doi:10.1177/001946467801500301

CWDS (2019): Women Migrating in India: Evidence from Odisha, Research Monograph (Collaboration with LSHTM), https://www.cwds.ac.in/wp-content/uploads/2019/10/Women-Migrating-in-Inida.pdf.

Davies, P and M Freedland (1983): *Kahn-Freund's Labour and the Law*, 3rd edition, London: Stevens & Sons.

Government India NSO (2019): *Annual Report: PLFS, 2017–18*.

Kahn-Freund, O (1972): *Labour and the Law*, Hamlyn Trust.

Kotiswaran, P (2017): "Law, Sex Work and Activism in India," King's College London Dickson Poon School of Law, Legal Studies Research Paper Series: Paper No 2017–30.

Mazumdar, I, RS Misra and A Kapur (2000): *Equal Remuneration in India, Research Monograph* (mimeo), Kriti.

Mazumdar, I, N Neetha and I Agnihotri (2013): "Migration and Gender in India," *Economic & Political Weekly*, Vol 48(10): 54–64.
NCEUS (2007): "Report on Conditions of Work and Promotion of Livelihoods in the Unorganised Sector," National Commission for Enterprises in the Unorganised Sector, Government of India, Academic Foundation, New Delhi.
Neetha, N (2014): "Crisis in Female Employment: Analysis across Social Groups," *Economic & Political Weekly*, Vol 49, No 47, 22 November, pp 50–59.
Pandit, A (2020): "Reporting of Crime a Must in New Anti-trafficking Bill," *Times of India*, 16 March.
Raveendran, G (2019): "Definitions and Statistics on Home-based Workers—Challenges, Gaps and the New ICLS Definition," Presentation at ILO, New Delhi, 18–19 November.
Srivastava, R (2005): "Bonded Labor in India: Its Incidence and Pattern," ILO Special Action Programme to Combat Forced Labour WP/ 43/2005, International Labour Office, Geneva.
Teerink, R (1995): "Migration and Its Impact on Khandeshi Women in the Sugar Cane Harvest," *Women and Seasonal Labour Migration*, L Schenk-Sandbergen (ed), 210–300. New Delhi: Sage.
Vaigai, R (2016): "Girl Workers in 'Sumangali Scheme' of Textile Industry, Tamil Nadu—Claiming Equality through Litigation," mimeo.

Part 3

The long march home

3.1 No train. No bus. Just a rickety cycle to cover 600 km – on an empty stomach[1]

Supriya Sharma

The unthinkable has become normal in India. With no help from the government, migrant workers march home on empty stomachs and empty pockets.

There are no speeding tourists on the Taj Expressway, only workers slowly cycling back home. They continue to cycle even after the government said on April 29 that it would run trains and buses to get them back. Many were on the road when the news came. Some hadn't heard it – their phones had run out of battery. Others didn't trust the government. They had already waited long enough, they said. One and a half months.

Around 9 am on May 2, I flagged down two young men, 50 km short of Agra.

"Your name?"
"Shivam".
"Your age?"
"Eighteen".
"Where are you coming from?"
"Karnal".
"Where are you going?"
"Etawah".

Of the nearly 600 km distance they estimated between their worksite in Karnal, Haryana, and their village in Uttar Pradesh, Shivam Rathore and his cousin, Ramanand Rathore, had already covered close to 400 km – in just four days.

"Raat din raat din chal liye". We walked day and night.

His face drained of emotion, he spoke softly and steadily, describing how they had been particularly unlucky. They had been offered work on a construction project in Karnal. "A building with seven-eight storeys", he said. "Possibly, a hotel". The wages were not great – Rs 400 a day. But

DOI: 10.4324/9781003291527-16

they accepted in the hope of stocking up some savings before the monsoon began.

They reached Karnal on March 19. Work came to a stop on March 22 – the day of the "janata curfew", a precursor to a seemingly interminable nationwide lockdown that began on March 24.

Instead of daily wages of Rs 400, the 20-odd workers were now getting an allowance of Rs 100 from the contractor, which they used to buy grain and vegetables to cook for themselves.

There was no help from the government. Food rations were being distributed among Karnal's regular residents, the young man said, but as migrants they were not eligible to get them. No one was running a community kitchen either – neither the government, nor social organisations. They were on their own.

On April 27, the contractor appeared outside their makeshift huts with folded hands. "Ab humare paas bhi nahi aa raha, hum kahan se dein, sorry". We are not earning any money, how do we pay you, we are sorry.

He did not give them any money but he arranged bicycles for them. "Three cycles between four of us", said Shivam Rathore, speaking of their small group of workers headed back to Etawah. Two sharing a bicycle had fallen behind, but would catch up by night, hopefully, he said. Other groups headed to villages in Bihar were already far ahead.

The bicycles were old and rusty. Their seats uncomfortable, their tyres worn out. But the young men were still glad to have them.

"What about food? How many times have you eaten in five days?" I asked.
"In five days, we have only been eating at night..."
"Only at night?"
"Not food, only snacks. Biscuits and namkeen".

They had passed through three states – Haryana, Delhi, and Uttar Pradesh. They had crossed past several toll booths. Not one state had made any arrangements on the highway to feed workers who were plodding their way home in the 42-degree heat. Over the past month, countless workers, including children, have died of hunger and dehydration before they could reach home.

In five days, only once did the young men cycling from Karnal get any help – policemen at the Taj Expressway toll booth gave them ten packets of biscuit, namkeen, and two dozen bananas.

"How are you able to cycle without food?" I asked.
"Slowly, slowly", said Shivam Rathore, in the same matter-of-fact way.

The only time the young man showed emotion was when I asked him whether his family back home knew he was on the road.

"Yes, I told them", he said. "They asked me not to come. They said 'we will send money, stay there.' But nothing came".

His eyes had turned moist.

"Who do you have back home?"
"Mummy and younger sister".
"What does your mother do? Does the family have agricultural land?"
"No land. She makes pooris".
"At a school?"
"No, at weddings".

He wiped the tears before they could spring up.

"Papa expire ho gaye", he said. His father had died when he was a child. He had been working since the age of seven. First, at a roadside eatery at the bus station near his village. Then, in Delhi, where he moved at the age of 12. He was 14 years old when he started working on construction sites.

In 18 years, he had seen a lifetime of struggle. But there had never been a time when he had gone to sleep hungry like he had in the past five days, he said.

"The government did wrong", he said, his steady voice betraying quiet anger. "They should have told us the lockdown was coming. We would have gone home".

Note

1 Reproduced with permission from Scroll.in where this article first appeared on May 3, 2020. https://scroll.in/article/960881/no-train-no-bus-just-a-rickety-cycle-to-cover-600-km-on-an-empty-stomach

3.2 Nightmare on Shramik Specials[1]

V. Sridhar

The Indian Railways' operation of the Shramik Express Special trains in May has been a national shame. The utter chaos resulted in trains being diverted far away from their supposed destinations, inflicting immense misery on passengers.

Nothing has shaken the conscience of the nation coping with COVID-19 as much as the plight of millions of its migrant workers setting off on cross-country journeys with children and the aged in tow. And no single Cabinet Minister in the Narendra Modi government, barring perhaps the Prime Minister himself and the Finance Minister, has drawn as much ire as Railway Minister Piyush Goyal has for sheer ineptitude and worse. No Railway Minister in independent India has drawn as much ire as Goyal has for his spectacular feat of reducing India's largest enterprise to a laughing stock. The litany of complaints against him is not confined to just ineptitude in using effectively the valuable assets under his command, but also focusses on the arrogance of his response to criticism. Indian Railways' utter inability to provide credible and timely information has made matters worse.

After doing absolutely nothing in the first 36 days of lockdown, Piyush Goyal suddenly decided to start running trains in May. Throughout the month, however, trains went "missing" or went on journeys hundreds of kilometres away from their intended destinations. These "ghost" trains carried thousands of passengers. These unscheduled journeys meant that passengers were provided only a fraction of the food and water that they ought to have been given, that is, if they were given anything at all. According to the Railways' own sources, at least 81 persons died while travelling, on trains or on railway platforms.

The latter half of May saw a spate of reports in the media, local and national, that trains were straying far away from their stated routes, often taking far longer than scheduled. For instance, a train supposed to travel from Vasai in Maharashtra to Gorakhpur in Uttar Pradesh ended up at Rourkela in Odisha.

DOI: 10.4324/9781003291527-17

Another train supposed to run from Bengaluru to Basti in Uttar Pradesh ended up at Ghaziabad, 675 km away by rail. A train that left Mumbai for Patna ended up at Purulia in West Bengal. Within the span of a few days after May 20, there were reports of 40 trains travelling to places hundreds of kilometres away from their scheduled destinations.

Lost trains, distressed passengers

The Railways initially maintained a stoic silence. But the gush of media reports, aided by enterprising reporters who found innovative ways to ferret out news, forced the government to issue denials. Reporters, using "contacts" among passengers travelling on these trains, gathered graphic accounts of the immense suffering that the migrant workers were undergoing.

One visual by a reporter showed desperately hungry passengers disembarking from a train while it was stationary, gathering maize from fields and roasting it on a fire. Others showed irate passengers packed into compartments with physical distancing norms abandoned. Common to most stories was the utter shortage of food and water for passengers, exacerbated by journey times that were double or even treble those in normal times. A journey that ought to have been completed in about 24 hours was taking more than 72 hours.

In fact, there were reports of journeys—from Surat in Gujarat to Siwan in Bihar, for instance—taking up to nine days. A loco pilot who steered a Shramik Special train from Bengaluru heading to a destination in northeastern India told *Frontline* that there were virtually no arrangements for food and water on the long journey.

The Indian Railways, despite its many failings, has always been well-regarded for its optimal use of resources; it has also been appreciated for operating efficiently despite severe resource constraints. So, how did the Railways manage to "lose" trains during the lockdown? "Trains cannot be lost in the Indian rail network. That is an impossibility", a former member of the Railway Board told *Frontline*. He explained that every trip that a train makes is planned well in advance, and the approval of every Railway Zone that the train traverses is taken before the journey is undertaken. This is not just a matter of complying with bureaucratic niceties but a necessary exercise because each zone needs to plan its traffic accordingly, the retired officer explained. So, what went wrong during the lockdown?

The Railways' initial explanation was that the traffic congestion on routes required the trains to be "diverted". But this was obviously a spurious explanation for several reasons. First, given that the Indian Railways runs more than 13,000 trains, about 6,500 of them passenger trains, every day in normal times, how could a daily average of about 200 trains cause congestion? True, most of these trains were converging towards particular destinations in some of the poorest States in the country. But railway officials say that even this ought not to have been a major problem.

One official said: "Better planning by staggering the departure of trains would have been eminently within the capability of the Railways, given its vast experience in handling much higher traffic volumes in normal times". Second, why should a "diversion" take a train hundreds of kilometres away, and towards a place that is not even in the same direction as the destination? How would it help the Railways to travel to Rourkela if the intended destination was Gorakhpur, about 530 km away? How could a "deviation" that accounts for almost one-third of the about 1,700-km journey be explained rationally? Would it not have made better sense to move the train closer to the intended destination even if "congestion" was a problem?

How the Railways managed to be so inept remains a question, one which we will turn to a little later. But the unprecedented tragedy that was unfolding on India's rail network was immediately obvious.

In his now-infamous presentation to the Supreme Court, in which he described the media as "vultures" preying on India's poorest, Solicitor General Tushar Mehta indulged in obfuscation. He triumphantly threw numbers at the court, without offering any context—a hallmark of the Modi regime in all matters concerning data. He said 80 lakh meals and 1 crore bottles of water (presumably one-litre bottles) had been provided to passengers on the Shramik Special trains. If the Railways had carried 50 lakh passengers, as Tushar Mehta claimed, this works out to about 1.6 meals per passenger and 2 water bottles per person. Mehta's own figures reveal the gross inadequacy of what the government provided. How could 1.6 meals and 2 litres of water be enough for a passenger for the four or more days he had to spend on a train in the height of the Indian summer?

In fact, the Railways had the capacity to deliver more and better. It is only that neither Piyush Goyal nor anyone else in the government felt the need to use this capacity. The Indian Railways has the capacity to deliver 12 lakh meals every day. In 2018, it announced that it was planning to expand its drinking water capacity to 16 lakh litres a day.

Indeed, when news of deaths in train toilets and on platforms caught media headlines, the Press Information Bureau, with its new-found penchant for catching "fake" news, dubbed these reports as false. The most dramatic one showed visuals of a toddler tugging at the bedsheet covering his dead mother at Muzzafarpur railway station; according to her relatives, she died of starvation and extreme dehydration on a train.

The Railways immediately dubbed this as fake news and said the woman had been sick when she boarded the train. Later, the PIB dubbed the news reports as "factually incorrect and misleading" and claimed that the woman, who was in her thirties, was mentally and physically ill.

The well-known fact-checking website Altnews investigated the case and concluded that the woman's distressed relatives were pressured soon after her death to say that she had died because she was already ill. A relative also said they had been forced to say that the woman was provided food and water during the journey. He said the PIB's claim that she was ill was utterly wrong and categorically asserted that she had died of hunger, food deprivation, and extreme exhaustion in the heat.

Faced with a barrage of criticism, the leadership of the Railways tied itself into knots. Addressing a press conference, the Chairman of the Railway Board, Vinod Kumar Yadav, made the preposterous claim that the routes of the trains were changed after ascertaining where the passengers wanted to go. This mocked every principle of scheduling rail traffic. Who was to tell the CRB that the railway service was not like a "share" auto in an Indian city that could go to a destination according to where passengers were headed?

Referring to the specific case of a train that went to Lucknow instead of Prayagraj, Vinod Kumar Yadav said: "These are not regular times and passengers told us where they were heading and how they wished to reach home". He added to this preposterous claim: When Railways staff "ascertained from passengers that there are fewer passengers heading to Allahabad, compared to Lucknow, after discussing with the State government, we changed the route to make it head to Lucknow".

Such statements from the highest levels of the Railway establishment mock every principle in traffic routing in a rail network and offend the sensibilities of those in the Railways who take pride in the work they do.

Frequent changes to rules

So what explains the failure of the Railways to manage a fraction of its normal traffic during the lockdown? To answer that question, one needs to look beyond the Railways' own operational parameters and examine the circumstances in which it was running the special services. The nature of the Indian lockdown provides clues to the question. The lockdown has been steered disastrously by the Union Home Ministry headed by Amit Shah. There have been at least eight travel orders issued by the Ministry in one month, each one adding to the confusion.

Rajendran Narayanan, academic at Azim Premji University and an activist with the Stranded Workers Action Network, pointed out that "barring one letter dated May 18 sent by Home Ministry to all Chief Secretaries, every order has been lacking in imagination and empathy".

The refusal to decentralise authority and decision making, reflected in the lack of any consultation with the States, has been a hallmark of the lockdown and of its utter failure.

The initial "rules" for deciding the routes and schedules for the Shramik Specials left them to be decided by the originating and destination States. However, through an innocuous amendment to the rules framed under the auspices of the National Disaster Management Authority (NDMA), which has choreographed the lockdown, the requirement of consent from the destination State was dropped. This was what prompted Jharkhand Chief Minister Hemant Soren, Kerala's Pinarayi Vijayan, and earlier West Bengal's Mamata Banerjee to register their protests.

The change that was effected was a sure recipe for disaster. There were two sets of factors that created problems. First, at the practical level, the destination States had to make preparations. Passengers had to be received at stations, screened, tested, and quarantined—at home or in institutional centres depending on individual cases. All this had to be done at a time when the State was already under great stress, financially and in terms of personnel and physical resources.

Second, the changes in the rules paid no heed to the capacity of the States on which the burden would fall. The Home Ministry was either oblivious to the brutality of the lockdown it was imposing or it simply did not care. The extreme distress and desperation it was causing in both originating and destination States where the migrants were heading imposed constraints on both sets of States. Originating States like Karnataka were increasingly under pressure from restive workers to let them go home. (The State Intelligence Department had apparently warned the administration that the workers' agitation might become too hot to handle.) But destination States faced an even bigger problem.

If Amit Shah or any of his Cabinet colleagues had shown some concern for these workers, they would have known that a significant portion of this workforce was heading to some of the poorest States in the Indian Union—Bihar, West Bengal, Uttar Pradesh, Odisha, Jharkhand, and Madhya Pradesh. To suddenly receive trainloads of passengers at a few days' notice was obviously beyond their means.

An East Central Railway officer, speaking to *Frontline*, said that it took about three hours just for passengers to disembark from the Shramik Specials; passengers had to be screened and organised depending on their health parameters and then transported to quarantine centres or to their homes.

"If it takes three hours for a train to be cleared, there is only so much we can do in a single day", he said. The Railways said that 256 trains were cancelled in May by various States—one of the highest numbers was reported from Maharashtra, which cancelled 105. Piyush Goyal was quick to make political capital of this in the midst of the Bharatiya Janata Party's (BJP) efforts to destabilise the Maharashtra government. What he forgot was that Gujarat, Karnataka, and Uttar Pradesh, all BJP-ruled States, cancelled 114 trains.

Destined towards chaos

It appears that the sheer scale of the problem at destination stations forced States to delay arrivals. And the Railways decided to let these trains run on and on in directions far away from where passengers thought they were heading. Outrageously, the Railways did not even bother to inform the passengers in which direction they were moving. The much longer journeys, mostly without food or water, also resulted in trains stopping for many hours in the middle of nowhere, parked in the peak of summer with temperatures sometimes hovering above 45 degrees centigrade. Given that trains have no autonomous source of electricity, this was neglect by design at its worst.

The entire saga of the way this crisis was handled exposed a government that never intended to care for this crucial but vulnerable segment of the working population. The reality is that it never intended to enable these workers to go back home, committed as it was to powerful lobbies that wished this workforce to stay tied to places far from home so that it would be available if and when the wheels of production turned again. It was only extreme pressure, from the media, as well as the workers themselves, that forced the government's hand. Not many media outlets reported that in Surat town alone, protesting migrant workers were tear-gassed at least five times during the lockdown.

It took more than a month for Piyush Goyal, perhaps much against his intent, to operate the special trains. But even this was done with not just shoddy planning but with scant regard for treating fellow citizens humanely. A volunteer who was assisting workers in Pune, for instance, said workers were given barely two hours' notice to leave, and then made to wait almost a day at the railway station before they set off on the long journey home. Many other activists alleged that the chaos caused by Piyush Goyal's unplanned schedules produced a thriving black market for train tickets. Of course, the pricing of the tickets was a scandal in itself.

If Piyush Goyal had really intended to send these desperate workers home, he would have started sending them before or soon after the lockdown was announced suddenly on March 24. That would have given him, the States, and the Railways the chance to stagger the traffic over a longer period and without all the panic and chaos that the country has witnessed.

India has had a tradition of Railway Ministers resigning in the past in acknowledgement of their failures. Indeed, Piyush Goyal's predecessor, Suresh Prabhu, resigned in 2017 after a series of major rail accidents. Those instances pale into insignificance in the context of the monumental ignominy that Piyush Goyal has heaped on the Indian Railways and the untold misery he has caused to millions of Indians during the lockdown.

Note

1 Reproduced with permission from *Frontline* magazine where this article first appeared on June 19, 2020. https://frontline.thehindu.com/cover-story/article31766697.ece

3.3 Not just the Aurangabad accident, 383 people have died due to the punitive lockdown[1]

Kabir Agarwal

From road and rail accidents to starvation, denial of medical care, police brutality, exhaustion, and suicides, there have been hundreds of reported non-coronavirus deaths.

On Friday, 16 migrant workers[2] were crushed to death by a goods train when they were attempting to make their way to Aurangabad railway station with the hope of catching a train to their homes in Madhya Pradesh. They were walking along the railway track to avoid being thrashed by the police on the roads and with the knowledge that trains weren't running.

After walking for several hours, the workers were exhausted. They sat down to rest and fell asleep. An oncoming goods train ran over them at around 5.20 am.

The migrants worked at a private steel company in Jalna in Maharashtra and had not been paid since the first lockdown began on March 24. Given the desperate situation and not knowing when they could work again, they wanted to get back home to be with their families and decided to walk in the hope of finding a train.

In another incident on Saturday night, at least 5 migrant labourers were killed and 13 others injured[3] when a truck in which they were travelling overturned in Madhya Pradesh's Narsinghpur district. The incident took place in Patha village in Narsinghpur. Around 18 labourers were travelling in a truck carrying mangoes from Telangana's Hyderabad city to Agra in Uttar Pradesh.

The workers killed in these two accidents are not the only people to have lost their lives during the lockdown due to reasons other than COVID-19.

Accidents take a toll

In fact, according to researchers Thejesh G.N., Kanika Sharma, and Aman,[4] till Saturday, 378 people had died since the lockdown was imposed due to reasons other than the disease. Of them, 69 people died in rail or road accidents while walking to their homes – the only mode of travel available

DOI: 10.4324/9781003291527-18

as public transport had been suspended by Prime Minister Narendra Modi's government, which gave notice of only four hours before the first lockdown came into effect.

Compiling information from news reports, the database[5] put together by the group, which describes itself as "freelance scholars and student volunteers interested in action-oriented research, socio-economic rights and related issues", shows that a large number of people have died due to reasons such as road accidents while walking back to their homes, starvation, denial of medical care, police brutality, exhaustion, suicides – all consequences of the lockdown.

The compilation began as a Twitter thread by Sharma on March 29.[6] "Immediately after the lockdown, we began seeing a lot of reports of deaths. People dying while walking back home, women dying due to denial of health care. These deaths were very distressing", Sharma, who is studying for a PhD in Sociology at Emory University in Atlanta in the United States of America, told *The Wire*.

According to their compilation, the death of the 16 migrant workers in Aurangabad was the largest number of people killed in a single incident. On March 28, a few days after the lockdown, eight migrants returning home were killed in a road accident in Karnataka's Raichur.[7]

The largest number of reported non-coronavirus deaths (83) so far have been due to suicides for reasons such as fear of infection, alcohol withdrawal symptoms, and due to loss of a job. A large number of people have also died due to starvation, denial of medical care, and exhaustion while walking home or queuing for rations or money.

To put the information together, the researchers have set up Google alerts in different languages, including Kannada, Marathi, Odia, Telugu, Bengali, Hindi, and English. "We do Google searches and people have also

Table 3.3.1 Deaths due to the lockdown as of May 14, 2020

Reason	*Number of deaths*
Starvation and financial distress	58
Exhaustion (walking, standing in queues)	29
Police brutality or state violence	12
Lack of medical care and attention to vulnerable groups (elderly or patients)	42
Suicides due to fear of infection, loneliness, and lack of freedom of movement	91
Alcohol withdrawal-related deaths and suicides	46
Road or train accidents due to walking/migration	89
Death by crimes associated with lockdown (not communal)	14
Unclassified (unable to categorise, need more details)	43

Source: Data compiled by Thejesh G.N., Kanika Sharma, and Aman

been sending reports to us. We verify them and volunteers help us translate them", Sharma said.

The researchers only take into account those deaths which have been reported by "credible" sources of news. "There are limitations. We can't do ground verification. We would also be missing a lot of deaths. Local media reports may not be reaching us. Also, a lot doesn't get reported", she said.

An 80-year-old man who lived near a bus stop in Tamil Nadu and was dependent on travellers for food died after the lockdown was imposed and there were no travellers.[8] A 12-year-old girl died due to exhaustion after walking 100 kilometres with her parents who had left for home after the lockdown was extended for the first time.[9]

Death and suicides

According to Sharma, a clear pattern that has emerged from the data is that those dying live on the margins.[10] "These are people of the working class. There are migrants and labourers. We have also seen that the reported deaths include more men than women because men go out working", she said.

A large number of women have also committed suicide, for instance, due to not being able to go to their parents' home. "These could be cases of women being in abusive relationships", said Sharma.

Another cause of death has been the denial of treatment by hospitals and doctors due to the fear of COVID-19. *The Times of India* reported in April that a pregnant woman in Telangana was turned away by six hospitals.[11] She was tested for COVID-19 and was admitted to a government maternity hospital only after the results came back negative. Due to the delay, the baby was born with complications and died. A day later, the woman also died.

In another similar incident, a woman pregnant with twins died in Jammu and Kashmir's Anantnag district as she was denied timely medical care.[12] She was a resident of an area which had been categorised as a "red zone" by the local administration and the doctors were hesitant to treat her.

The researchers point out that their compilation does not include all deaths that have occurred as a consequence of the lockdown. "It must be underscored that these deaths are likely an underestimate: only a fraction of deaths are reported by the media and we may have missed some deaths reported in local media as well", they said in a press note on Friday.

Notes

1 Reproduced with permission from *The Wire* where this article first appeared on May 10, 2020. https://thewire.in/rights/migrant-workers-non-coronavirus-lockdown-deaths

2 "Walked all night on tracks, left behind as I couldn't keep up" says Aurangabad tragedy survivor; 16 migrants who died were fatigued, fell asleep: cop, *Firstpost*, May 09, 2020. Retrieved from https://www.firstpost.com/india/walked-on

-tracks-to-avoid-police-check-posts-were-in-too-deep-sleep-to-hear-goods-train-coming-says-aurangabad-tragedy-survivor-8350121.html. Last accessed on October 10, 2021.

3 "Five Migrant Workers Killed, 13 Injured as Truck Carrying Them Overturns in MP", *The Wire*, May 10, 2020. Retrieved from https://thewire.in/rights/madhya-pradesh-migrant-workers-killed-truck. Last accessed on October 10, 2021.

4 "Non Virus Deaths", *Thejesh GN*, July 30, 2020. Retrieved from https://thejeshgn.com/projects/covid19-india/non-virus-deaths/. Last accessed on October 10, 2021.

5 "Non Virus Deaths", *Thejesh GN*.

6 See https://twitter.com/_kanikas_/status/1244118676594233346?s=20

7 "Hyderabad: Eight Migrants Returning Home Killed in Road Accident", *The Indian Express*, March 28, 2020. Retrieved from https://indianexpress.com/article/cities/hyderabad/india-lockdown-hyderabad-migrant-labourers-accident-6335807/?fbclid=IwAR3cSta5cPjibyt52giqm76vJRx9_Thuxjo39SmdBPkYnQmvbyYWTjEAN2M. Last accessed on October 10, 2021.

8 "ஊரடங்கால் உணவு தர யாருமில்லை" - பட்டினி கிடந்து உயிரிழந்த முதியவர் - அதிர்ச்சி தகவல்! #CORONALOCKDOWN", *Kalaignarseithigal*, April 11, 2020. Retrieved from https://www.kalaignarseithigal.com/tamilnadu/2020/04/11/old-man-hunger-death-during-corona-lockdown. Last accessed on October 10, 2021.

9 "12-Year-Old Walks 100 km, Dies Just Short of Bijapur Home", *The Indian Express*, April 21, 2020. Retrieved from https://indianexpress.com/article/india/12-yr-old-walks-100-km-dies-just-short-of-bijapur-home-6371779/. Last accessed on October 10, 2021.

10 "Lockdown में मायके नहीं भेजे जाने से परेशान विवाहिता ने की खुदकुशी", *IndiaTV*, April 17, 2020. Retrieved from https://www.indiatv.in/india/uttar-pradesh-married-woman-commits-suicide-due-to-not-being-sent-to-her-mothers-home-in-lock-down-704009. Last accessed on October 10, 2021.

11 "TSHRC Seeks Reports on Death of Woman, Her Newborn Baby", *The Times of India*, April 28, 2020. Retrieved from https://timesofindia.indiatimes.com/city/hyderabad/tshrc-seeks-reports-on-death-of-woman-her-new-born-baby/articleshow/75431954.cms. Last accessed on October 10, 2021.

12 "Pregnant Woman Dies in Anantnag Hospital, Inquiry Ordered", *The Deccan Herald*, April 26, 2020. Retrieved from https://www.deccanherald.com/national/pregnant-woman-dies-in-anantnag-hospital-inquiry-ordered-830031.html. Last accessed on October 10, 2021.

3.4 As Manipuri workers return home from Goa, what does the future hold for Baby Emmanuel Quarentino?[1]

Nandita Haksar

It isn't just the virus that has shattered the dreams of migrant workers – it's the response to it.

Prime Minister Narendra Modi has been wearing a *leirum phee*, a traditional Manipuri scarf, in place of a face mask. The *leirum phee* has been produced in Manipur since the ninth or tenth century and was mandatory during the wedding ceremonies of the Metei community. Did Modi want to show that the state has a special place in his heart? The problem is that Manipuris are up in arms because a textile mill in Barabanki in Uttar Pradesh is mass producing the Metei pattern and selling it as the Modi gamsha.

The idea that cultural artefacts can be appropriated to make up a national culture belies the fact that people in each part of India experience citizenship very differently. In Manipur, the thousands of young men and women who have been migrating to the towns and cities of India in search of work may have begun to feel a sense of being Indian. Despite innumerable difficulties, they have adjusted to different cultures across the country even though they dreamt of returning home one day.

I do not think anyone imagined that they would be returning so soon; put in Shramik trains, travelling without food or water. No one had in their worst nightmare thought there would be such an exodus back home after the government on March 25 imposed a total lockdown to curtail the spread of the coronavirus.

Returning empty-handed

Even worse, they were returning empty-handed, without the gifts they usually took home. In fact, many of their families had encouraged them to remain where they were out of fear that their sons and daughters would bring the coronavirus back with them from the cities.

This journey back to the village will mark an important moment in the history of Manipur, as it has for the rest of the country. I wanted to

DOI: 10.4324/9781003291527-19

document the journey of the migrants returning from Goa to Manipur. This was not going to be easy.

To begin with, the North-East people, across communities, have been brought up to remain stoic in the face of all situations. It is simply not done to speak of your pain when you know everyone else too is suffering. Adults, both men and women, are expected to bear it with a smile.

On one occasion in the 1990s, when I was fighting a case against security forces for torturing villagers in Senapati district of Manipur, the village headman, and my witness, gave his long deposition about how the armed forces had tortured and even killed men in his village. Later, I learnt his own child had died in the operation. I asked him why he had not told the court this. "How could I talk about my suffering when everyone has been through the same pain?" he asked.

When the journeys home were finally allowed, the Goa government on May 23 released a video of the train that left Madgaon in Goa for Jiribam in Manipur.[2] I recognised one of the Tangkhul Naga women in it; Ruth. She smiled and said she was grateful to the government of Goa for everything they had done for her and the others. No one bothered to ask her why she was leaving if things had been so good in Goa.

The months of hard work, the humiliations of being treated as an outsider, the horror she encountered when she had her first baby – Ruth's polite smile belied the growing homesickness that had driven her to the decision to leave her two small children with her husband and go home to Ukhrul.

No one on the train was sure what the future would hold. For the time being, the only thought was of going home. But getting home was not going to be easy even when they reached Jiribam, the final destination: the train arrived at its destination nearly 48 hours late, a journey marked by irregular meals, scanty drinking water, and filthy toilets.

Everyone was exhausted and climbed into the waiting bus ready to sleep for a few hours till they reached Imphal. But even the bus ride was not smooth. On the way, the bus had to stop because a truck lay across the road. I do not know how it was cleared. My citizen journalists were too tired to report. The second time the bus broke down it was at Noney. It was already dark, and they waited for an hour or more while the driver put it right.

Noney is the site of the world's tallest railway bridge, being built at a cost of more than Rs 12,000 crore, in violation of forest and environment laws. The tracks will ultimately connect South Asia with South East Asia. But for the local people, the train project had taken away their banana farms and many had been displaced. I wondered whether some of those displaced had become migrant workers.

By the time the bus reached Imphal, everyone was exhausted but the warmth of the welcome woke them up. They were given some refreshments but it was only in the morning they were sent back to the districts.

Those who arrived in Ukhrul, the district headquarters, were overwhelmed by the welcome. Many were quarantined in the Pettigrew College, including the group from Goa. For the next few days I got pictures of food: the pork, the egg curry, the beef fried, and organic green vegetables. It was good that they were being fed well.

One friend in Ukhrul, Lemyaola, an amateur photographer, said the migrants were well looked after. She said a bucket of good pork was calculated to feed eight people. She added: "Aunty, I have not had pork for months".

A meal at a quarantine centre.

But those who were put in other quarantine centres in Ukhrul did not have access to toilets and had to go out in the open even in the bitter cold nights. There were slippery roads and no electricity. Those who were quarantined in their villages lived in shelters made of tin sheets given to tribals as a part of a housing subsidy. The food did not include meat or even egg, and the cold got into the bones.

Where had all the money gone? The crores collected by the prime minister in the name of the most vulnerable victims of the pandemic? What about the Chief Minister's Relief Fund? Why could the funds not be used to build toilets in the villages – something that in any case should not have needed special funds?

In Manipur, like in other parts of India, almost all development projects or even the building of infrastructure had resulted in displacement of the people from the villages. The gap between the rich and poor had grown. Now, the migrant workers who had returned would be at the bottom of the hierarchy along with the landless.

It will take a lot more to convince the people of Manipur, especially the poor in both the Valley and in the Hills, that the government really cares than Prime Minister Modi wearing a traditional Meitei muffler.

I wonder what the migrants themselves are planning. Like all poor people they take comfort and solace in the family. I have been getting pictures of baby Haothangin Emmanuel Quarentino, born to a Kuki couple who worked in a spa in Goa. The baby's parents, Seilungthang and Nengnihat, had been excited about the coming of their baby. They could not have imagined that he would be born in the middle of the pandemic. Now Emmanuel will grow up with more cases of coronavirus coming up in Manipur. The fear in the villages has become palpable.

What does the future hold for little Emmanuel and his generation of those born in the midst of a virus that killed so many dreams; simple dreams of returning to the village with money to build a home, surrounded by a garden full of flowers and a kitchen garden with fresh vegetables; maybe a pig or two and a few clucking chickens. Of course, it is not just the virus that is to be blamed – it is the response to it that is responsible.

Notes

1 Reproduced with permission from *Scroll.in* where this article first appeared on June 16, 2020. https://scroll.in/article/964694/as-manipuri-workers-return-home-from-goa-what-does-the-future-hold-for-baby-emmanuel-quarentino
2 See https://www.facebook.com/DrPramodPSawant/videos/939888896469712/, last accessed October 10, 2021.

3.5 COVID-19

Odia women migrants suffer mental stress, feel nobody heeds their plight[1]

Rakhi Ghosh

For the last few years, young women from poor and impoverished families of Odisha, Jharkhand, Bihar, West Bengal, and Assam started replacing local workers in Bengaluru.

Golap Swain, 30, from Siko village of Odisha's Khordha district, has been waiting desperately to return home. She and other women migrants, who work in a garment factory in Bengaluru, have registered on the Odisha government's portal, but there is no sign of their travel arrangements.

> We are only waiting to go home and stay with our family. We are not interested in work. The company owner keeps us to meet the target. The rising number of Covid-19 cases creates anxiety and fear within us. If anything happens and we die, our bodies will be left unnoticed,

says Golap with a mix of tears and anger.

The desperate women migrant workers working in the garment, spinning, and textile factories of Tamil Nadu and Karnataka states made videos pleading with the Odisha Chief Minister to listen to their plights. Since the lockdown, they have been making distress calls to families, friends, village representatives, and activists in Odisha to take them back to the state.

> We think the Odisha government is not willing to take us. There is a nexus between employer, recruitment agencies in Odisha and the local police here. Now factories have started operating and we are forced to work. We are even asked to work 12 hours for two days in a week,

says Chinmayee Sahu, another migrant worker.

Odisha Distress Mapping and Mitigation Initiative (ODMMI), a WhatsApp group of volunteers working for stranded Odia migrants,

DOI: 10.4324/9781003291527-20

received a number of videos and distress calls from these migrants. Rajaram Sundaresan, a volunteer with ODMMI, with the help of AICCTU intervened and spoke with these migrants in Coimbatore.

> The Covid-19 situation is creating fear, anxiety and panic among them and they want to return. The Odisha government should discuss with the destination states and factory owners to arrange their travel. If delayed they may take some drastic steps,

he says.

Largest women migrant workforce

Earlier local young women were recruited in these garment and textile industries. But for the last few years, young women aged between 18 and 30 from poor and impoverished families of Odisha, Jharkhand, Bihar, West Bengal, and Assam started replacing local workers. According to a study, more than 5 lakh workers from these states are recruited to work in 1,200 factories in Karnataka. In Odisha, young women from tribal, Dalit, and other marginalised communities are mobilised, trained, and recruited under the government's Skill India scheme. Besides this, single women through friends and relatives are recruited to work in these factories.

Once recruited they have to face difficulties of long working hours, low wages, restricted mobility, language problems, physical, verbal, and mental harassment, and regular threats of being laid off from work. "These women are forced to work in semi-bondage conditions and being poor and hailing from rural areas, they are forced to be voiceless at their workplaces", says Sunderasan, adding that language problems and restricted mobility keep them away from joining unions.

They are usually first-generation migrants. The reasons for migration are lack of employment in their villages, an opportunity of a livelihood, the burden of feeding family, the need to pay off dowries, and aspirations of city life. The decision of their migration is taken by their family, not by them. The field staff of Project Implementation Agencies (PIAs) convince parents that their daughters are working in safer places. "In this pandemic situation, both family and their daughters are in fear and anxiety. When all stranded migrants are retuning homes, these women also want to return and Odisha government should intervene to bring them back", says an employee of one PIA who didn't want to be named.

Forced work, unpaid dues

In Coimbatore, some workers alleged they were forced to work during the lockdown.

> Since we stay in hostels inside the factory campus we were asked to work during the lockdown. They forced us to work even when we were not well. They said your machine will remain idle and who will operate it,

says Jharana Sahu, another migrant from Nabarangpur.

Now the factories have opened, and they are asked to do 12 hours for 2 days a week. "To meet the target demand the company owners are keeping us here and not willing to send us back", says Sumati Munda. In Tirupur, the women migrants protested against forced work and non-payment. They made videos and sent them to activists and media houses in Odisha. Later, with interventions of the state administrations, they boarded the train back home.

Sukumari Munda, 20, says they are yet to receive their dues since March. "We are working in a small factory and due to lockdown, the work was stopped. The factory has started operating only a few days back, once they clear our dues we will return", she says.

Karuppusamy Raman, Director, READ, an NGO that works for the rights of underprivileged in Tamil Nadu, says: "There is a complete lack of coordination between the source and destination states and factory owners. It is the right of women workers to go home. But before they leave their due wages need to be settled".

Violation of COVID protection norms

The Factories Act 1948 deals with occupational safety and health conditions at work. Under the Act, employers are required to take adequate measures to ensure the safety and health of workers. With the COVID-19 pandemic around, Golap says: "We are maintaining physical distancing, wearing masks and using sanitiser at the factory. During the screening, if the body temperature shows higher than the prescribed limit we are asked to go". On the other hand, Sukumari says they are working in a small factory and don't have enough space to maintain physical distancing; they are only wearing masks to protect themselves.

Prof Asha Hans, who did a study on women migrant workers, says:

> During our visit to Tirupur and Bengaluru we noticed there were 10–15 women staying in one small room with the regular scarcity of water. Thus, it would not be possible for them to follow physical distancing and regular hand wash.

Some factories don't have sufficient toilets and clean drinking water facilities for women workers. There is no sick leave, government holidays, or compensatory days off. If they go home and take leave for nearly a month they are replaced by another worker. "When they are not allowed to go to the washroom to avoid wasting time how they will be allowed to clean hands at regular intervals to avoid infection", she asks.

Challenges of reverse migration

Prof Chinmay Tumbe, Assistant Professor, Economics Area, IIM, Ahmedabad, and author of the book *India Moving* says:

> There is going to be a large labour gap and employers will have to provide better assurances on workers safety and better wages in order to induce migrants to come back. They will eventually come back as wages start to spiral up, reflecting the shortfall.

Activist Sneha Mishra, who has been counselling these women, says: "Almost all of them want to return. At least for the next few months, they want to stay with their families", adding, the pandemic will have a larger adverse impact on women migrants than men. Families may not allow them to migrate again which will lead to job loss, and make them prone to early marriage, domestic violence, and trafficking.

Umi Daniel, Director, Aide et Action, says

> Government should evacuate them on a priority basis, counsel them and provide financial incentives for next 2–3 months to sustain them. These young women are trained in certain skills and are supporting their families. If they want to return government should ensure them to reclaim their jobs in the factories they were working.

Most of the women migrants will decide whether to return or not when the situation eases. Right now, all they want to do is go back home.

Note

1 Reproduced with permission from *Outlook* magazine where this article first appeared on May 22, 2020. https://www.outlookindia.com/website/story/india-news-covid-19-odia-women-migrants-suffer-mental-stress-feel-nobody-heeds-to-their-plight/353325

3.6 Between household abuse and employer apathy, domestic workers bear the brunt of lockdown[1]

Deepanshu Mohan, Kensiya Kennedy, Mansi Singh, and Shivani Agarwal

The nature of their work has exposed female workers to a higher degree of abuse and exploitation in the absence of an underlying social or economic safety net.

An indifferent government's response to the current pandemic and its economic impact is now presenting a set of scenarios that is likely to exacerbate deep-rooted inequities, otherwise entrenched in different socio-political, economic forms.[2]

One particular group worst affected by the economic crisis, particularly within the unorganised or unsecured worker space, has been that of the domestic workers. The plight of the domestic working class (mostly women), toiling hard in India's rich urban metropolises, often at the risk of higher exploitation and indignation by the elite class (of higher-income urban households), is widely known and written about.[3]

Noted sociologist Dipankar Gupta has often written and spoken about the inherent failure of the elite middle-class residing in urban metros to empathise with the lives of female workers, both experientially and in terms of understanding their material state of being, calling it the problem of intersubjectivity.[4]

Such concerns around "intersubjectivity", as part of the troubled modern relationship between the elite and the (lower) working class, existed long before the pandemic, and now it seems, the divide has only been further intensified.

According to an ILO report of April (2020),[5] estimates show that the economic crisis arising from COVID-19 and the government's response to it is likely to further push almost 40 crore informal (unsecured) workers into absolute poverty. This estimate includes more than 200 million women employed as domestic workers. The actual numbers may be far worse due to (pre-existing) concerns in the statistical accounting of unpaid, care workers.[6]

In making sense of the micro-scenario, as part of a recent study undertaken by the Centre for New Economics Studies[7] over the last few months, we made

DOI: 10.4324/9781003291527-21

an attempt to understand the extent to which women working as domestic workers (across different cities) were impacted during the weeks of a curfew-style lockdown (and since the unlocking process began in some areas).

During our study, we spoke to over a dozen female domestic workers across the cities of Bhopal, Chandigarh, and Jhansi – those being hometowns of our team members who interviewed the domestic workers employed by households in their own respective residential colonies.

Our research team, conducting a mini-ethnographic survey over seven to eight weeks, explored how a pandemic-induced lockdown affected female domestic workers (of different ages), to what extent the government's response and aid support (in the form of food rations) affected their intra-household consumption patterns, and, given the unsecured nature of work, what some of the psycho-social costs faced by these women domestic workers are (in terms of domestic abuse and violence). Whatever direct assistance was offered to the workers by the government in the form of food aid and ration-support involved serious administrative (and distributive) concerns in implementing the aid schemes at the ground level (see Figure 3.7.1).

Here, we share some key observations from the survey.

Lives and livelihoods

As the lockdown was enforced across the nation, many resident welfare associations (RWAs) exercised absolute discretion in restricting the entry (and mobility) of domestic workers in (urban) residential colonies and apartments. This made many workers lose out on day-to-day work with very few receiving any cash (or in-kind) support from their respective employers.

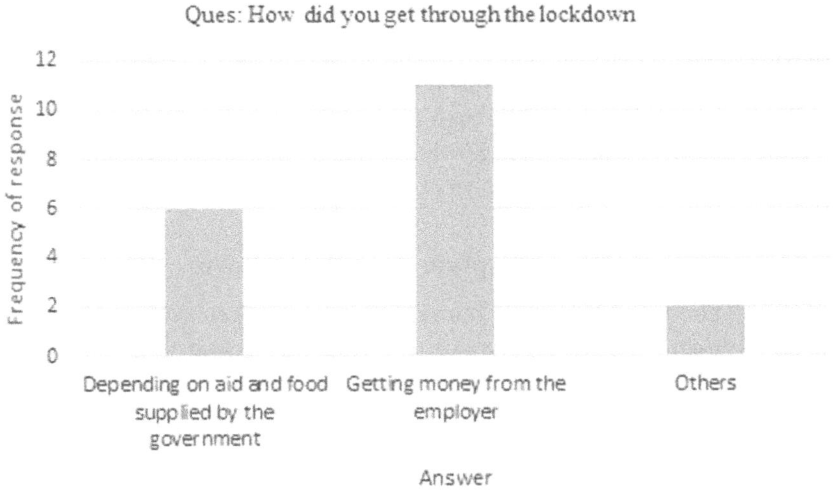

Figure 3.7.1 Source of direct support for domestic workers during lockdown.

When asked whether she received her wages from employers during the lockdown period, 40-year-old Babita from Chandigarh said, "my employer provided me with gas and money along with some other employers giving some cash money, and our family barely made it through".

Amongst all respondents interviewed, 85% responded by saying that like Babita they had received some cash-support from their respective employers which had helped tide them over for the first two months of the lockdown period. Without the cash-support, and without any safety net, they didn't have any other alternative channel for soliciting any help (whether from the government or anyone else).

Most workers felt that the increased sense of social responsibility amongst the elite, higher-middle income class employers was largely because of the observed inefficiencies in the government's response to the pandemic. The glaring visuals of the migrant labour crisis across cities, according to some respondents like Babita, made most employers pay salaries even if the workers couldn't enter their homes to work.

However, on the other hand, many who couldn't manage to get cash-support or were rendered jobless because of the lockdown were left at the mercy of the state to receive food and ration-support.

Thirty-five-year-old Asha from Bhopal said that as a single wage earner in her household, it became very exhausting for her to stand in long queues for ration packages without receiving any help from her husband. She had to return empty-handed on most days. As a result, she ended up borrowing most of her food ration on credit from the local *kirana* store close to her house.

Similar narratives emerged from Chandigarh and Jhansi, where most respondents (like Asha) could not avail of food aid provided by the government either because they lacked a ration card, or had a ration card with the address of their native village, or could not put up with long queues daily which made it difficult for them to get access even when supplies could be made available.

It was also interesting to note how most female domestic worker respondents said that they were asked by their husbands and other family members to stand in crowded queues and get the ration which made them more vulnerable to being infected with the virus itself.

Patterns in household consumption during lockdown

When asked about how her daily household consumption level was affected by the lockdown, 37-year-old Priya from Chandigarh said that her family and children had skipped many meals across days and were able to have only 1 decent meal in a 2-day period.

She, and her family, survived on the food-packets they had received from social organisations and other community-outreach efforts (near her residence). Her inability to receive state-provided food aid was because of her ration card address, which was of her native village and made her "ineligible" to get rations.

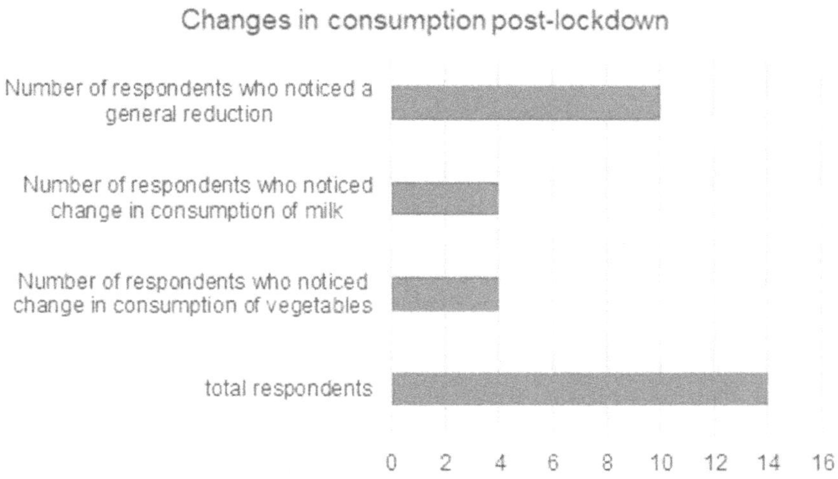

Figure 3.7.2 Patterns in household consumption during lockdown.

Asha also echoed a similar concern about not being able to receive food aid despite pleading with the distribution centres. "I think the people in charge of the ration centres were taking advantage of helpless people like us and hoarding government aid for themselves", she said.

While studying the change in consumption patterns during the pandemic for most domestic workers, the most noticeable change (as seen in Figure 3.7.2) was observed in the consumption of milk, milk-related products, and vegetables. There was an observed reduction of up to 50% in the consumption of milk in most households.

While for many urban and semi-urban households across India, milk and vegetables are part of the staple or essential diet, we observed how these became a "luxury" during the lockdown because of broken supply-chains. As a result, many female respondents with children of one or less than one year found it difficult to provide basic nutrition and milk to their children. Most had to borrow money from people nearby to buy milk (at higher prices) for their children while many couldn't afford to do even that.

Forty-five-year-old Aarti from Jhansi said that the lockdown period saw an exponential rise in her basic household expenses. This added to her family's plight when she and her husband couldn't earn anything.

The psycho-social cost of being vulnerable

Apart from the exacerbated vulnerabilities from external factors or the outbreak of the pandemic, this group of workers also face serious concerns in terms of mediating their own intra-household relations (with their spouse and families). Three of our respondents, from Bhopal, Chandigarh, and Jhansi, reported an increased incidence of abusive environments in their respective homes and were desperately looking to return to work despite the risk of getting infected or breaching the enforced lockdown restrictions.

Rashmi from Jhansi injured her right arm during the lockdown while driving her two-wheeler. However, she could not find any assistance from her spouse or her family to get her arm treated at a clinic or a nearby hospital. She faced abuse from her own spouse and attributed his behaviour to "lack of a stable job". She has been the sole-earning member in her family and takes care of her children from her earnings as a domestic worker. During the lockdown, that became difficult and also led to a higher incidence of domestic violence from her spouse.

Rajni from Jhansi said that she couldn't disclose to her own family that her employer had given her wages in advance for the period of the lockdown. This was because every month her husband and other family members would take her income without giving her much to manage her personal expenses. She feared that the wages she had received in advance would again be spent on some frivolous expenditure. She stayed with her employer – at her place of work – for the duration of the lockdown as she was scared of the abuse she would face at home from her spouse and family.

Two other respondents, Asha and Priya (from Bhopal and Chandigarh respectively), narrated a similar pattern of domestic violence and abuse that they faced during the lockdown and shared experiences similar to that of Rajni. In all cases, three points were common: the abuser was their husband or his family members; their husbands didn't have a job; and they (husbands) were alcoholics and would beat them for money.

Asha said that her husband was borrowing money from her ex-employer – whose household she had escaped with great difficulty after facing abuse. Now, with her husband borrowing money from the same person, the debt was being added to her name and had imposed a huge financial burden on her.

"COVID-19 may not kill us but hunger and debt definitely will", she said.

The US and Western European countries along with developing nations like Brazil, South Africa, etc., have acknowledged the depth of this problem and the pandemic's disproportional impact on the unsecured working class. It has implored them to expand coverage of state-funded emergency lending plans to cover contractual workers, gig-workers, and others in the unorganised workforce.

However, India, on the other hand, has largely left almost all of these workers – including domestic workers – to be hung out to dry, offering little to no actual support. The vulnerability of women, working as domestic workers or in other informal forms of work, has left them without any underlying social or economic safety net.

Moreover, as seen in the cases of Rashmi, Rajni, Asha, and Priya, the nature of their work has exposed each one of them to a higher incidence of abuse and exploitation at the hands of both their "employer", and their household members. This crisis has exposed them to higher vulnerability while challenging their basic livelihood and survival.

As the number of COVID-19 cases continues to surge even now in most tier 2 and tier 3 cities across India, the plight of domestic workers and others who are a part of India's large informal, unorganised workforce may further worsen, pushing many into states of extreme poverty.

Notes

1 Reproduced with permission from *The Wire* where this article first appeared on July 24, 2020. https://thewire.in/labour/lockdown-female-domestic-workers-covid-19-lockdown
2 Mohan, Deepanshu. "How Women Get a Raw Deal in Pandemic", *Daily O*, June 6, 2020. Retrieved from https://www.dailyo.in/variety/women-empowerment-unemployement-gender-equality-covid-19-lockdown/story/1/33039.html. Last accessed on October 10, 2021.
3 Mahanta, Upasana and Gupta, Indranath. *Recognition of the Rights of Domestic Workers in India*. Singapore: Springer. 2019.
4 Joshi, Poornima. "Our Middle Class is Actually the Elite", *The Hindu Business Line*, August 15, 2018. Retrieved from https://www.thehindubusinessline.com/specials/india-file/our-middle-class-is-actually-the-elite/article24692967.ece. Last accessed on October 10, 2021.
5 "Covid-19 Can Push 40 Crore Informal Sector Workers in India Deeper into Poverty: ILO", *The Print*, April 7, 2020. Retrieved from https://theprint.in/india/covid-19-can-push-40-crore-informal-sector-workers-in-india-deeper-into-poverty-ilo/397355/. Last accessed on October 10, 2021.
6 Deepanshu. "How Women Get a Raw Deal in Pandemic".
7 See https://jgu.edu.in/jslh/centre-for-new-economics-studies/. Last accessed on October 10, 2021.

3.7 Social distancing and sex workers in India[1]

Priyanka Tripathi and Chhandita Das

The deplorable condition of sex workers in India amidst the COVID-19 lockdown is discussed. Prostitution, now called sex work, has been a historical reality with cultural connotations. However, a significant amount of shame and stigma is attached to the profession wherein it is not even seen as work. Social distancing and the lockdown have left sex workers across the country in poverty and hunger. There is a need to address the issues of this section of society from a human rights' perspective.

With an intention to break the chain of the novel coronavirus spread in India, Prime Minister Narendra Modi announced the "Janata Curfew" on 22 March 2020, coupled with a complete nationwide lockdown from 24 March 2020. Even though the nation is in the unlocking phase now, the lockdown in India has disproportionately affected various sections/classes of society.

While the comparatively rich and privileged class can afford to be locked down, it is primarily the poor and the vulnerable that have been driven by the distress of survival. Diseases and disasters may not differentiate much while infecting human bodies, but the uneven social structures do render a non-uniformity of pandemic impacts upon people, and this has already been witnessed in the recent past during epidemics across developing nations, like the crises of human immunodeficiency virus (HIV) in 1999, severe acute respiratory syndrome (SARS) in 2003, the Ebola outbreak in 2014, the major spread of Zika in 2016, and others. The present pandemic of COVID-19, particularly in India, allows a revisiting of those grim realities where the poor and the marginalised sections suffered, being denied their rights and entitlements amidst a crisis.

During this COVID-19 pandemic, one becomes a witness to how social distancing has intensified the already existing class inequalities, wherein there is a larger section of people desperate to sustain their livelihoods. Amidst the practice of "social distancing", and "self-quarantine" becoming an important phrase in our vocabulary and practice, there are various measures taken by the government for virus prevention. However, at the grass-roots level, they do not appear to be very inclusive of the marginalised

DOI: 10.4324/9781003291527-22

sections in terms of their strategies of pandemic management. To identify the effect of this COVID-19 pandemic, the government identifies Indian states as red, orange, and green zones. They are channelised and extensively advertised by the government and non-government agencies for mass awareness and virus prevention, but in between the stakes of these coloured zones, theexistence of the red-light areas is ghettoed and ignored by the socially insensitive narratives of the COVID-19 crisis. The case in discussion here is of the sex workers who reside in these red-light areas, and their profession is considered as "a contact job" (Hurst et al 2020). The ravenous and derailed condition of the sex workers in every corner of India during the lockdown period reinforces these questions of uneven social foundations, and again, their missing link in the government's relief packages compels one to wonder if sex workers have been denied their human rights.

Several reports across the world indicate that whether it is a developing or developed country, sex workers are at the cliff, holding on to life with the bare minimum. A recent report by the International Committee on the Rights of Sex Workers in Europe (ICRSWE) highlights the discriminatory and exclusive nature of governments' pandemic-recovery schemes across continents (Wheeler 2020). Officially, there are over six lakh sex workers[2] in India, while the unofficial numbers may be higher. Many of them continue their profession from the narrow, dingy lanes of the urban metropolises like Delhi's GB Road, Mumbai's Kamathipura, Kolkata's Sonagachi, Varanasi's Shivdaspur, Pune's Budhwar Peth, etc., and there are more than 1,100 red-light areas in India, falling within the range of plausible hotspots of the ongoing pandemic (Parthsarathi 2020). These areas under complete lockdown have been denied any income.

Irony of "social distancing"

The entire concept of "sex work", particularly in India, is at the relative juncture of economic, social, and cultural engagement. Although, Indian history witnessed the categorically esteemed institution of sex work within the brief accounts of Vedas, Puranas, Mahabharata, Buddhist literature, Kautilya's Arthashastra, etc., under the colonial hegemony of moral politics, sex workers were relegated to the margins. Our society continues to use their professional services but casts them out publicly under the garb of a gentlemanly outlook playing upon the politics of "shame". One iconic text that can be noted here is George Bernard Shaw's *Mrs Warren's Profession* (1893), which was a reflection of Shaw's discussion with sex workers, of course to no avail as far as the change of the mindset towards the profession is concerned. Sex work became a derogatory *dhanda* for them, making them *dhandewalis*.[3] The COVID-19 pandemic may now add "social distancing" to sex workers' existing vocabulary, but each one of them has already felt and imbibed the nuanced distance that society maintains with them. In "normal" or pre-COVID-19 days, this distancing may not be of much concern to them, but since the virus tightened its grip over India and the government announced the safeguard of "social distancing", the distance between sex workers and mainstream society has widened., Most of them work from brothels, while some as call girls provide services in places of demand, but due to the lockdown, the majority of them are stuck in their residential red-light areas.

Considering their places of residence as "home", the entire sacrosanct ethos of the tag line "Stay Home, Stay Safe" promoted by state agencies and social media raises a big question mark in the context of the sex workers' plight. Their places of residence are located mostly in the jam-packed lanes of red-light areas where practising social distance is close to impossible. In Delhi's GB Road, over 3,000 sex workers share 80 small brothels. There are similar types of congested residences in Kolkata's Sonagachi, from where more than 10,000 sex workers continue their living. As many as 15–20 people share 1 bathroom with limited water supply; therefore, "hand sanitisation", "self-quarantine", and overall hygiene are altogether very are difficult to follow. The recent joint report of the Global Network of Sex Workers Project and the Joint United Nations Programme on HIV/AIDS (UNAIDS) has already sounded the grave threats that the COVID-19 pandemic will cast upon sex workers due to the combined effect of patriarchy, poverty, and social discrimination. Being "excluded from COVID-19 social protection responses, sex workers are faced with putting their safety, their health, and their lives at increased risk just to survive" (UNAIDS 2020a). The lockdown has put them in the midst of the worst reality ever. Even as they respond to the government's call by deciding to stay indoors at their residences with no WORK, the "Laxman Rekha" between private and public spaces drawn by India's Prime Minister in his nationwide lockdown announcement hardly guarantees the safety of these sex workers either from disease or hunger.

Futility of laws and codes

The socially and economically precarious position of sex workers that this pandemic crisis only exacerbates is duly rooted in their ambiguous position in Indian laws and codes. Most of the anti-sex work policies and policing practices do cause hurdles in accessing their rights to earn from rendering their sexual-activity contingent services. The entire industry of commercialised sex was criminalised soon after India's independence in 1956 under the Suppression of Immoral Traffic Act (SITA). Under the pressure of constitutional challenges regarding the right to the profession, this Act was amended in 1986 as the Immoral Traffic (Prevention) Act (ITPA), and it partially decriminalised sex as a profession for adults, putting sex workers across India in a legally vague position. The activities needed for sex work like keeping a brothel, "soliciting in public places", "living off the earnings of prostitutes", "seduction of persons in custody", etc., are all under criminal provisions (Reddy 2004). The Union Cabinet of the Government of India's recently approved Trafficking of Persons (Prevention, Protection and Rehabilitation) Bill, 2018, is also not clear and comprehensive about sex workers' rights, since the bill is coupled with the ITPA 1986 with extensive emphasis on the strategies of raids and rescue that hardly pay heed to the consenting sex between adults resulting in "human rights violations" (Pai et al 2018). Although the Supreme Court of India recommends entitlement rights of sex workers and as per the norms of Article 21 of the Constitution, which urges states to provide willing sex workers a conducive situation in which to continue their profession, there are several instances under which sex workers often face harassment and are abused by police, agents, clients, goons, and whoever sees them at work. Even a decade ago, a Supreme Court panel did recommend the central government and Election Commission to issue sex workers voter ID cards, relaxing verification, and appealed to states and local institutions to promote ration cards for them.[4] Under stigma, till date, sex workers are often denied the basic entitlements of ration cards and health cards, and, if they ask, they are routinely silenced at the end of legal questions. Apart from prostitution policies, this lack of documentation provides grounds to exclude them in broader forms of social and economic sectors and increases the level of vulnerabilities amidst this COVID-19 pandemic.

Economic fallout

Sex work in India is one of the unrecognised economic sectors where most of the work is informal and unprotected (Agarwala 2013). Under dominant discourses of developing nations, sex workers are either "exploited victims" or "fallen women" and are rarely in the broader spectrum counted as workers. In recent times, by valorising the term "sex worker" rather than "prostitute", efforts are being shown towards their inclusion in the labour markets of India, and, for financial inclusion, the need to link their profession with formal banking systems has already been highlighted by various scholarly insights, yet the results are still not satisfactory (Chakrabarty and Sharma 2018). Still, their profession is outside the loop of standard labour-protection measures, and thereby, both in the long and short term, their work is the most "informal" among India's informal economy where the ongoing pandemic crisis hits hard, and overnight, they are left with no income. India's quick imposition of lockdown as a precaution as well as a preventive measure for the deadly COVID-19 pandemic receives international appreciation. In reality, it costs the country's economic growth, and each section has to undergo its cascading impact more or less. However, it is the daily wage earners working in the unorganised sectors who are instantly bearing the brunt of the crisis. The lack of a far-sighted plan during the lockdown became visible with the plight of migrant workers in their desperate attempts to reach home. Lucknow had witnessed an accident of a migrant worker's family in their desperate attempt to go back home over 750 km on a cycle (Pandey 2020). Recently, 16 migrant workers were run over by a freight train near Aurangabad, who were also walking back towards home (Banerjee and Mahale 2020). These incidents make visible the real disparity between the decision of an unforeseen lockdown and hunger in the country, which is reflected on social media, with the picture of pieces of bread scattered over that railway track. The irony of discourse is that while the public exhibits its concerns for migrant labourers over social media, there is rarely any concern shown over the troubles of sex workers amidst the lockdown, although their condition is grimmer than other wage earners. Quite a few attempts have been made by some non-governmental organisations at the local scale to distribute foods and other necessary items temporarily to the sex workers in red-light areas, such as by the Kat-Katha in Delhi, Durbar Mahila Samanwaya Committee in Kolkata, Kranti in Mumbai, etc. While such initiatives are highly commendable, they are barely enough for the sustenance of the entire sex workers' community amidst the extended time this pandemic crisis continues.

Finance Minister of India Nirmala Sitharaman, in response to the pandemic lockdown, announced relief packages for the benefit of people in informal sectors. In brief, these include the doubling of ration entitlements free of cost to the beneficiaries under the National Food Security Act, giving `500 per month directly to the "Jan Dhan Yojana" bank accounts of female customers, and disbursing a pension amount of `1,000 for the coming three months to widows, old persons, and persons with disabilities. The government has also announced free liquefied petroleum gas cylinders for three months to the beneficiaries of "Ujjwala Yojana".

However, nowhere is it clearly mentioned as to how much these relief packages are going to benefit the socio-economically excluded groups like sex workers. To avail of the benefits of the government's relief packages, the Aadhaar number has been made mandatory, which most sex workers lack, and they also do not have bank accounts since they live mostly on cash due to the highly informal nature of their profession. Their clientele mostly includes truck drivers, migrant workers, and others who are also facing an economic challenge amidst lockdown that has decreased their footfall at a noticeable rate in red-light areas. Since sex workers often have no savings and the lockdown has blocked their source of income, they are unable to pay their residential rents and are left at the stake of hunger and anxiety. Even if the lockdown is entirely lifted soon, it is a matter of debate as to how much they will be allowed to continue the profession, for "social distancing" has become the new normal.

Conclusions

The trajectory of the COVID-19 crisis in India and its intersection with political decisions setting up new sociocultural norms have placed sex workers of India in a state of high anxiety. Over and again, it puts their human rights in question, although the executive director of UNAIDS, Winnie Byanyima (24 April 2020b), continuously reminded countries to be inclusive of sex workers in their pandemic management schemes, since human rights are universal, inalienable, and interdependent. The roots and layers of sex workers' problems attuned to the broader spectrum of the social, economic, political, and legislative contexts of India are densely exclusionary so that inventing their antidote may even be more challenging than discovering the vaccine for COVID-19. Should not some immediate infrastructure be arranged for this marginal section of women, at least to sustain them amidst this pandemic? At a point when imagining an agency for the marginalised in this kind of a state of crisis is quite utopian, it surely points towards an opportunity to rethink the existing norms and practices collectively.

Notes

1 Reproduced with permission from *Economic and Political Weekly* (Volume 55, Issue Number 31) where it first appeared on 1 August 2020. https://www.epw.in/journal/2020/31/commentary/social-distancing-and-sex-workers-india.html
2 As per the UNAIDS survey in 2016, there are 657,800 sex workers present in India.
3 *Dhandewali* is a native Hindi word for sex workers which is considered to be derogatory.
4 In 2011, the Supreme Court of India, in its interim order, urged the rehabilitation of sex workers. For further details, see: http://indialawyers.wordpress.com/2011/09/16/sex-workers- rehabilitation-case.

References

Agarwala, R (2013): *Informal Labor, Formal Politics, And Dignified Discontent in India*, New York: Cambridge University Press.

Banerjee, S and A Mahale (2020): "16 Migrant Workers Run Over by Goods Train Near Aurangabad in Maharashtra," *Hindu*, 8 May, viewed on 9 May, https://www.thehindu.com/ news/national/other-states/16-migrant-workers-run-over-by-goods-train-near-aurangabad- in-maharashtra/article31531352.ece.

Chakrabarty, A and V Sharma (2018): "Financial Inclusion of Female Sex Workers: A Study from Andhra Pradesh," *Economic & Political Weekly*, Vol 53, No 44, 3 November, pp 30–35.

Hurst, L, M Martinez and L Monella (2020): "'It's a Contact Job': Sex Workers Struggle Amid the Coronavirus Crisis," *Euronews*, 16 April, viewed on 9 May, https://www.euronews.com/2020/ 04/16/it-s-a-contact-job-sex-workers-struggle- amid-the-coronavirus-crisis.

Pai, A, M Seshu and L Murthy (2018): "In Its Haste to Rescue Sex Workers, 'Anti-Trafficking' Is Increasing Their Vulnerability," *EPW Engage*, Vol 53, No 28, 14 July, https://www.epw.in/en- gage/article/raid-and-rescue-how-anti-trafficking-strategies-increase-sex-workers-vulnerability-to-exploitative-practices.

Pandey, A (2020): "Migrant Couple on 700-km Cycle Journey Home Run Over, Children Injured," *NDTV*, 8 May, viewed on 9 May, https://www. ndtv.com

/india-news/coronavirus-lockdown- in-up-migrant-couple-trying-to-cycle-home- amid-lockdown-run-over-by-car-2225355.

Parthsarathi, M (2020): “No Money, Food or Medicines, Delhi’s Sex Workers Struggle to Survive in Lockdown,” *Outlook*, 6 April, viewed on 28 April, https://www.outlookindia.com/newsscroll/ no-money-food-or-medicines-delhis-sex-work- ers-struggle-to-survive-in-lockdown/1793198.

Reddy, GB (2004): *Prevention of Immoral Traffic and Law*, Hyderabad: Gogia Law Agency.

Shaw, GB (1893): *Mrs WARREN’S Profession*, L W Conolly (ed), Toronto: Broadview Press, 2005.

UNAIDS (2020a): “Sex Workers Must Not be Left Behind in the Response to COVID-19,” 8 April, viewed on 2 May 2020, https://www.unaids. org/en/resources/presscentre/pressreleasean- dstatementarchive/2020/april/20200408_sex- workers-covid-19.

UNAIDS (2020b): “COVID-19 Responses Must Uphold and Protect the Human Rights of Sex Workers,” 24 April, viewed on 4 May 2020, https://www. unaids .org/en/resources/presscentre/feature- stories/2020/april/20200424_sex-work.

Wheeler, S (2020): “Sex Workers Struggle to Sur- vive Covid-19 Pandemic: Criminalisation Makes a Bad Situation Worse,” *Human Rights Watch*, 4 May, viewed on 8 May, https://www. hrw.org/news/2020/05/04/sex-workers-struggle-survive-covid-19-pandemic.

Part 4

No wages, no jobs, no food

4.1 Can the State let employers walk away from lockdown wages?[1]

Bharat Bhushan

If the government is serious about standing with the migrant workers, then it cannot leave them to the vagaries of unequal negotiations with employers.

"Dear migrant labourers and daily wage earners ... the country stands with you!" proclaims a Central government advertisement in the newspapers. Notwithstanding this public protestation of solidarity with migrant workers, the government is ready to remove the mandatory wage protection it had offered earlier for the pandemic-induced lockdown period. Attorney General K. K. Venugopal has requested the Supreme Court to suspend the government's earlier order on full lockdown wages. Eventual payments, he suggested, could be settled through negotiations between workers and employers.

Government ads enumerating its welfare measures for migrant workers list over Rs.1 lakh crore allocation under MGNREGA for employment generation. They also list access to food grain for two months without a ration card and a proposal to set up "Affordable Rental Housing Complexes" in cities so that should such crises recur migrant workers will not have to return to their villages because of unaffordable rents. There is not a word about assured lockdown wages.

On March 29, the Union Home Secretary issued an order saying,

> All the employers, be it in industry or in shops and commercial establishments, shall make payment of wages of their workers at their workplace, on the due date, without any deduction, for the period their establishments are under closure during the lockdown.

Non-compliance with the order would invite action. By mandatorily protecting the wages of the workers during the lockdown the government took a major decision to protect the incomes of the vulnerable.

Section 51 (1)(b) of the Disaster Management Act mandates punishment up to one year or a fine or both for non-compliance. Further if non-compliance results in loss of life or imminent danger thereof, then the punishment

DOI: 10.4324/9781003291527-24

may extend to two years. In other words, if any worker forced to flee the city due to non-payment of wages died on the way home, the liability for the death could, in principle, be fixed.

The government has not yet put any detailed information into the public domain about numbers of job losses by urban workers or estimates of lost income. A study in "India Forum", by Noman Majid of the ILO's Decent Work Team for South Asia, has estimated migrant job losses using data from two recent studies. While the Centre for Monitoring Indian Economy estimates that 91.3 million labourers and small traders (corresponding to the categories of casual workers and self-employed) lost their jobs in April, a survey by Azim Premji University showed that 81% of casual workers, 84% of self-employed, and 76% of regular salaried workers had lost their jobs by mid-May.

Applying these figures to the population-adjusted estimates of the government's Periodic Labour Force Survey 2017–18, Majid concludes that 15.35 million casual workers would have lost their jobs by mid-May. Adjust this to the population of 2020 instead of 2017–18 and the number is likely to climb.

The massive shock to the livelihoods of migrant workers is also underlined by a survey of 15,000 households conducted by researchers at the Indian Statistical Institute, Delhi. Nearly 77% of households reported job losses in their family and 72% within their social network of family, relatives, and friends. Respondents reported greater job losses in Phase 2 of the lockdown (74%) than in Phase 1 (66%). The ISI survey's job loss perception is in the same high range as that of Azim Premji University.

A different study by Jayan Jose Thomas of the Economics Department of the Indian Institute of Technology, Delhi, estimates income lost by migrant workers at about Rs. 4 lakh crore for two months – nearly 2% of the GDP.

The government began to retreat from its March 29 order when Lockdown 4.0 began. On May 17, the Union Home Ministry rescinded its order on full lockdown wages. It soon became clear that this did not apply only to future wages but also retrospectively to the period from March 25 to May 17.

The Attorney General clarified this on June 5 to the Supreme Court.

> If the notification (of March 29) was not issued at that time, there would have been a much larger exodus of the migrant workers. Now the government wants to start economic activity. Please keep in abeyance the scrutiny of the March 29 notification for two months and let employers and employees reach a settlement on payment of wages under the Industrial Disputes Act.

His arguments suggest that the March 29 order was never meant to ensure workers' wages but was just a tactic to retain workers in the cities.

Some employers have argued in the Supreme Court that the government was not empowered under the Disaster Management Act to direct the private sector to pay full wages to workers. The court has itself raised the same doubt. Employers have suggested that the government pay wages for the lockdown period from the excess funds of the Employees' State Insurance Corporation (ESIC). They obviously took their cue from media reports that ESIC funds which stood at over Rs. 68,000 crore at FY2019-end could be used to give livelihood support to workers hit by the lockdown.

However, the government has not taken this position before the Supreme Court which will pronounce its order on June 12. The apex court's own attitude was telling. Chief Justice Sharad Arvind Bobde shocked the nation by asking why migrant workers living in temporary government shelters and given free food needed to be paid wages!

If the government is serious about standing with the migrant workers, then it must come forward with a positive plan of its own instead of leaving workers to the vagaries of unequal negotiations especially when labour laws have been diluted in many states.

If it wants to let employers and companies off the hook on lockdown wages, then it must find other ways of putting cash in the hands of the workers to compensate them. Additionally, it must launch public works – building infrastructure in rural areas – to provide employment and avoid the livelihood crisis staring them in the face.

Note

1 Reproduced with permission from business-standard.com where the article first appeared on June 8, 2020. https://www.business-standard.com/article/opinion/can-the-state-let-employers-walk-away-from-lockdown-wages-120060800087_1.html

4.2 Hunger grows as India's lockdown kills jobs[1]

Rahul Lahoti, Amit Basole, Rosa Abraham, Surbhi Kesar, and Paaritosh Nath

The lockdown has devastated livelihoods at unprecedented levels, causing widespread job losses and hunger. The measures so far will not solve the crisis. India should universalise the PDS, expand cash transfers, and create a national job guarantee scheme.

The COVID-19 global pandemic and its associated containment measures have taken a heavy toll on economies and societies worldwide. In India, the national lockdown, imposed on 24 March and subsequently extended three times to 31 May, has had a profound effect on employment and earnings.

Livelihoods have been devastated at unprecedented levels. Food insecurity and economic vulnerability have increased to staggering proportions. Hunger deaths and suicides linked to economic stress are being reported from various parts of the country.

Any recovery from this crisis will be slow and very painful. The immediate relief measures do not appear to be in proportion to the severity of the situation on the ground.

In a survey of nearly 5,000 self-employed, casual, and regular wage workers across 12 states of India, conducted between 13 April and 23 May in collaboration with civil society organisations, we have found a massive increase in unemployment and an equally dramatic fall in earnings.[2]

Two-thirds of our respondents have lost work. The few informal workers who were still employed during the lockdown saw their earnings drop by more than half. Almost eight in ten are eating less food than before. The impact of job losses and food insecurity has been higher for certain groups of people: Muslims, Dalits, women, and those with lower levels of education.

As late as May, even the grossly inadequate government relief measures, in the form of cash transfers or increased rations, had not reached large sections of the economically vulnerable population. Half of our respondents reported not receiving any cash transfers.

Three structural characteristics of the Indian economy and decades of underinvestment in public goods have combined with the sudden and severe lockdown to generate widespread misery.

DOI: 10.4324/9781003291527-25

First, for India's predominantly informal labour force, which earns income day-to-day, any stoppage of economic activity instantly destroys employment and earnings. Second, the lopsided nature of economic growth has created a large divide between rich and poor states. Third, the same uneven growth process has created employment opportunities in larger cities much faster than in smaller towns and villages.

This unequal development manifests as migration flows of millions of workers, creating dense populations of the urban poor. When these long-run factors are put together with India's persistent underinvestment in health and housing, our vulnerabilities to the present crisis become painfully clear.

The vulnerable population in urban areas has been severely impacted, but relief measures have not reached them. The union government should follow the lead of states such as Odisha and Himachal Pradesh, which are trying out an urban employment generation programme, or of Kerala, which already has such a programme running. State finances may not allow effective urban employment guarantees, but the central government can certainly do this.

The measures recently announced by the government go some way in addressing the crisis. But they fall well short of what is required, since the bulk of the stimulus package focuses on increasing liquidity rather than direct spending.

Survey coverage

We partnered with 10 civil society organisations for phone surveys in 12 major states of India. They provided us a list of telephone numbers from their databases, from which we randomly selected households for the organisations to interview.

The sample is purposive and non-representative of the states and regions it covers. However, we ensured that the sample is diverse by selecting respondents across rural administrative blocks and by talking to respondents across diverse occupations. In total, we completed 4,879 interviews across rural and urban areas in 12 states.[3] Our survey covered 161 districts and 7 large cities (Ahmedabad, Ajmer, Bengaluru, Bhubaneshwar, Delhi, Jaipur, and Pune). Respondents interviewed in urban areas spanned over 30 different occupations. Our findings are broadly consistent with what other similar surveys reveal.

Since our respondents are in the network of civil society organisations, they are more aware and have more access to government schemes. They are not among the most economically vulnerable sections in the country. Hence our results are a conservative estimate of what the most vulnerable population might be experiencing. The results presented are not weighted, and the conclusions below are not generalisable. But with the paucity of representative data, they present a useful broad picture to guide policy.

In some of the states, our sample is predominantly rural or largely urban, and is indicated in the labels in Figure 4.2.1.

Overall, 58% of our respondents were in rural areas, 52% were women, 79% were married, and the average age was 38 years.[4] About half of the sample was illiterate or had only primary education. Of those interviewed, 85% were either the main income earners of the household or spouses of the main income earners. More than eight in ten households had a monthly income of less than Rs 10,000 in February.

In rural areas, more than half of our respondents were either farmers or casual workers. About seven in ten households in rural areas owned some cultivable land. In urban areas, more than four in ten respondents had in February been non-agricultural casual workers (Figure 4.2.2). A majority of workers in urban areas were service providers or construction workers. They worked as rag pickers, domestic helps, tailors, sanitation workers, street vendors, plumbers, painters, carpenters, taxi or auto

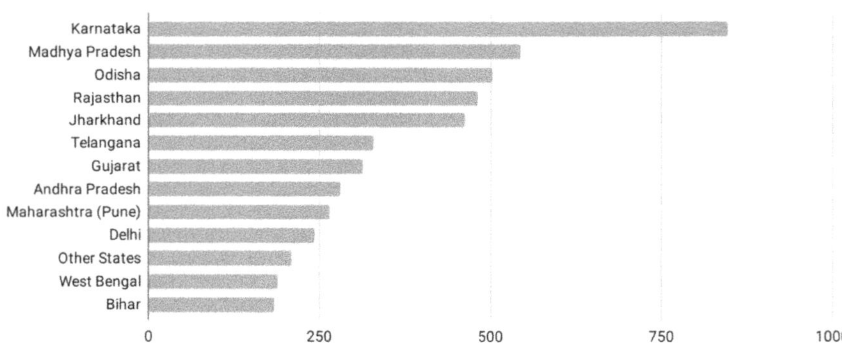

Figure 4.2.1 State-wise distribution of respondents.

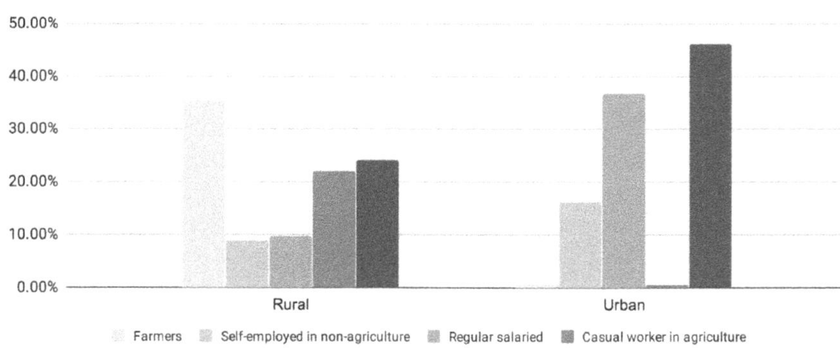

Figure 4.2.2 Work activity status of respondents prior to lockdown.

drivers, balloon sellers, cleaners, beedi makers, construction labourers, or security guards.

Impact on livelihoods

The lockdown has resulted in unprecedented losses in livelihoods and earnings.[5]

Amongst those who had been working in February, 66% reported they lost employment during the lockdown. They could not find even a single day's work during the lockdown or had to completely stop their self-employment activities. The loss of employment was more severe in urban areas, with almost eight in ten respondents reporting losing work, compared with just over half in rural areas (Figure 4.2.3).

About half of regular wage workers contacted by us received a reduced salary or no salary during the lockdown period. This was higher for those in urban areas (54%) than those in rural areas (39%).

"I have worked for so many years in the factory, I should get paid at least a little amount for now. The government should also help. Otherwise how will we bear daily expenses?" asked a 39-year-old male regular-salary worker from Uttarakhand.[6]

The non-agricultural sector had more job losses than the agriculture sector, with casual workers and the self-employed being the worst-off (Figure 4.2.4).

Individuals who had some degree or diploma seem to have experienced relatively lower loss in employment. Members of the Other Backward Castes experienced relatively lower loss in employment compared with those from the Scheduled Castes or the Scheduled Tribes. Muslims in our sample have experienced substantially larger losses in employment than Hindus, at 81% versus 65%.

Respondents living in vulnerable urban households—those with monthly income of less than Rs 10,000 in February—have seen greater levels of loss

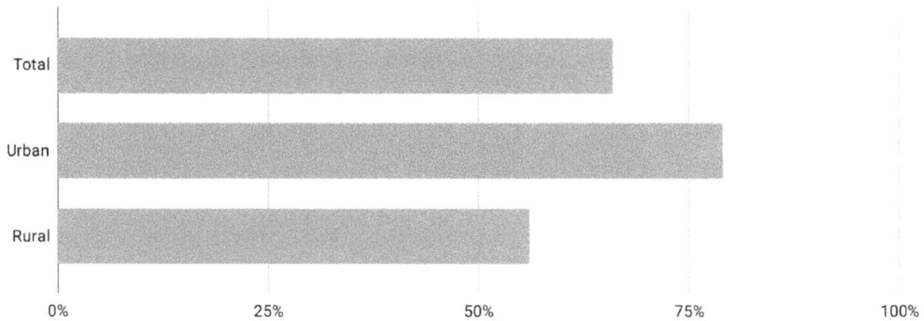

Figure 4.2.3 Loss of employment for those who were working in February.

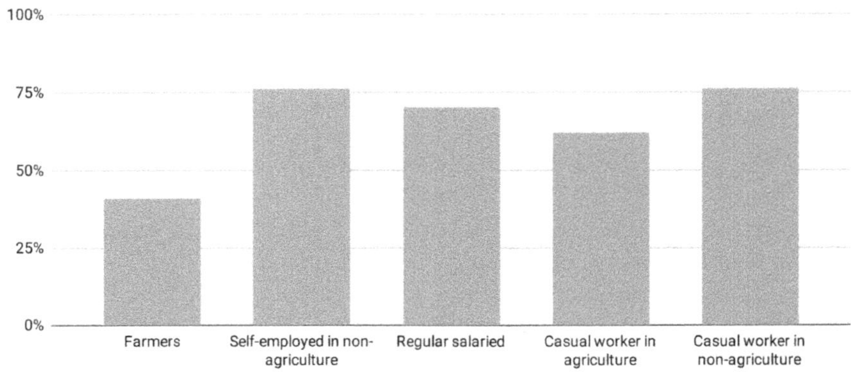

Figure 4.2.4 Employment loss by work activity status in February.

of employment (79%) than those in higher-income households (76%). In rural areas, fewer respondents from land-owning households reported loss of work, relative to those from landless households: 67% versus 51%.

For those who managed to retain work during the lockdown, incomes were more than halved. For casual workers, median monthly earnings dropped to Rs 1,727 from Rs 3,750, and for the self-employed in the non-agriculture sectors, to Rs 2,165 from Rs 5,000. The median earnings drop was higher in rural areas than in urban areas. Among farmers, as many as 85% faced severe difficulties in harvesting and selling crops. They were unable to harvest due to lack of machinery or labour. They could not sell their harvest or had to sell at reduced prices due to lack of transportation.

Impact on households

The lockdown has led to severe levels of food insecurity, depleted savings, and increased household borrowing. In urban areas, 83% reported consuming less food than before. In rural areas, the corresponding figure was 73%. Food insecurity was higher among women, Muslims, Scheduled Castes, people with lower educational qualifications, and in vulnerable households.

"Living has become hard. We have two children and are unable to provide them three meals a day. During many instances, we go hungry or eat one meal to give food to them", said a 31-year-old female casual worker from Karnataka.

"There is no help from the government".

Almost half of our respondents reported not having enough money to buy even a week's basic essentials. The contrast here between rural and urban areas is stark: the lack was reported by 65% of urban respondents but just

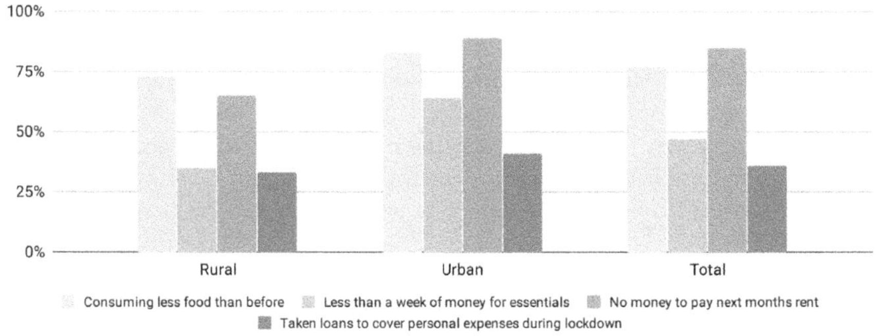

Figure 4.2.5 Impacts on households.

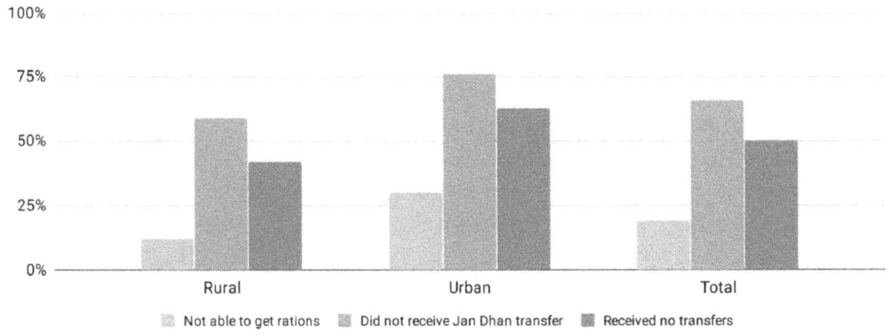

Figure 4.2.6 Reach on relief measures.

35% of rural respondents. This probably reflects the greater dependence of urban respondents on market-provided goods and services.

More than eight in ten respondents did not have money to pay the following month's rent. More than a third were taking loans to cover daily personal expenses during the lockdown. The median size of such loans was Rs 5,000. Urban respondents were more likely to take loans (41%) than rural (33%) (Figure 4.2.5). Less than a tenth of these loans were taken from formal sources, indicating the limits of banks to reach out at times of distress. Half of the respondents borrowed from friends and family. About two in ten borrowed from moneylenders.

Reach of relief measures

Large sections of the economically vulnerable population had not received any government relief (Figure 4.2.6). Almost two in ten vulnerable households were unable to get any rations. Muslim respondents were also more likely to not be able to procure rations than Hindus: 27% versus 17%. The median quantity of grains obtained by those able to access rations was 5 kg per person, far less than the promised quantity.

"The villages are in bad shape. We can't buy essentials even. And we can't go to the town for work or for buying items for daily needs", said a 37-year-old male self-employed worker from Rajasthan.

"Savings are also getting depleted. It will be difficult to keep going for months like this".

Since our respondents are connected to civil society organisations, they are more likely to be able to access the ration system than other socio-economically similar households. The inability to get rations is likely to be worse for other groups.

The saga is far worse when we examine the reach and extent of the promised cash transfers. Half of our respondents reported not receiving any cash transfer under central or state-specific schemes.[7] The reach of cash transfers was particularly weak in urban areas, where 63% did not get even a single cash transfer.

In absolute terms, on average, our respondents had lost Rs 2,000–3,000 of income per month. The announced cash transfer that is supposed to reach most households is grossly inadequate to compensate for this loss.

For instance, the central government announced cash transfers of Rs 500 per month for three months to every woman with a Jan Dhan bank account. This translates to Rs 4 per person per day, assuming the eligible woman has a family of four. Compare this to the poverty line of Rs 50 per person per day in rural areas and Rs 73 in urban areas (based on the Rangarajan committee estimates of 2011–12, converted to current prices).

Even the reach of Jan Dhan accounts is very limited. Only one in three vulnerable households reported receiving the promised cash transfer. This was mostly because a large majority did not have Jan Dhan accounts. Overall, six in ten vulnerable households did not have Jan Dhan accounts.

The suspension of MGNREGA work has deprived the vulnerable of a safety net. "We want to work in MGNREGA but no work is available … The contractor has not started work this year", said a 40-year-old female casual worker from Jharkhand.

"My payment from last year's work is also pending, it was wrongly deposited in someone else's account".

Recommendations

The disruption from COVID-19 and the lockdown in the economy and the labour markets is enormous. Any relief measures for this crisis should at minimum consist of three prongs: a universalisation of the Public Distribution System (PDS), the expansion of direct cash transfers, and an expansion of the rural employment guarantee scheme and its introduction in urban areas. We expand on these recommendations here.

The PDS has the widest reach in providing relief. But there still are a large number of households, especially amongst the most vulnerable groups, that do not receive rations due to lack of ration cards. Governments should issue temporary ration cards or through other means universalise PDS for the next six months. India has enough food reserves for this. Governments should also open cooked meal centres for the hungry. The mid-day meal scheme in schools, anganwadi centres, and public feeding programmes existing in several states can be utilised for this effort.

To cover the income losses, governments should provide a monthly cash transfer of at least Rs 7,000 for the next three months to households by combining administrative lists of welfare schemes such as MGNREGA, PDS, and Ujjwala. To relieve pressure on the rural banking system, panchayats could be used for cash transfers, as is being done in Odisha.

There is large demand for work, both from returning migrants and from those who have lost jobs. Large-scale worksites under MGNREGA should be started immediately. The allocation for MGNREGA work should be increased by at least Rs 1 lakh crore. The number of days of guaranteed work per household should be raised to 150 days. MGNREGA workers should be paid without delays, preferably with cash in hand, and their past dues should be cleared. To provide relief to the urban poor, a nationwide large-scale employment guarantee programme should be launched, expanding on the experiments in some states with urban wage employment programmes.[8]

The pandemic and the resultant economic distress are likely to stay with us for some time. This unfortunate situation has already caused a lot of suffering for many. We as a society need to realise the scale of the problem, be empathetic to the plight of the underprivileged, plan for it, and provide much-needed direct and immediate relief.

Acknowledgements

The survey was conducted by a team of researchers at the Center for Sustainable Employment at Azim Premji University. The team includes Mridhula Mohan, Sanjana Rajashekar, Zaeen D'Souza, Sravan Pallapothu, Neha Joshi, and Adithi Rao. We greatly acknowledge their efforts in the project and several others who advised us at numerous stages of the project. We also acknowledge support and funding for the project from the research centre at Azim Premji University and the Azim Premji Philanthropic Initiative. We thank the staff at the various civil society organisations that did the interviews and the numerous students volunteers from Azim Premji University. For any further questions get in touch with us at rahul.lahoti AT gmail.com.

Notes

1 Reproduced with permission from *The India Forum* where the article first appeared on 29 May 2020. https://www.theindiaforum.in/article/hunger-grows-india-s-lockdown-kills-jobs
2 The data and details of the survey and of the organisations are available at https://cse.azimpremjiuniversity.edu.in/covid19-analysis-of-impact-and-relief-measures/
3 We made 7,000 telephone calls and our response rate was close to 70%. This response rate is far higher than response rates obtained in random number telephone dialling. This was partly because respondents were called by organisations with whom they had a prior relationship. We have 12 states where more than 180 respondents each were interviewed. Overall we have observations from 15 states.
4 The distribution of sample by sex is not uniform across states. In a few states like Gujarat, our sample is mostly women, while for some others it is dominated by men.
5 The findings reported here differ slightly from the ones presented in a webinar on 12 May conducted by the Center for Sustainable Employment at Azim Premji University, as they have been updated with results from about 1,000 households that have been surveyed since then. The broad patterns remain the same.
6 Respondents were interviewed on conditions of anonymity; hence they are not named here.
7 Detailed results for each cash transfer scheme are available at https://cse.azimpremjiuniversity.edu.in/covid19-analysis-of-impact-and-relief-measures/
8 A detailed proposal has been made by the Center for Sustainable Employment. https://cse.azimpremjiuniversity.edu.in/wp-content/uploads/2019/04/SWI2019_Urban_Job_Guarantee.pdf

4.3 COVID-19

Intra-state migrants marooned too[1]

Bhanupriya Rao

Thousands of intra-state migrants from other districts in AP who work as seasonal farm labourers are stranded in their workplaces with little or no support from the government.

Peddapalem (Guntur district), Andhra Pradesh: Thousands of families of intra-state migrants are stranded on the margins of Guntur's world-renowned chilli farms, scrambling to live on a meagre supply of grains and other provisions, and sheltering from 40-degree Celsius temperatures under tarpaulin, as they wait for the lockdown to end.

The continuing ordeal of these chilli-farm workers—hailing mostly from Andhra Pradesh's drought-ravaged Kurnool district—who have neither been accommodated in buildings nor received timely rations and cash from the district administration, suggests that poor migrants within states may be even worse off during the lockdown than inter-state migrants whose home states have been taking up their plight with the states where they are marooned.

The national lockdown[2] to contain COVID-19, announced by the central government with four hours' notice on the evening of March 24, 2020, triggered massive reverse migration,[3] with millions of migrants trying to return to their home states, and intra-state migrants also trying to return to their home districts, triggering concerns of contagion spreading to rural areas through these returning migrants. As borders between states, and even between districts within states, were sealed, millions remained trapped in their workplaces, including intra-state migrants, no reliable estimates of whose numbers are available.

Even in a pandemic, intra-state migrants appear to be invisible. While the Andhra Pradesh government issued detailed instructions on April 4, 2020,[4] regarding inter-state migrants, saying "no person belonging to other state stranded in Andhra Pradesh should complain about non-availability of food and other basic amenities", it had little to say on intra-state migrants, beyond stating that they should be allowed to get rations using portability in an electronic-Public Distribution System. Even these rations have not

DOI: 10.4324/9781003291527-26

reached many of the intra-state farm workers in the district, according to voluntary groups in Guntur.

Chilli pickers stopped halfway home

Husseni (he uses only one name) was in a group of 70 who were stopped by police on March 27, 2020, while travelling in a hired open truck from the chilli farm where they worked to their homes in Alavam village in Kurnool's Kosigi mandal (block). They were halfway home on the roughly 320-km journey southwest, when they were ordered to turn back.

After returning to the farm in Peddapalem, the group of men, women, and children sat with their belongings for two days under the open sky without food or water. "Our kids have turned pale with hunger, but no one is bothering about us", Husseni told IndiaSpend in a phone interview on the morning of March 29, 2020.

The seasonal migrants, though anxious to get home on account of COVID-19 and the lockdown[5] announced by the Andhra Pradesh government from March 23 to March 31, 2020 (extended to April 14, 2020, as part of the national lockdown), were due to leave anyway. Their work had ended, and the tents housing them had been dismantled.

Each worker having earned Rs 350 a day during the three-month season that began in January 2020, they were not destitute. But their food had run out, and villagers did not allow them into local shops, fearing they had been infected with COVID-19 during their attempt to go home.

"I am so hungry, but they are not even allowing us to buy a packet of biscuits", said eight-year-old Najma (uses only one name), weeping.

"They have threatened to drive us out of the farm if anyone tests positive in the village", Venkanna (uses only one name), another worker, told IndiaSpend.

Later that afternoon, after a local NGO arranged dry rations, the farm workers were able to feed themselves and their children. The farmer whose chilli farm they worked on arranged tattered tarpaulin sheets to erect makeshift tents.

Several thousand stranded

Several thousand seasonal migrants, about half of them women and children, may be stranded in Guntur, farmers' rights activists suggest. On just the evening of March 27, 2020, about 3,000 migrant workers heading home in open trucks were turned back at the border between Guntur and Prakasam districts, which they would have had to cross to reach their homes in Kurnool.

Atchampeta, one of Guntur's 58 mandals (blocks), had 6,846 seasonal farm workers—around 3,200 from Kurnool—according to data collected[6] by the state government for relief purposes. Data for other mandals are not yet available, revealing poor record-keeping on seasonal migrants, who have been coming to this prosperous district for two decades from arid western Andhra Pradesh (AP).

Volunteers from local NGOs distribute food and sanitation items to stranded migrant workers on Guntur's chilli farms. As the state of AP sets up relief mechanisms for inter-state migrants, intra-state migrants continue to rely on local NGOs for food.

Andhra Pradesh began distributing free rations—5 kg rice and 1 kg dal per family—on March 29, 2020, as part of the welfare measures[7] it announced during the lockdown, but this is yet to reach many of the seasonal migrants. Even among groups that have received these rations, those without ration cards have been left out, say local volunteers who are feeding about 500 families.

"We left our ration cards at home in Kurnool for our family there. Now we have been asked to wait for a few more days to get the free rice and dal promised by the Jagan government", Venkanna told IndiaSpend, referring to chief minister Y. S. Jagan Mohan Reddy.

"In normal times, those living in villages have always received rations distributed by the state before workers living on farms", said Sikha Narasimha, who runs LEAF,[8] a local NGO that has been distributing food. "We have been appealing to the district administration to at least prioritise these migrant workers on farms during the pandemic, because they are completely without supplies".

The chilli pickers have also not been given the Rs 1,000 per family promised by the state government during the lockdown. They have been told they would get this only when they return to their villages.

"Our kids will die of heatstroke"

While the district administration maintains it is working towards delivering rations to all migrants, it has been silent on the question of providing shelter. When asked, twice, about plans for proper shelters for the migrant workers, the district collector of Guntur, I. Samuel Anand Kumar, told IndiaSpend that it had been arranged. However, NGOs and the farm workers themselves said this was not the case.

"If not hunger, heatstroke will kill us and our children", said Easweramma, alluding to the soaring temperatures. Besides, there is a severe lack of privacy, water, and sanitation facilities, making life especially difficult for women.

Narasimha said he had asked the mandal revenue officer to house the chilli-farm workers in empty schools, but was told "village people will not allow them to stay there for fear of contracting coronavirus from them".

"During the day, they sit under trees for shade, mothers protecting small babies from the heat by keeping them in makeshift cradles made with sticks and sarees", he said.

They also have to worry about being evicted once farmers begin to prepare their fields for the kharif (monsoon) crop. In a farm in Neeleswarapalem village in Atchampeta mandal, a group of seasonal workers was asked to vacate a farm for this reason. Local officials had to persuade the farmer to let the group stay.

IndiaSpend has written to the state nodal officer in charge of humanitarian aid during the pandemic, and the district nodal officer for Guntur district, asking about shelter arrangements for migrant workers. This report will be updated with their responses.

Kerala and Telangana ahead of AP

Like most Indian states, Andhra Pradesh was slow to respond to the crisis of migrant workers stranded in the state, activists say.

"AP was no different from any state, except Kerala, in imagining how a lockdown would affect the most marginalised", said Kavitha Kuruganti, farmers' rights activist and a convenor of the Alliance for Sustainable and Holistic Agriculture. "Governments are showing how apathetic they can be unless they are alerted, harangued, pursued and prodded". Kuruganti has been leading migrant relief work and coordinating with senior bureaucrats in Andhra Pradesh and Telangana to mitigate the distress of stranded migrants.

By March 27, 2020, Kerala had already opened 4,603 relief camps[9] to house 144,145 migrant labourers, referring to them as "guest workers". In contrast, Andhra Pradesh's chief secretary issued orders[10] to identify stranded migrant workers, arrange shelters for them, and provide them with food, drinking water, and sanitisers, on March 29, 2020, a week after its lockdown was announced.

Even after these belated instructions, relief work at the district level was uneven, and at the discretion of district collectors, activists say. Neighbouring Telangana, which announced free rations and Rs 500 cash relief for each of the 335,669 migrant workers enumerated by the state on March 29, 2020,[11] performed better, they point out.

Furthermore, on April 4, 2020, the Andhra Pradesh government, as we said, directed[12] the district to make arrangements for food and shelter for migrant workers from other states along with homeless people and beggars, but had little to say about stranded migrants from within the state.

"This crisis has revealed two things—one, that the state has no place for intra-state seasonal migrant labour in its imagination. Second, the much touted systems like biometrics are a failure", Kuruganti said, referring to the migrants' inability to access rations.

Lack of credible information

Lack of credible information about the pandemic and lockdown has worsened the trauma of the seasonal workers living and working in relative isolation on the chilli farms. They did not get their news from television or smart phones, but from relatives they spoke to on their basic phones. The state's lack of communication on how it was going to enforce its lockdown, and the suddenness of the national lockdown, added to their bewilderment.

"We were told about the Janata Curfew on March 22, 2020, and we observed it properly. No one told us that we would not be able to travel after that", Husseni said.

Groups that had left before March 27, 2020, had not been turned back at the district's border, so the migrants who left that day were shocked to experience this. "We paid Rs 30,000 to hire a truck to take us home. The transporter refused to give us back our money when we had to turn back", said Anjanamma (uses only one name), one of the workers.

Even worse is the ostracisation faced by the farm workers, who make a significant contribution to Guntur's status as a hub[13] of the international chilli trade. Barricades have been put up not just between villages but even between streets within the villages, to impede the free movement of anyone the villagers perceive as an "outsider".

"Rural India is grappling with rumours and prejudices without a clear understanding of what the pandemic is about", said Kuruganti. "It's not that hard for the government to run an awareness campaign about the pandemic and to assure migrant workers it is there for them".

"We do know that staying back is the best option for us right now. But not once has the government told us, 'We will take care of you'", said Husseni.

Migrants worry about those at home

Successive droughts over 15 years in Rayalaseema, the arid western region of Andhra Pradesh consisting of the four districts of Kurnool, Anantapur, YSR Kadapa, and Chittoor, have forced farmers to turn to daily wage labour, as IndiaSpend reported[14] in April 2019. Between 2014 and 2018, continuous drought has impacted close to 3.2 million farmers[15] resulting in losses of up to Rs 3,216 crore ($509 million), according to the latest available data.

Recurring droughts and depleting groundwater resources have forced not just landless, small farmers and marginal farmers but big landowners, too, to give up agriculture and migrate to prosperous places for daily-wage jobs in agriculture or construction, both within and outside the state.

In the absence of official estimates, farmers' rights activists say that 60,000 to 100,000 people from Kurnool come to work annually on Guntur's chilli farms, about 30 to 70 people per farm. Between January and April, they earn just about enough to tide them through the rest of the year. Some bring their children with them, to help with chilli picking and boost their earnings, while those better off leave their children behind with their elderly parents so that they can go to school.

"Our children and parents back home are worried about us", said Easwaramma (uses only one name), another migrant worker from Kosigi stranded in Guntur. "They are crying and begging us to come home. We all want to be together in these difficult times".

The growing number of positive cases in both Andhra Pradesh and Telangana has made families anxious about their relatives stuck in Guntur: The district has seen a rising number of COVID-19 cases with 33 positive cases,[16] the third highest after Kurnool (74) and Nellore (42), as of 11 am on April 7, 2020.

Migrant workers who have left their children behind with elderly relatives are worried that they will go hungry in the absence of cooked mid-day meals due to school closures. Cooked school meals are often the only source of food for the children of seasonal migrants during the months that their parents are away, as we reported earlier.[17]

"My old mother-in-law can barely see. What will she cook?" asked an anxious Anjaneyamma. "Neighbours are giving them food right now. But for how long? How can we be at peace when our kids are hungry?"

Notes

1 Reproduced with permission from *IndiaSpend* where the article first appeared on April 8, 2020. https://www.indiaspend.com/covid-19-intra-state-migrants-marooned-too/
2 Ministry of Home Affairs. "Government of India Issues Orders Prescribing Lockdown for Containment of COVID-19 Epidemic in the Country". March 24, 2020. PIB Delhi. Retrieved from https://pib.gov.in/PressReleseDetail.aspx?PRID=1607997. Last accessed on December 10, 2021.
3 Varun Aggarwal, Priyansha Singh, and Prachi Salve. "Migrants Returning Home to Ill-Equipped Healthcare Systems". *IndiaSpend.com*. March 28, 2020. Retrieved from https://www.indiaspend.com/migrants-returning-home-to-ill-equipped-healthcare-systems/. Last accessed on December 10, 2021.
4 See https://www.indiaspend.com/wp-content/uploads/2020/04/GO-1.pdf. Last accessed on December 10, 2021.
5 V. Raghavendra. "War on COVID: Andhra Pradesh Announces State-Wide Lockdown". *The Hindu*. March 23, 2020. Retrieved from https://www.thehindu.com/news/national/andhra-pradesh/ap-announces-lockdown/article31141012.ece. Last accessed on December 10, 2021.
6 See https://www.indiaspend.com/wp-content/uploads/2020/04/Data-Table-1-Sheet1-2.pdf. Last accessed on December 10, 2021.
7 See https://twitter.com/AndhraPradeshCM/status/1243907796615090177?s=20
8 See https://saveleaf.org/. Last accessed on December 10, 2021.
9 Nidheesh M. K. "Kerala Opens 4603 Relief Camps for Over One Lakh Migrant 'Guest' Workers". *The Mint*. March 27, 2020. Retrieved from https://www.livemint.com/news/india/kerala-opens-4603-relief-camps-for-over-one-lakh-migrant-guest-workers-11585330696675.html. Last accessed on December 10, 2021.
10 See https://www.indiaspend.com/wp-content/uploads/2020/04/GO-3.pdf. Last accessed on December 10, 2021.

11 Yunus Y. Lasania. "Migrant Workers in Telangana to Get Rs 500 Cash and 12kg of Rice Each". *The Mint*. March 29, 2020. Retrieved from https://www.livemint.com/news/india/coronavirus-migrant-workers-in-telangana-to-get-rs-500-cash-and-12-kg-rice-each-11585501239262.html. Last accessed on December 10, 2021.

12 See https://www.indiaspend.com/wp-content/uploads/2020/04/GO-1.pdf. Last accessed on December 10, 2021.

13 P. Samuel Jonathan. "Chilli Prices Crash by 20% in Guntur". *The Hindu*. February 10, 2020. Retrieved from https://www.thehindu.com/news/national/andhra-pradesh/chilli-prices-crash-by-20-in-guntur/article30785796.ece. Last accessed on December 10, 2021.

14 Bhanupriya Rao. "Losing Their Fields and All Hope, Andhra Farmers Turn Daily Wagers". *India Spend*. April 06, 2019. Retrieved from https://www.indiaspend.com/losing-their-fields-and-all-hope-andhra-farmers-turning-daily-wagers/. Last accessed on December 10, 2021.

15 G. V. R Subba Rao. "Drought Continues Its March in Andhra Pradesh". *The Hindu*. August 10, 2018. Retrieved from https://www.thehindu.com/news/national/andhra-pradesh/drought-continues-its-march-in-andhra-pradesh/article24647303.ece. Last accessed on December 10, 2021.

16 See http://hmfw.ap.gov.in/

17 Bhanupriya Rao. "Losing Their Fields and All Hope".

4.4 Bihar's migrants return to face stigma, under-prepared medical facilities[1]

Parul Agrawal

Migrant workers returning to Bihar are shocked to find that they are presumed to be carriers of the virus and are being ostracised. Some villages have put up barricades as well posters asking "outsiders" to stay away.

Lakhisarai (Bihar) and Bengaluru: On March 24, 2020, Ramgarh police station received a phone call from the village of Durdih in Lakhisarai district in southern Bihar, 140 km from the state's capital, Patna. The person on the line said that someone had come from the "city" and had "coronavirus", said Dhirendra Kumar Pathak, the police station in-charge. The police reached the house at around 8 pm, but there was no one there, Pathak said. A member of the family told the police that the person, their son-in-law, had already left.

Such calls have been frequent in recent days, Pathak said, ever since a government-imposed 21-day lockdown[2] led to an exodus of migrants from large cities back to their home towns and villages. Several incidents where migrants are not being allowed to enter their villages or being handed over to the police have been reported from Patna, Rajasthan, and West Bengal.[3,4]

The stigma associated with being a COVID-19 patient could hinder those with symptoms from reaching out for help, experts told *IndiaSpend*. Some migrants could be unknowing carriers of COVID-19 and spread the infection, as not all districts are equipped to screen and quarantine them.

Public healthcare systems in the migrants' home state are under-equipped to deal with the challenge of COVID-19, and experts warn that many of the migrants might well be infected and take the pandemic with them, as *IndiaSpend* reported[5] on March 28, 2020.

Ostracism

People have been calling up hospitals, the police stations, and district government officials to report COVID-19-related issues. In most cases, an ambulance accompanies the police officer or government official. "When we reach the spot, it is usually a case of travel from other districts or states ...

DOI: 10.4324/9781003291527-27

We try to tell them not to panic and explain the symptoms of the disease", Pathak said.

In Durdih, the family of the returnee are continuing to face ostracism even after his departure, the father-in-law told *IndiaSpend*, requesting not to be named. They had food stored at home but were "not being allowed to take water from the local hand pump", he said. After some social workers and villagers intervened, the family are now being "allowed" to fetch water from the animals' water source.

Pathak said the family has not reported this ostracism to the police.

Bihar's first case of a COVID-19 death, a contagious viral respiratory disease, was of a person from Munger, the region where Lakhisarai district is located, according[6] to media reports.[7] The person died at the All India Institute for Medical Sciences in Patna.

The World Health Organization (WHO) declared[8] COVID-19 a pandemic on March 11, 2020. In India, it had infected 1,397 and killed 35, as of 8:30 pm on March 31, 2020, when data were last released by the Ministry of Health and Family Welfare, according to Coronavirus Monitor, a HealthCheck database.[9] Bihar had 15 cases and 1 death.

An estimated 2.2 million from Bihar migrate to other states, according to data from the 2001 census.[10] Some of them work in Kerala (which now has 234 COVID-19 cases), Delhi (97 cases), Rajasthan (74 cases), and Maharashtra (216 cases). Many migrate overseas, often to the Middle East.

"Outsiders not allowed"

In many villages around Lakhisarai district, inhabitants and local leaders have barricaded the entry and exit points of villages, and placed posters that say: "Outsiders are not allowed", asking those who return to self-report. If they do not self-report, other villagers report them to the authorities, residents told *IndiaSpend*.

The fear that outsiders will bring COVID-19 is rampant across villages.

"Most villagers think that anyone who has come from outside is a coronavirus patient", said Ravi Ranjan, the block development officer at Dhamdaha in Purnea district, in northern Bihar. Even if workers who have travelled from afar have a mild cough or are sneezing, people panic and report them as cases of coronavirus on our helpline, he said. "The teams have been running around day and night due to this. Since the last two to three days, we are appealing to people to fight with the disease but not distort the social fabric of the villages", said Ranjan.

"The stigma around COVID-19 is not specific to rural areas and even cities and urban areas are witnessing this", said Soumitra Pathare, a consulting psychiatrist and director of the Centre for Mental Health Law and Policy in Pune.[11] "If you have more stigma, the people are more afraid to come out and seek help or treatment", he said, giving the example of stigma around the human immunodeficiency virus (HIV) which causes acquired immunodeficiency syndrome (AIDS) in some patients.

The problem is not community surveillance but a lack of understanding of the disease as well as of community surveillance, experts told *IndiaSpend*. It means different things to different people—doctors, police, and the common man, said Pathare. "Surveillance is not vigilantism but maybe that is how it has got through", he added.

"Our authorities have relied on this notion of fear to get everybody to act but the danger of that is it results in stigma", he said, adding that "ensuring the information flow, open communication and dealing with misconceptions is what is required" as most people do not understand what the disease is.

Screening, tracking, quarantining

Not all districts in Bihar are adequately prepared to handle the return of these migrants. Although some have facilities for quarantining and door-to-door visits by healthcare workers, others are unable to track and screen migrants or quarantine them properly, our investigation found.

More than 400,000 people had been screened at transit points and over 21,000 at airports and 221 passengers had completed the 14-day quarantine, as of March 30, 2020, according to the State Health Society of Bihar, under the National Health Mission. The data do not clarify whether this includes migrants returning from other Indian states.

About 2,570 "passengers" were under observation in various districts as of March 30, 2020, data show. Most (648) were in Siwan, a district in north-western Bihar.

Vigilantism by villagers is partly an outcome of inadequate awareness and partly a lack of comprehensive government screening of returning migrants, our investigation showed.

In some cases, returnees are mingling freely with their families, never having been tested for symptoms.

Villagers do not know what quarantine means and there is no mechanism to ensure that they quarantine themselves, said a Patna-based social activist, working with an international organisation on climate change in Bihar, requesting anonymity. "Issuing instructions on paper does not work in our kind of setup", he said. "Returning workers are both scared and careless and do not want to go and stay in government buildings".

The Bihar government issued a circular on March 22, 2020,[12] instructing district magistrates to make temporary arrangements in government schools and community centres to quarantine returning workers. The government has sanctioned Rs 100 crore from the chief minister's relief fund for food and other arrangements at such locations, according to this statement[13] by the Bihar government.

"Nobody is staying in our facility as of now but we have enough space", said Lakhisarai block development officer Pushpa Lakda, when *IndiaSpend* spoke to her on March 28, 2020. She said schools have been prepared for quarantining of the returning migrants, water is available as most schools have a hand pump, but food will have to be brought by their families. "Each school has two to three rooms and all the people coming back from such places will be kept together so we can handle a large number of people", she said.

In Siwan district, the local administration is focusing on the 648 people who are under observation and on international migrant workers, said Amit Kumar Pandey, the district magistrate. When asked about the measures the administration is taking, he said he had no details since the sub-divisional magistrate was in charge.

Siwan had its first COVID-19 case on March 26, 2020, when a person returning from Dubai tested positive, according to Ashesh Kumar, the civil surgeon at Sadar Hospital in Siwan.

Home quarantine, door-to-door visits

Some districts are doing better than others in handling returnees.

In Sheohar district, in northern Bihar, the administration decided that they would quarantine migrants at home since getting the schools and community centres ready at short notice seemed impossible, said Rakesh Singh, a social activist from the area, who was part of the meetings with local leaders.

The district has counted 563 migrants so far who have come back, said Avaneesh Kumar Singh, the district magistrate. A pamphlet has been put outside their homes to indicate they are under quarantine but many are hiding details of their travel history, he said. The medical team now goes door-to-door, responds to phone calls, and makes sure that no one with symptoms comes to the health centre, he said.

Someone who has symptoms should not go to the health centre but call the helpline and a medical team will visit them at home, officials said.

Lack of public health, testing facilities

Overall, Bihar's health infrastructure is poor. It ranked 20th of 21 states on the Niti Aayog's Health Index report published in June 2019.[14] For its 120 million population, it currently has four operational COVID-19 test centres, three in Patna and one in Darbhanga, according to Coronavirus Monitor.

By March 30, 2020, the state had tested 869 samples, of which 15 were found positive, data show.

Hospitals have been asked to increase the number of beds and set up isolation wards, but many do not have the capacity to expand.

Siwan has a 110-bed hospital and the government has ordered that 6 isolation wards be created for potential COVID-19 cases, said Kumar, the civil surgeon at Siwan's Sadar Hospital. "But just creating only a ward does not help ... there is a lack of space, manpower and the medical supply is very limited", he said, citing the example of the expansion of the hospital from 30 beds some time ago without a corresponding increase in other medical facilities as a futile step.

The hospital is also facing a shortage of protective equipment for health workers. "We have to offer everything to the team in the field since they are examining the patients", Kumar said. "So, I do not have enough for the other staff or myself".

For other districts, such as Gopalganj, well-equipped hospitals are few and far between.

For any serious treatment, people in Gopalganj rely on Baba Raghav Das Medical College in Gorakhpur (120 km west) or the government hospitals in Patna (150 km southeast), said Nand Kishore, the civil surgeon at the Sadar hospital in Gopalganj. "I am meeting the district magistrate to see what system can be put in place", he said. "The tests are being done in Patna but in case of a crisis, the ambulances will be allowed to go to Gorakhpur". Special permission is needed as the central government has ordered that state borders be closed during the lockdown.[15]

Protective gear for grassroots workers

The government has said that grassroot health workers such as accredited social health activists (ASHAs) will conduct door-to-door campaigns to educate people about the need to identify high-risk cases and quarantine them.

But unlike in Siwan, not all districts are able to provide protective gear to their health workers.

"We have not been given any masks or gloves or anything to protect ourselves when we go out and visit families where people have returned from other areas", said Anita Devi, an ASHA worker with the Ramgarh primary health centre (PHC) in Lakhisarai. "How are we supposed to go and meet people without any protection?"

Asha Devi said she had heard about a person who had come from outside the district with flu-like symptoms. "We do not know what happened to him or where he was taken", she said, highlighting the lack of information on what happens when someone is detected with symptoms similar to those of COVID-19. Such incidents made her fearful of going out in the field without protective equipment, she said.

The Ramgarh PHC team is ready to handle cases, said Kanchan Kumar, who is in charge there, but "we are also receiving many unnecessary calls". "We were given eight kits with masks and gowns to test such patients and they have almost all been used up. We are trying to do whatever we can, but the resources are limited".

IndiaSpend reached out to officials of Bihar's health ministry, including principal secretary Sanjay Kumar, by phone multiple times on March

30 and March 31, 2020, and emailed Bihar's health department. We also called Arvinder Singh, the special secretary, Manoj Kumar, additional secretary of the State Health Society, and Lokesh Kumar Singh, secretary of the Swasthya Suraksha Samiti. This story will be updated when we receive a response.

(Kumar Neeraj, founder-director of Khetee, an agroforestry non-profit, contributed to this story from Lakhisarai district.)

Notes

1 Reproduced with permission from *IndiaSpend* where the article first appeared on April 1, 2020. https://www.indiaspend.com/bihars-migrants-return-to-face-stigma-under-prepared-medical-facilities/
2 Press Information Bureau, Government of India. *PM Calls for Complete Lockdown of Entire Nation for 21 Days*. March 24, 2020. Retrieved from https://pib.gov.in/PressReleseDetail.aspx?PRID=1608009. Last accessed on December 10, 2021.
3 "Migrant Labourers Return Home, Only to Face 'boycott'". *Indian Express*. March 30, 2020. Retrieved from https://www.newindianexpress.com/nation/2020/mar/30/they-return-home-only-to-face-boycott-2123241.html. Last accessed on December 10, 2021.
4 "Coronavirus in India: Migrant Workers Returning to Villages in Bihar Handed over to Police, Medics". *India Today*. March 29, 2020. Retrieved from https://www.indiatoday.in/india/story/coronavirus-india-migrant-workers-returning-villages-bihar-handed-over-police-medics-1661027-2020-03-29. Last accessed on December 10, 2021.
5 Varun Aggarwal, Priyansha Singh and Prachi Salve. "Migrants Returning Home to Ill-Equipped Healthcare Systems". *IndiaSpend*. March 28, 2020. Retrieved from https://www.indiaspend.com/migrants-returning-home-to-ill-equipped-healthcare-systems/. Last accessed on December 10, 2021.
6 "38-Year-Old Man Having Coronavirus Dies in Patna's AIIMS Hospital". *The Economic Times*. March 22, 2020. Retrieved from https://economictimes.indiatimes.com/news/politics-and-nation/38-year-old-man-having-coronavirus-dies-in-patnas-aiims-hospital/articleshow/74757682.cms?from=mdr. Last accessed on December 10, 2021.
7 "First Coronavirus Death in Bihar: Man with Travel History to Qatar Dies at AIIMS, Patna". *Business Line*. March 22, 2020. Retrieved from https://www.thehindubusinessline.com/news/first-coronavirus-death-in-bihar-man-with-travel-history-to-qatar-dies-at-aiims-patna/article31134822.ece. Last accessed on December 10, 2021.
8 "WHO Director-General's Opening Remarks at the Media Briefing on COVID-19 – 11 March 2020". Retrieved from https://www.who.int/director-general/speeches/detail/who-director-general-s-opening-remarks-at-the-media-briefing-on-covid-19---11-march-2020. Last accessed on December 10, 2021.
9 See https://corona.health-check.in/
10 Census of India 2001, Migration data, Highlights. Retrieved from https://censusindia.gov.in/Data_Products/Data_Highlights/Data_Highlights_link/data_highlights_D1D2D3.pdf. Last accessed on December 10, 2021.
See https://corona.health-check.in/
11 See https://cmhlp.org/

12 See https://www.indiaspend.com/wp-content/uploads/2020/03/School-buildings-circular.jpg
13 See http://210.212.23.61/AdminPanel/Files/PressRelease/2020/208.pdf
14 Health Index 2019, published by the Niti Ayog. See http://social.niti.gov.in/uploads/sample/health_index_report.pdf
15 Ministry of Information and Broadcasting, Government of India. "Center Directs States to Ensure No Movement of People across Cities". March 29, 2020. Retrieved from https://pib.gov.in/PressReleaseIframePage.aspx?PRID=1608984. Last accessed on December 10, 2021.

4.5 Across India, workers complain that employers used lockdown to defraud them of wages they are owed[1]

Rajiv Khandelwal

It is imperative that this money is reclaimed and not treated as an unavoidable collateral loss in the fight against COVID-19.

On March 25, my colleagues and I at the Aajeevika Bureau, which tries to address the economic and socio-legal problems of migrant workers in Gujarat and Rajasthan, woke up to dozens of messages of utter distress, both on our personal phones and on our toll-free Labour Line.

Among the people who phoned was Devaram. He told us how, minutes after Prime Minister Narendra Modi had announced a 21-day lockdown to contain the spread of the COVID-19 epidemic the previous night, he and 12 co-workers were told to pack their bags immediately. They were ordered to leave the textile factory premises in Ahmedabad that had doubled as their night sleeping spot for over six years.

Between them they barely had Rs 500. When they asked their contractor for the money they were owed, which worked out to about Rs 12,000 each, he threatened them – and then fled.

Another caller told us that 200 fellow workers in his Jaipur factory were brusquely informed that business had shut down and they would only be paid once the lockdown had finished. They were offered Rs 1,000 each as an interim payment and told not to return in a hurry.

From Mumbai, Suraj and his group told us that they had been made to sign blank papers in lieu of half the wages for March. They later realised that they had signed off on resignation letters.

Supreme Court indifference

These callers were among an estimated 400 million Indians who earn daily wages or are casually employed in construction, small manufacturing, transportation, head loading, and agriculture markets. They are the section that has been hit hardest by loss of the wages and jobs losses because of the lockdown.

DOI: 10.4324/9781003291527-28

Yet a public interest litigation filed in the Supreme Court by activists Harsh Mander and Anjali Bhardwaj seeking immediate government action in the payment of minimum wages attracted a surprisingly indifferent response from the Supreme Court bench on April 7. Not only did the bench observe that policy decisions are the prerogative of the government, it also said that wage payments need not be a high priority since adequate arrangements to provide shelter and food for migrant workers have been put in place.

Nothing could be further from reality. Evidence coming in from everywhere suggests that migrant workers and daily-wage earners face an unprecedented livelihood disaster. At our Labour Line, over 200 calls of stranded workers just in the first four days of the lockdown indicated the mass abandonment of workers. Contractors pleaded that they had not received their own payments from people up the line and fled work sites without paying any wages or offering paltry sums.

Another 300 calls reported that they were denied their wages outright or given vague promises that they would be paid when the lockdown was lifted. We have heard hundreds of cases from every part of the country where workers left for their homes virtually penniless.

Like wages, jobs have been suspended everywhere in informal labour markets. At one branch of a well-known hotel chain, the staff was made to sign pre-drafted resignation letters as soon as the lockdown was announced. We were told about workers also receiving expulsion notices on WhatsApp and SMS. Their attempts to make inquiries were met with switched-off phones and locked doors.

Possibly the worst blow was delivered to the large numbers of invisible migrant workers who lived inside factory premises or construction sites. Not only did they lose wages, but also the dingy roofs over their heads – turning them out to join the exodus returning to rural homes.

Of course, this isn't as unusual as it sounds. Wage denial, salary forfeitures, forced retrenchments, and bonded work are deeply normalised in India's informal economy. The aftermath of lockdown is an amplified reminder of this reality. A study by Aajeevika Bureau conducted in 2018 estimated wage frauds in the construction sector to be in the range of Rs 6,400 crores per annum – and that is likely to be an underestimate.

Just from our presence in the Rajasthan-Gujarat labour corridor, we have registered an average of 2,000 cases of wage denials and frauds a year for the past 3 years. These are cases that pass without formal legal recourse not because the workers do not know better, but because a legal response needs representation and evidence – both of which are scarcely available in the world of informal work.

Unrealistically low wages

These problems cannot be delinked from the fact that India's current real wages are simply too low to a support dignified life. We have neglected with scathing impunity the idea of a living wage that, according to the International Labour Organization, allows "workers and their families to afford a basic, but decent, lifestyle that is considered acceptable by society and allows them to live above the poverty level, and be able to participate in social and cultural life".

The ILO's India Wage Report confirms that almost a third of waged workers in India are paid less than the national minimum wage. Rural wages are less than half of urban wages and a gender gap of 34% keeps the average wages of female workers in rural areas as low as Rs 104 a day.

Not surprisingly, the early evidence from our relief operation in migration-dependent adivasi villages of south Rajasthan has found that they are sliding into penury, facing acute shortages and hunger within a few days of the lockdown. A recently released report by Jan Sahas, a rights organisation with a special focus on women, said that of its rapid survey sample of over 3,000 construction workers, over 90% reported that they have no savings to feed their families beyond one week of lockdown.

Notwithstanding the relief measures announced by the government, it is imperative that workers' wages are reclaimed and not treated as an unavoidable collateral loss in the fight against COVID-19. This requires a commitment to treating wages and work as an inviolable right and a radical repurposing of the legal aid machinery.

An astonishing Rs 1,800 crores remains unpaid to workers under the government's Mahatma Gandhi National Rural Employment Guarantee Scheme across the country. Many have been waiting for well over four months to collect their dues. The government must immediately disburse these wages and establish exemplary precedence by crediting another month of wages in advance into accounts.

Second, a call must be made to migrant workers and daily wagers to self-declare and attest their wage arrears as of March. Workers should be asked to furnish whatever information is available to them on their employers/contractors and on the wages. This mass of worker-generated evidence must be collated and sent to workers' facilitation centres run by workers' collectives, unions, and civil society organisations. These centres must have the backing of an urgently resourced labour administration and be charged with the task of following up with employers and conveying states' intent to take legal action.

The amount of lost wages and jobs is sufficient to establish special status fast-track wage and employment mediation cells and courts in all major cities and industrial clusters.

Third, all packages to bail out industry and businesses must lay down exemplary protocols of labour practice and make these conditional to institutional support – written contracts, documentation, adherence to fair and equal wages, social security, and workers' safety. A wage compensation fund for workers in medium and small-scale enterprises must be announced as this is the hardest hit economic space. This is the opportunity to re-inject the value of labour rights and welfare as central to the recovery of the collapsing economy.

Fourth, there should be an urgent re-examination of labour codes that are likely to compromise the claims of workers in the informal economy. The Labour Code on Wages (2019), for instance, has diluted the responsibility of the principal employer for the payment of wages. It does so by broadening the definition of "principal employer" to include contractors and site managers as well. Such a definition creates difficulties in fixing accountability on the principal employer in cases of wages being denied, especially where there are long chains of intermediaries with multiple labour contractors involved.

It also weakens institutions responsible for enforcing wage protection, by replacing labour inspectors with labour facilitators who can give concessions to employers for wage violations, with only compounded offences leading to penalties. The hollowing out of institutional mechanisms under the labour codes must be revoked.

National minimum wage

A national floor minimum wage must be declared under the Labour Code on Wages, based on the recommendations of the Anoop Satpathy-led expert committee, which proposed Rs 375 per day. This protection under minimum wages legislation must also be extended to home-based or own-account workers, as well as domestic workers, who have multiple employers and are facing the cancellation of orders or loss of work due to the pandemic and lockdown.

In addition, it is essential to establish tripartite bodies based on the Industrial Disputes Act (1947) to allow the government to broker negotiations between employers and workers in sectors such as garments and textiles. This is necessary to ensure that the enforcement of minimum wage regulations reaches sectors where workers' bargaining power is low.

The confidence and morale of the Indian worker are at their lowest. Even as many among us have sought to provide immediate relief in terms of food and supplies, this is not sufficient. Workers not only need food, but are also due their rightful wages – both during this crisis and after. Decades of a lack of commitment to minimum wage standards and institutional protection against wage fraud have made workers increasing vulnerable, leading up to this collapse under the pandemic and lockdown.

The Supreme Court must not stop at applauding the government's relief measures – it can empower waged workers to seize this epochal opportunity to belatedly remedy long-standing unjust wage norms and offer a hope for dignified life as they find their way out of the lockdown.

Note

1 Reproduced with permission from *Scroll.in* where the article first appeared on April 17, 2020. https://scroll.in/article/959428/across-india-workers-complain-that-employers-used-lockdown-to-defraud-them-of-wages-they-are-owed

4.6 India cannot fight a pandemic with police *lathis*. It must ensure people have food – and dignity[1]

Supriya Sharma

India's lockdown has been harsh and the worst-affected are millions of Indians who live on subsistence-level wages.

"You can speak to him in English", said a rickshaw puller who was eating his first morsel of food for the day around 1 pm on Saturday. He was among more than a hundred people who had lined up in the heat outside a government school in South Delhi's Jangpura neighbourhood to get a scoop of dal over a small plate of rice.

The rickshaw puller pointed to another man – who presumably spoke English – to underline how even educated workers could not afford to buy food during the lockdown. Embarrassed at the attention, the man moved away, indicating he did not want to speak to this reporter.

"Please tell the government that the public is starving", the rickshaw puller said. "I haven't even had tea since morning, forget breakfast. On top of it, the police are swinging their lathis at us". He did not want to be identified by name: "You will go away, the police will come and trouble us".

Further down the line were a group of women squatting on the road with empty steel vessels.

They had come to Delhi with their husbands in December from their village in Madhya Pradesh's Tikamgarh district to live and work on a construction site. The contractor last paid them wages in February. "Since then, he gave us money for kharcha paani, which we used to buy rations, but he has disappeared after the lockdown began", Meena Vanshkar said. Now, stranded in the national capital, unable to return home, these workers were running out of money to buy essentials like tea and milk.

They had even run out of soap – the most reliable weapon to fight the coronavirus. "We bathe and wash our clothes in water, what to do", Vanshkar said.

As they spoke to this reporter, a policeman came and banged his lathi on the road in front of the women. "Stand up", he said. "Why are you sitting? Keep distance".

DOI: 10.4324/9781003291527-29

When this reporter pointed out that distance could not be maintained even while sitting on the road, the policeman walked away without a response.

"We won't die of Covid", Mohammad Ali Khan, a middle-aged man, had wryly remarked while waiting for the food distribution to begin. "We will die of lathis and hunger".

With the novel coronavirus pandemic sweeping the globe, countries have closed down transport and economic activities to contain its spread. But India's lockdown has been the harshest – with the public spending needed to soften the blow among the smallest in the world.[2]

The worst-affected are millions of Indians who live on subsistence-level wages. Casual labourers make up one-third of the country's workforce and have no social security to fall back on.[3]

In rural areas, at least people have the cushion of home and community. Some have a patch of land to grow food. Three-quarters of the rural population is eligible for food rations under the National Food Security Act. While there are gaps in the public distribution system, at least there is a mechanism for state governments to deliver grain.

For many urban migrants, even this basic safety net is missing.

Captive and hungry

This is why lakhs of people hit the roads to walk hundreds of miles home even though Prime Minister Narendra Modi asked them to stay. But many could not make it. The police stopped them on the way and herded them into shelters. While prisoners were being released from jails to avoid the spread of disease, migrants were taken captive.

Last week, the central government told the Supreme Court that over six lakh people were staying in these shelters. Reports from Uttar Pradesh[4] to Telangana[5] reveal many are staying against their will.

On Saturday, three men reportedly jumped into the river Yamuna to escape from a shelter in Delhi – one drowned to death. Heated arguments broke out over food, lack of space, and mosquitoes, reports say.[6] By the end of the day, three shelters had been set on fire.

Even outside the shelters, migrant workers are captive and hungry.

While the government asked all private establishments to pay full salaries to even contractual workers, a small survey in Haryana's automobile-making hub of Manesar found more than two-thirds of workers had gone unpaid. The government asked landlords to waive rents, but few did. Many auto-sector workers sent us pictures of the last food stocks remaining in their kitchens.[7]

With food stocks depleting, on Friday evening, hundreds of workers employed in the textile industry of Surat in Gujarat poured out on the streets to demand that the government restore transport and allow them to go back to their villages in North and East India. Watch how young men rioted and set road-carts ablaze.[8] The police arrested 80 workers that night.

But if worker unrest were to spread in India, how many people can the police arrest?

A police crackdown cannot help contain a pandemic. Expanding social welfare to ensure food and dignity for the poorest Indians stands a better chance.

In the early days of the lockdown, economist Reetika Khera proposed 30 ideas,[9] including allocating double the quantity of food rations and providing them free through the public distribution system. Some states have already announced such measures. But implementation is weak. In Jharkhand, for instance, the chief minister declared even households who do not have ration cards will get 10 kg of food grains. However, Right to Food activists visited 50 blocks and found few were receiving them.

To strengthen the capacity of states to give universal food rations, economist Jean Dreze argued the Centre needs to release the millions of tonnes of excess food stocks lying in its warehouses.[10] "In economic terms, releasing excess stocks is costless, and even saves money", he wrote in the *Indian Express*, explaining why cash transfers announced by the government had severe limitations.

In urban areas, for those who aren't covered by the public distribution system, Khera suggested the government supply grains and dal to migrants, allowing them to run their own community kitchens.

Recognising the agency of workers and giving them freedom makes a big difference, as the contrast between two shelters in Telangana shows.[11] In a shelter run by a non-profit organisation, migrants cook their own food. They walk out and return, unguarded. In another shelter, migrants have been kept behind locked gates, with the police watching over them. The atmosphere here is more oppressive and food cooked by volunteers is tasteless, migrants said.

The workers in Delhi's Jangpura neighbourhood had similar complaints. "Taste the food the government gives us", said Sanjay Singh, 50, a worker from Bulandshahr, Uttar Pradesh. "There is salt and haldi, but nothing else". Food packets distributed by private groups were better, he said, but they were erratic.

The absence of choice meant an hour before the food truck arrived, the workers had started gathering on the pavement outside the school. One elderly worker, Rakesh Shukla, fell asleep in exhaustion.

Mohammad Ali Khan sat on the pavement, reading the morning's newspaper. He had picked it off the road. "Modi is meeting chief ministers today and will make an announcement on the lockdown", he told the others.

"When corona [virus] was spreading in China, then itself the prime minister should have become alert", he continued, his voice ringing sharp and clear. "The entry of tourists should have been stopped. But nothing happened, the tourists continued to flock to see the Taj, Humayun's Tomb, Red Fort. They went away and they left corona [virus] in India".

Had the government been sensitive, it would have allowed migrants to go home before shutting off all transport, he said. But wouldn't that have resulted in the disease spreading to rural areas? "Those coming from outside on flights can be screened, so why can't those travelling within the country?" asked Khan.

Khan, 49, is from Adilabad in Telangana. He had run away from home as a teenager, living in Mumbai before moving to Delhi. He worked in the "shaadi-party" business, or tent and catering services. He had no permanent home in the city, he said. He slept where work took him. In the offseason, when weddings and events dipped, he lived around the railway tracks near Nizamuddin, picking up odd jobs. Despite the itinerant existence, he said there was never a time when he ran out of soap – like he had now. "I haven't taken a bath since the lockdown began", Khan said. "Only I know what condition I'm in".

Dinesh Ram, a scrawny, neatly dressed man from Bihar, who worked in the "events business", serving people at glitzy parties, said: "There is no money left. Even beggars have no one to beg from". Seated on the same pavement was a family of beggars. They nodded their heads in agreement.

The government had made Rs 500 transfers into the bank accounts of women opened under the Jan Dhan Yojana. But nearly no one on the pavement had a bank account. One man said he had opened an account under the Jan Dhan Yojana but closed it after money was deducted from it mysteriously. "No money would come into the account, money would only go", he said. This was perhaps a reference to the deductions made for government insurance schemes, which some account holders complained was done without their knowledge.

In the town of Bhind in Madhya Pradesh, women who had gone to encash the Rs 500-transfers were fined Rs 10,000 by the police after they were held for violating "social distancing norms".[12]

Almost everyone on the Delhi pavement had a story to share about police brutality. "I had gone to the dispensary to buy medicines, but there were no stocks. As I was returning, the police hit me with a lathi", Khan said, showing the dispensary slip.

But more than the violence what had shocked them was the duplicity that they alleged the authorities used to get people off the streets on the evening of the Shab-e-Barat festival. "They came in buses and said we are going to distribute food, come with us", recounted Dinesh Ram. "Some people fell for it. They were bundled into buses and taken away. They haven't come back. God knows where they have been taken, to the jungle, or to those hellish shelters".

The government must ensure the working class doesn't starve, he said. Otherwise, who will run the city?

"When work needs to be done, it is the chote log [small people] who will do it, the bade log [the rich] won't even step out of their house", Ram said. "Don't just make announcements. Give us rations. Help everyone, whether rich or poor".

Notes

1 Reproduced with permission from *Scroll.in* where this article first appeared on April 17, 2020. https://scroll.in/article/958993/india-cannot-fight-a-pandemic-with-police-lathis-it-must-ensure-people-have-food-and-dignity
2 Nikita Kwatra and Pramit Bhattacharya. "Migrants Returning Home to Ill-Equipped Healthcare Systems". *Mint*. April 11, 2020. Retrieved from https://www.livemint.com/news/india/to-ride-out-great-lockdown-india-needs-an-emergency-basic-income-11586544661099.html. Last accessed on December 10, 2021.
3 Ministry of Labour and Employment, Labour Bureau Chandigarh. Government of India. Retrieved from http://labourbureaunew.gov.in/UserContent/EUS_5th_1.pdf. Last accessed on December 10, 2021.
4 Asad Rehman. "Desperate to Get Home, Migrants at UP Shelters Ask: 'Are We Criminals?'". *The Indian Express*. April 9, 2020. Retrieved from https://indianexpress.com/article/india/coronavirus-india-lockdown-desperate-to-get-home-migrants-at-up-shelters-ask-are-we-criminals-6353919/. Last accessed on December 10, 2021.
5 Malini Subramaniam and Padmaja Shaw. "Locked up in the Coronavirus Lockdown, Migrant Workers in Telangana Pin Hopes on WhatsApp Rumours". *Scroll.in*. April 11, 2020. Retrieved from https://scroll.in/article/958849/locked-up-in-the-coronavirus-lockdown-migrant-workers-in-telangana-pin-hopes-on-whatsapp-rumours. Last accessed on December 10, 2021.
6 Jignasa Sinha and Somya Lakhani. "Fire at Crowded Delhi Shelters, Residents Held". *The Indian Express*. April 12, 2020. Retrieved from https://indianexpress.com/article/cities/delhi/fire-at-crowded-delhi-shelters-residents-held-6358451/. Last accessed on December 10, 2021.
7 Vijayta Lalwani. "'We Are Trapped': Hunger Is on the Rise in Haryana's Industrial Belt". *Scroll.in*. April 12, 2020. Retrieved from https://scroll.in/article/958838/we-are-trapped-hunger-is-on-the-rise-in-haryanas-industrial-belt. Last accessed on December 10, 2021.
8 Scroll Staff. "Coronavirus: Migrant Workers in Gujarat's Surat Block Roads Over Fears of Extended Lockdown". *Scroll.in*. April 11, 2020. Retrieved from https://scroll.in/latest/958877/coronavirus-migrant-workers-in-gujarats-surat-resort-to-violence-over-fears-of-extended-lockdown. Last accessed on December 10, 2021.
9 Reetika Khera. "Coronavirus Lockdown: 30 Steps Government Should Take to Ease the Suffering of the Poorest Indians". *Scroll.in*. March 26, 2020. Retrieved from https://scroll.in/article/957352/coronavirus-lockdown-30-steps-government-should-take-to-ease-the-suffering-of-the-poorest-indians. Last accessed on December 10, 2021.
10 Jean Dreze. "Excess Stocks of the Food Corporation of India Must Be Released to the Poor". *The Indian Express*. April 9, 2020. Retrieved from https://indianexpress.com/article/opinion/columns/coronavirus-lockdown-food-for-poor-migrants-mass-exodus-jean-dreze-6353790/. Last accessed on December 10, 2021.
11 Subramaniam and Shaw. "Locked up in the Coronavirus Lockdown". *Scroll.in*.
12 अनुराग द्वारी, edited by सूर्यकांत पाठक. 'महिलाएं 500 रुपये जनधन खाते से लेने गईं, 10000 रुपये का मुचलका भरकर लौटीं!' *NDTV.in*. April 9, 2020. Retrieved from https://ndtv.in/india-news/mp-lockdown-women-went-to-collect-rs-500-from-jan-dhan-account-returned-with-a-bond-of-rs-10-000-2209084. Last accessed on December 10, 2021.

4.7 Differently abled migrant women workers grapple with the pandemic[1]

Vedika Kakar

The complexities of vulnerabilities of marginalised sections have been propelled further by the socio-economic impact of COVID-19. Differently abled women workers are the most vulnerable and deprived amongst the migrant workers.

When Anita Ghai, a prominent disability rights advocate, said that the heterogeneity of disability is often ignored in terms of governance and policymaking, she had a point.

Despite existing policies, there are loopholes in their implementation. The political economy of disability needs to be understood. The attitude of the governments seems to be that if they invest in infrastructure for persons with disability, they would be losing money.[2]

Women and the differently abled form one of the most vulnerable sections in society. To understand the struggle of differently abled migrant women in India, we should closely look at the political economy and their social deprivation.

Political economy of disability

The recent migrant exodus has caused a wave of reverse migration in the country where the migrant workers are returning to their native states. This is a direct result of the national lockdown imposed in India, due to the COVID-19 pandemic that has resulted in an economic recession.

It has forced businesses to shut down and has driven migrant workers out of jobs and means of livelihood. This has prompted migrants to travel long distances and cross state borders on foot due to transportation restrictions and economic deprivation.

Unfortunately, government mechanisms to protect labour rights have been disregarded and ignored. The Inter-State Migrant Workmen Act stipulates an additional displacement allowance of 50% of monthly wages at the time of recruitment and journey wages for the migrant to return back to their residence in the other state. This act has been one of the most unregulated

DOI: 10.4324/9781003291527-30

labour rights in recent times. Other social welfare schemes are unable to reach the migrant workers as their current residence is different from their residence registered in their PAN cards and Adhaar cards.

Women bear the larger brunt of the inter-state migrant crisis. They are underpaid, and their gender-specific needs are unaccounted for.

Unskilled and semi-skilled most vulnerable

The most vulnerable of migrant women labour are those employed in unskilled to semi-skilled jobs. They usually come from rural areas and migrate with their families to work in factories and construction sites in urban areas.

A study found that 78% of rural and 59% of urban women migrant workers were working as unskilled manual labour; 16% and 18% were in skilled manual work in rural and urban areas respectively.[3] They have reported poverty, debt, lack of local employment, and migration of their husbands as the main reasons for inter-state migration.

Reports suggest that the rate of suicide among female migrant workers is on the rise and the irregularity of their immigration status is directly proportionate to the amount of abuse they suffer.[4] Apart from working in factories and in households as domestic help female migrant workers also have the responsibility to take care of their household, which is not economically accountable.

A large number of inter-state migrating families presently do not have access to food and medication. In these excruciating circumstances, menstrual health and hygiene have been ignored, specifically because sanitary products were not even counted as essential goods (till March 30).

Pregnant migrant women were forced to give birth on highways and were relying solely on cloth and ash to deal with their menstrual cycles. Without medical aid and essential healthcare mechanisms, giving birth to a child while malnourished and dehydrated is a risk many women take. Existing legal mechanisms like the Maternity Benefit Amendment Act fail to serve their purpose in such situations.

"Invisible Victims of Sexual Violence"

Differently abled migrant women face the larger disproportionate brunt of lockdown. Apart from the migration crisis, women also become victims of domestic violence. Human Rights Watch refers to them as "Invisible Victims of Sexual Violence". Domestic violence can include physical violence, the threat of abandonment, verbal abuse, and so on. Domestic violence cases usually go unreported due to the stigmatisation and social isolation the woman needs to go through and lack of economic standing. Even though several sexual harassment reforms have been amended on paper, their lack of enforcement has prevented women from having easy access to justice.

According to the Disability Guidelines issued by the Health Ministry: "Special care should be taken with respect to women and children with disabilities". Even so, there have been several reports of violence and domestic abuse towards differently abled women and children, labelling them as a burden on the household and society.

Images of differently abled and elderly being carried around on the back of their co-workers and family have flooded the internet. It is important to note that visually and mentally impaired migrants need constant support to navigate their daily lives.

In the current pandemic and the social-distancing norm, they fear for their jobs and lives. A report by People's Archive of Rural India (PARI) discussed two visually impaired migrants who begged on streets and worked in the railway station, wondering who would help them down from trains and buses or buy from their street-side shops. The lack of inclusivity infrastructure in the country prevents them from having easy access to information and transportation.

"Their complex intersectional identity and society's ignorance towards their needs have hindered them from equality and forbid them to be empowered and independent".

One migrant worker noted that to even read Braille signage they need to constantly touch things which put them at high risk for contracting the virus. Unlike most of us, differently abled migrant women cannot work virtually and earn for them or their families. As there is a dearth of information focusing on differently abled women migrants and their grievances are not covered by mainstream media, it is hard to expect any rapid change in government policy or amendments to the existing acts. Their complex intersectional identity and society's ignorance of their needs have hindered them from equality and forbid them to be empowered and independent.

The government needs to create effective door-to-door delivery mechanisms of essential items for differently abled people. Now that lockdown restrictions have been removed in most states, the government needs to make sure that people get back on their feet and are provided with essentials.

The government is generating cards for differently abled people which will allow them to derive benefit from a number of schemes. The lockdown has generated a rise in local entrepreneurship, and it is anticipated that it will increase local employment. This may benefit differently abled rural women as they can keep earning and be with their families, without the need to migrate.

Notes

1 Reproduced with permission from *The Leaflet* where this article first appeared on July 21, 2020. https://theleaflet.in/differently-abled-migrant-women-workers-grapple-with-the-pandemic/

2 Ritwika Mitra. "Lockdown Comes as Double Bummer for Differently-Abled as They Struggle to Secure Basics". *The Indian Express*. June 12, 2020. Retrieved from https://www.newindianexpress.com/nation/2020/jun/12/lockdown-comes-as-double-bummer-for-differently-abled-as-they-struggle-to-secure-basics-2155673.html. Last accessed on December 10, 2021.
3 Indrani Mazumdar, Indu Agnihotri, and N. Neetha. "Migration and Gender in India". Vol. 48, Issue No. 10, March 9, 2013. *EPW*. Retrieved from https://www.epw.in/journal/2013/10/special-articles/migration-and-gender-india.html. Last accessed on December 10, 2021.
4 Prasad Kariyawasam. "Protecting the Rights of Women Migrant Workers". *The Wire*. January 28, 2017. Retrieved from https://thewire.in/women/migrant-women-workers. Last accessed on December 10, 2021.

4.8 Pandemic crisis

"Migrant home-based women workers work 8 hours/day for Rs 10–15"[1]

Cenny Thomas and Nivedita Jayaram[2]

Migrant home-based women workers, the lowest rungs of India's textiles and garments industry, are working for as little as Rs 10–15 for more than eight hours of work, after the COVID-19-induced lockdown. They are struggling for their families' sustenance due to employers' apathy and a lack of access to urban welfare schemes due to lack of documentation.

Ahmedabad: Migrant home-based women workers, who form the lowest rungs of India's labour chain, are working for as little as Rs 10–15 for over eight hours a day during the pandemic, in the face of employers' apathy and the lack of access to urban welfare schemes, a study by labour rights organisation Aajeevika Bureau[3] has found.

While public attention has remained focused on the worker exodus during the lockdown,[4] the distress of migrant families that chose to remain in India's cities remains undocumented. In Ahmedabad, one of India's textiles hubs, women from many such families are employed as home-based workers by domestic and global businesses. Many of them told researchers they were struggling to survive because their wages had gone unpaid and debts were mounting.

Home-based workers, who usually perform subcontracted work on a piece-rate basis, are dealing with twin vulnerabilities—of being migrants and women—the study found. Homenet South Asia,[5] a network of home-based workers across eight countries, defines these workers as "informal sector workers who carry out remunerative work from their own homes or adjacent grounds or premises".

In the textiles and garments hub of Ahmedabad, for example, most home-based workers are employed to perform small but critical tasks—snip loose threads in embroideries, stick embellishments such as rhinestones and glitter on sarees and lehengas, sew collars and cuffs on outfits, and stitch cloth bags. A few are also employed by incense units to roll agarbattis.[6]

Women workers now cannot find any home-based work except garland-making, said Aditi, 18, who hails from Sultanpur district in Uttar Pradesh and lives in Narol, Ahmedabad.

DOI: 10.4324/9781003291527-31

> Ek din mushkil se do-teen maala bana sakte hain aur ek se paanch rupaye milenge. Pura din kaam karke bhi dus-pandrah rupaye hi milenge [It is impossible to make more than two to three garlands a day and we are paid Rs 5 per piece. Even if we work an entire day, we will not make more than Rs 10–15],

she said.

The textile and garments industry,[7] where most of these women were employed, contributes 2.3% to India's gross domestic product, 7% to its manufacturing output, and 13% to its export earnings. The contribution of home-based women workers to this sector and the national economy remains invisible and unrecognised.[8] They are without formal or standard employment contracts, work from home, are often described as "marriage migrants"—they usually move to urban areas with their husbands—and have no means to assert their rights as workers.

India had 7.3 million women home-based workers in urban areas, as of 2012, as per the latest data available from Women in Informal Employment Globalizing and Organizing,[9] a global network focused on women workers in the informal economy. Their numbers are steadily rising, with 20%[10] of urban women workers being home-based workers.

Product outsourcing from large to small firms and home-based workers is increasing, stated the 2007 report of the National Commission for Enterprises in the Unorganised Sector.

In interviews with over 50 home-based women workers across the Narol and Vatva areas of Ahmedabad, the study found that the workers are not entitled to any public provisioning or basic labour rights, including food, shelter, wage, health, and employment security. This is because they lack the identity and residence documents essential for accessing welfare schemes. Their rental and employment agreements are all informal. Over 95% of the households surveyed had no documents to be eligible for the public distribution system,[11] pushing them to near-starvation during the lockdown.

The pandemic has pushed their families even further into the margins, they said. Until the disease hit the city, the women were earning an average daily wage of Rs 40–50. Then the industrial units shut down and now, few have resumed production though the lockdown has been lifted. Many women told the researchers they were waiting for pending wages; they had no means to pay rent or buy essentials and food even after the lockdown was lifted.

The preference for home-based work is rooted in the social preference for married women to work from home. But the survey found that many women are now seeking work in nearby factories and manufacturing units. The search is mostly futile because industries prefer to recruit from the regular pool of experienced male workers, they said.

Men from these households have also lost their jobs and wages, and mounting frustration and need are resulting in increasing cases of domestic violence, as we explain later.

No power to demand or negotiate wages

The industrial peripheries of Ahmedabad, one of the world's fastest growing cities[12] of the decade, is home to hundreds of thousands of home-based women workers. The work they do is central to the fashion and jewellery sector—they receive orders from agents who aggregate their products and then supply to export houses or retail brands for sale in national and international markets.

However, migrant home-based workers have no means to prove their employment links with their contractors or companies that outsource work to them. They have no power to negotiate wages, as prescribed by the Supreme Court in its recent ruling on recovering workers' wages.[13]

Women from the migrant households in the industrial area of Rangoli Nagar in Narol in eastern Ahmedabad come from the rural pockets of Rajasthan, Uttar Pradesh, and Bihar, Aajeevika Bureau's engagement with migrant communities in Ahmedabad revealed. Most of them moved to Ahmedabad to join their husbands' families who have been living here for at least 15–20 years. Their husbands work as skilled workers in the manufacturing units as daily-wage or contractual workers.

These families largely belong to Other Backward Classes (OBC) or general caste categories. They visit their villages once a year, mostly during festivals, and their families have saved their marginal incomes to build a few assets and they are invested in social relationships and networks to access work and provisions.

In Janiyapir, another neighbourhood in eastern Ahmedabad, women home-based workers live in a settlement different from Rangoli Nagar due to its disputed land ownership. This semi-urban plot next to an industrial dumping yard in Vatva has chalis, settlements with low-ceiling tenements typical of shanty towns, occupied by migrant families from Uttar Pradesh and Bihar. They are worse off than the community in Rangoli Nagar, the survey found—they belong to oppressed caste groups and have not been able to build enough assets and social networks in the city. The men work as unskilled labour in chemical and dye factories where minimum daily wages are as low as Rs 300 and the women take on home-based jobs.

"We can ensure that rents are paid"

In both these neighbourhoods, women do not get to relax after their husbands, sons, or younger children set off for work or school. In Rangoli Nagar, their homes double as workplaces—they sit by the only window in their one-room-and-a-kitchen apartments, working for six to eight hours. They make as little as Rs 40 to 50 a day, they said, in non-lockdown times.

Women workers in Janiyapir are only able to access cheaper work—they make maalas and bags, while the children engage in small tasks such as the sorting of disposable cutlery. They have to work longer hours to make

Rs 40 to 50 daily at rates as low as Rs 2 per piece. When the 8 × 10 feet homes feel too cramped, the women move to the grounds outside. Limited mobility and lack of networks outside Janiyapir force women to settle for these poorly paid options where the contractor brings the raw material to their doorsteps.

Since the piece-rate system forces the women to work long hours, bent over their tasks and eyes straining, we also heard complaints of poor health. This work is considered menial, underpaid, and taxing, but the women said they take it on because the jobs held by the men are often insecure and poorly paid. Quite often their wages ensure that their families do not lose their rented accommodation. "Kam se kam, bhaada toh ho jaata hai [At least our rent gets paid with these earnings]", was a common reasoning across interviews.

Often, women are forced to involve their children to complete their orders on time or produce enough to meet their daily earnings targets. In festival season, such as Navratri or Diwali, work is plentiful and even friends and neighbours are called in to help for a share of the earnings. For the retailer, the cost of production remains the same but for the home-based workers, incomes are further depleted despite the long working hours.

Maaya* and her 15-year-old daughter take turns between cooking and cleaning to finish as many pieces as they can so they can procure more work. A few weeks before the lockdown, they were working on an elaborate ghagra-choli, sticking stones and glitter to it. The 10–12 hours of labour spent on the skirt would fetch them Rs 40.

Classified as "self-employed"

Home-based workers' earnings are so low that buying raw material leaves them with little for their households. The consequent absence of savings has hit their families hard during the days of no work, the women said.

Atmaben*, who sews cloth bags for a popular "ethical" retailer in the city, receives Rs 10 per bag. She has to spend on material and the maintenance of her sewing machine to be ready for the next order. Nirbharaben*, who lives in the same building, sews together pre-cut pieces of women's kurtis and nightgowns at Rs 15 a piece. Though she has been working for ten years, her earnings and her value in the labour market have remained stagnant. She is now teaching her daughter-in-law to stitch so that the household earnings can improve.

Most home-based workers are employed by the garments industry to perform a range of critical tasks—snip loose threads in embroidery, stick embellishments such as rhinestones and glitter on sarees and lehengas, sew collars and cuffs on outfits, stitch cloth bags, and so on.

Maaya, Atmaben, and Nirbharaben are categorised as "subcontracted workers", a sub-group within "self-employed home-based workers", but not as "employees" with standard employment relations or rights, according to the National Sample Survey Office.[14] As per their work arrangements, many of these women are expected to bear the risk and cost of production—invest in the purchase and upkeep of sewing machines, buy raw material such as fabric, needle, thread, glue, beads, and so on, and pay for the electricity used while working.

The contractor provides the design and instructions and since these vary, the women cannot reuse all the material they invest in. Over and above their work hours, they also spend time organising production. Some of the women receive raw materials from their contractors, and are much closer to the category of "employees" than "self-employed", but they still do not have access to this status or associated rights.

Work availability in the garments and other fast-fashion supply chains is heavily dependent on seasonal demand,[15] and workers said they were constantly anxious about the loss of compensation or work. They are expected to absorb the costs for the entire product or piece in case of any flaws. They are also responsible for protecting their raw material and finished goods so that they are not stained or damaged in the cramped tenements where they live.

No bargaining power, "gratitude" for work

We found that women owning sewing machines, especially electric ones, had better standards of income, earning up to Rs 100–150 daily. However, investing in a machine is not easy for women given the income capacity of their households.

Methods of distribution and collection, and the mode and frequency of payments differ from contractor to contractor—some collect finished products at workers' doorsteps and others at a designated collection point. The payments are mostly in cash and on a weekly or monthly basis.

Surveyed workers said they did not have any bargaining power, and often spoke in terms of "respect and gratitude" for the contractor for "giving" them work. This means that rather than asking for more wages, they rely on requesting the contractors for more work or extending their work hours even as payment remains poor. The contractors themselves are marginal players in long and opaque supply chains with little power to negotiate with their employers—their strength lies in remaining competitive and offering the cheapest options in the market. They have limited information about where their product will be sold, and no means to hold the retailer accountable.

Work, wages during the pandemic

Many of the surveyed women said they were dealing with the emotional and psychological impact of the pandemic. Men in their families are stressed and enraged by the loss of income, mobility, and access to alcohol and tobacco.

Cases of domestic violence in Narol have been rising since the lockdown, they said. Arguments over dowry have increased in almost all homes, said Aditi.

Home-based workers also bear gender-based responsibilities—of feeding their families, organising milk, vegetables, and arranging for rations that cost at least Rs 50 daily. Even during times of severe income shock, women are expected to manage these costs, and they do this by reaching out to each other or using up their meagre savings. Many of them have ended up mortgaging small amounts of gold jewellery, their only assets, for which they will have to pay an interest of Rs 400 to 500 every month until they repay the principal amount.

One of the main reasons they are willing to work for as little as Rs 10–15 per day following the lockdown, the women said, is the fear of backlash from the men in their households for not fulfilling their gendered role of putting food on the table.

No state support

While these migrant families are believed to have better access to cities compared to the more temporary migrant groups[16] such as tribal construction workers, their urban experience during the lockdown has proved otherwise. The families here are dependent on the local kirana stores where the shopkeepers know that they have no option but to buy provisions even at exorbitant prices.

Migrant families are dependent on rental settlements in disputed, informal lands that appear blurred in maps of urban governance, with extractive rental arrangements. Homeowners in Rangoli Nagar belong to similar socio-economic backgrounds and live in the same building or neighbourhood. Despite being equally vulnerable during the pandemic, many of them have allowed their tenants to defer payments, the surveyed women said.

With growing debts and rent arrears, and forced to sell their few assets—mostly household appliances and goods that reduce the time spent on domestic labour—the workers are now back to where they began, the survey showed.

"I called a government helpline for free rations—but I was asked to walk 6 km with my two young children to the homeless shelter for each meal", said Pushpa, a home-based worker. There were no government facilities for provisioning in their neighbourhood. Hemlata Maheriya, a community leader in Narol and Vatva, argues that, despite this, government workers arrive to conduct fumigation and vaccinations because migrant workers are perceived as threats to public health.

The families of home-based workers have no land holdings or assets in the village and are now losing their grip on the city as well.

> Ration card aur voting card paisewallon ko hi milenge ... sarkari suvidhayen bhi. Gaon me bhi hamare liye kuch nahin hai. Wahan ja

> ke bhookhe marne se achha hai idhar rehna [Only those with money get ration cards and voter IDs and government services too. We have no assets in the village. It is better to stay here than to die of hunger in the village],

said Aditi.

Citizenship and labour rights

Home-based workers and their families are forced to remain "migrants" in the city because they are unable to procure city-based domicile documents that would allow them to vote or access the benefits available to urban residents. The city administration does not enumerate or recognise their settlements for public provisioning, because they do not have city-based domicile documents to make claims of urban authorities.

The Affordable Rental Housing Scheme approved[17] by the Union cabinet under the Prime Minister's Awas Yojana promises to resolve migrant workers' housing crisis in urban areas. The Rs 600 crore approved for the scheme focuses on developing vacant, government-owned housing complexes into rental housing complexes through private developers. However, the announcement does not acknowledge the large number of migrant women for whom informal rental housing acts as a workplace as well. The overwhelming response by the women we interviewed to the proposed scheme was on its lack of relevance to them. Relocating from their existing neighbourhoods to access affordable rental accommodation would cut them off from the connections and networks they use to access work, they said.

"Labour is brought by industry, let them provide for them", said a senior official in the Ahmedabad Municipal Corporation who chose to remain anonymous when asked about the local bodies' responsibility towards the migrant workers. "We only serve tax-paying, voting residents, these are labour", said a local elected representative who did not wish to be named. These responses are part of face-to-face interviews conducted by Aajeevika Bureau's research team during October–November 2019.

However, the industry and the employers cannot be held legally responsible for the conditions of home-based workers either—they do not have formal work contracts and are not covered by labour protective legislations.

Several states[18] as well as the central[19] government's strategy for economic revival following the lockdown is the proposed dilution of existing labour protection laws. Far from extending the scope of labour laws to include those in vulnerable employment, such as home-based workers, it has shrunk their scope, experts say.

"There is nothing in the offing that can help in reviving India's economy in the next six months to a year", said Ravi Srivastava, former professor of economics and chairperson, Centre for the Study of Regional Development, Jawaharlal Nehru University, during a webinar in May 2020.[20] "What it has put in place instead is a set of labour law changes ... to attract investments through lengthening of the labour day, and demolishing labour laws". He added that the result would be sharply declining rates of female labour force participation, combined with a severe impact on the wages and earnings of the bottom-most segment of women workers.

This was echoed by Renana Jhabvala from the Self Employed Women's Association, who said[21] that the desire to keep workers—particularly home-based workers—as an "unidentified mass" with low wages and poor conditions of work informs the proposed shifts in labour legislations.

**Names of interviewees have been changed to protect their identity.*

Notes

1 Reproduced with permission from *IndiaSpend* where this article first appeared on July 23, 2020. https://www.indiaspend.com/pandemic-crisis-migrant-home-based-women-workers-work-8-hours-day-for-rs-10-15/

2 The authors wish to thank Hemlata Maheriya, Geeta Parmar, Mukesh Parmar, and Durgaram for their insights and assistance with interviews.

3 See http://www.aajeevika.org/

4 Sushant Singh and Aanchal Magazine. "Explained: Indian Migrants, across India". *The Indian Express*. April 6, 2020. Retrieved from https://indianexpress.com/article/explained/coronavirus-india-lockdown-migran-workers-mass-exodus-6348834/. Last accessed on December 10, 2021.

5 https://hnsa.org.in/home-based-workers

6 See https://www.wiego.org/sites/default/files/publications/files/IEMS-Ahmedabad-Home-Based-Workers-City-Report.pdf

7 "India – Knitting the Future". *Invest India*. Retrieved from https://www.investindia.gov.in/sector/textiles-apparel#:~:text=The%20domestic%20textiles%20and%20apparel,employment%20to%2045%20million%20people. Last accessed on December 10, 2021.

8 Shalini Sinha. "Rights of Home-Based Workers". National Human Rights Commission. Retrieved from https://www.ihrc.in/wp-content/uploads/2018/06/Home-based.pdf. Last accessed on December 10, 2021.

9 Govindan Raveendran, Ratna M. Sudarshan, and Joann Vanek. "Home-Based Workers in India: Statistics and Trends". *WIEGO Statistical Brief No 10*. December 2013. Retrieved from https://www.wiego.org/sites/default/files/publications/files/Raveendran-HBW-India-WIEGO-SB10.pdf. Last accessed on December 10, 2021.

10 Indrani Mazumdar and Neetha N. "Crossroads and Boundaries". Vol. 55, Issue No. 20, May 16, 2020. *EPW*. December 2013. Retrieved from https://www.epw.in/journal/2020/20/review-womens-studies/crossroads-and-boundaries.html. Last accessed on December 10, 2021.

11 See https://dfpd.gov.in/pd-Introduction.htm

12 Joel Kotkin. "In Pictures: The Next Decade's Fastest-Growing Cities". *Forbes.com*. October 7, 2010. Retrieved from https://www.forbes.com/2010/10/07/cities-china-chicago-opinions-columnists-joel-kotkin_slide.html?sh=1dd8252062bf. Last accessed on December 10, 2021.

13 See https://main.sci.gov.in/supremecourt/2020/10983/10983_2020_36_1502_22526_Order_12-Jun-2020.pdf

14 Raveendran, Sudarshan, and Vanek. "Home-Based Workers in India".

15 Shalini Sinha, Firoza Mehrotra, HNSA with the HomeNet South Asia (HNSA) Team. Working in the Shadows: Women Home Workers in the Global Supply Chain. September 2016. Retrieved from https://hnsa.org.in/sites/default/files/Working%20in%20the%20Shadows%2C%20Nepal.pdf. Last accessed on December 10, 2021.
16 See http://www.aajeevika.org/assets/pdfs/Unlocking%20the%20Urban.pdf
17 Ministry of Housing & Urban Affairs. "Cabinet Approves Developing of Affordable Rental Housing Complexes for Urban Migrants/Poor". July 8, 2020. Retrieved from https://pib.gov.in/PressReleasePage.aspx?PRID=1637218. Last accessed on December 10, 2021.
18 Udit Misra and Nushaiba Iqbal. "Explained: What Labour Law Changes by States Mean". *The Indian Express*. May 16, 2020. Retrieved from https://indianexpress.com/article/explained/what-labour-law-changes-mean-coronavirus-6403611/. Last accessed on December 10, 2021.
19 Yogima Sharma. "Centre Likely to Fast-Track Changes for Uniform Flexi Labour Laws". *The Economic Times*. May 25, 2020. Retrieved from https://economictimes.indiatimes.com/news/economy/policy/centre-for-uniform-flexi-labour-laws/articleshow/75958644.cms?from=mdr. Last accessed on December 10, 2021.
20 See https://www.youtube.com/watch?v=i7wZlnDuy3g&t=3449s
21 See https://www.youtube.com/watch?v=i7wZlnDuy3g&t=1260s

4.9 Pandemic-induced return of the migrant workers

Response of West Bengal[1]

Debashis Aich

Migrants who returned penniless to West Bengal find that there are no jobs available and prepare to return to cities. They are eager to go back although initially they had expressed reluctance to go back.

Migrants begin return to cities

The migrant workers are on the move again. They are leaving for the cities again. Mahibul Biswas of Raninagar in Murshidabad district of West Bengal has also gone back. At 18 years old, Mahibul is responsible for looking after his entire family. His father sells knick-knacks in the streets, his mother suffers from ulcers, and he has three younger siblings – two sisters and a brother.

Four months before the lockdown, Mahibul had gone to Kerala in search of work. On May 7, however, he managed to return home with great difficulty and after spending a large sum of money.

I met Mahibul in Domkal on August 3. Nur Islam Mandal from Domkal has arranged a bus that will take workers back to Kerala. Nur had distributed handbills, pasted posters around town. They carried the message – "Dear, brothers and friends, a bus will leave Laskarpur for Kerala on Thursday, August 7, 2020. You have to carry your voter ID card and Aadhar card with you. To book your ticket today, contact this number".

Mahibul had come to book his return ticket to Kerala. Three months have passed, and he is still without any job. There is no work for him in the village. His father managed to get work for a few days under NREGA. But Mahibul has spent all his savings. "I have to leave. There is no other way. I have to leave for the sake of my brother and sisters", he said. Mustakin Mandal of Laskarpur village in Domkal, and Enamul Malitha of Sahebrampur in Jalangi have left as well. No jobs are available in the villages for workers like Mahibul or Mustakin.

The Anandabazar Patrika on June 25 quoted government sources that according to a preliminary list, 12.5 lakh migrant workers have returned

DOI: 10.4324/9781003291527-32

to Bengal and about 80 percent of them do not want to go back to other states,[2] but my fieldwork tells a different story.

I visited the migrant workers in Ashina village in Falta block of South 24 Parganas on July 26, in East Gurguria in Kultali block of South 24 Parganas on July 26 and 27, in Domkal in Murshidabad district on August 2 and 3, and in Changail in Howrah district on August 19. I met and talked to the workers and artisans who have returned due to the pandemic. I did not get the impression that 80 percent of the migrant workers were reluctant to go back. Rather, I found that they had begun the process of migration again and were eager to go back.

Migration began before PM announced national lockdown

Prime Minister Narendra Modi announced a nationwide lockdown on March 24 at 8 pm in a televised speech to the nation. Even before the Prime Minister's announcement of a nationwide lockdown, lockdown was declared by many state governments by enforcing the Epidemic Diseases Act 1896. In West Bengal, a four-day shutdown or "mini lockdown", from March 23 to March 26, was declared with the state government asking people to "stay at home". After a day, the lockdown period was extended till March 31. In Punjab, the lockdown started from March 22 and in Telangana, Andhra Pradesh, Delhi, and Kerala from March 23.[3] The State Government of Maharashtra had announced on March 20 that everything except the essential services and institutions would be closed till March 31.

And from the evening of that day, people, including the migrant workers, began flooding the railway stations in Pune, Kalyan, and in Mumbai. The rush to board trains and return home was such that in addition to the 48 scheduled trains, the officials of Central Railway had to run 16 additional special trains.[4] Habibur Rahaman Mullick, a resident of Chaingail, Howrah, told me how he reached the CST station on a local train from Baikulla at 4 am. Even at that time the station was so crowded that it was not even possible to move. Somehow he made his way through the crowd, reached the platform, and boarded the train. And although he had reserved a seat in a Sleeper class coach in advance, he had to sit and stay up for the entire journey back home.

Within a few hours of the Prime Minister's announcement of a 21-day countrywide lockdown, all the trains stood cancelled. Thousands were stuck at the train stations. Those travelling by road were detained at the borders and on the highways.

Majid Ali Mollah of East Gurgurai in Kultali and 29 others from West Bengal were among those detained. Amalesh Bhuiyan of the same village, however, was able to return home. He had left Telangana by train on March 21. He reached home on March 23, after enduring indescribable hardships. Similarly, Basudev Basanta, a resident of Manasatla in East Gurguria village of Kultali, South 24 Parganas, returned home from Washim in Maharashtra.

He, along with five other workers from West Bengal, left Washim on March 19 boarding a train from Akola station the same day. He had purchased a General Compartment ticket for Rs. 360. He travelled for about a day and a half, standing most of the time, meeting hunger pangs by swallowing dried bread and gram-flour with water, and returned home on March 21.

Rafiqul Sheikh, 26, a resident of Ashina, Falta, who used to stitch jeans for children at a factory in Badarpur, Delhi, had a similar experience. The factory was shut down four days before the lockdown. His wages amounting to Rs. 3000 were due. "I didn't get my due wages even after a lot of pleading. I purchased a train ticket and came back travelling in an unreserved compartment", said Rafiqul. He reached home on March 24.

It would thus seem that migrant workers began their journey home because of the panic induced by the pandemic, at least seven to ten days before the formal announcement of the countrywide lockdown by the Prime Minister.

Case studies: Migrant workers return home penniless

Majid Ali Mollah (36)

Purba Gurguria, Kultali South 24 Parganas.

Work and wages

Majid and his wife Ajmira went to Kerala through a labour contractor from Nadia. He rented a room for Rs. 3500 per month. His working time was from 8 am to 4 pm. The wage rate was Rs. 350 per day and Rs. 60 per hour for overtime. For a skilled worker this wage was quite low. Majid agreed and said, "I've been doing this for just two years. Since I was new, perhaps I was getting less".

Ajmira used to work as a domestic help in a Malayali household. She did household chores from 8 am to 2 pm and was paid Rs. 300 a day, in addition to tiffin once a day. Since both Majid and Ajmira were employed through a contractor, he handled their wages. They suspect that they were paid less by the contractor. While Ajmira received full wages at the time of leaving work, Majid was owed Rs. 16,000 by the contractor in back wages for 48 days or about one and a half months.

Return home

On March 21, Majid and Ajmira, along with 27 others, from West Bengal, left for Chennai to return to their homes. When they arrived at Chennai Central Station the next day, they found out that trains had stopped running. Then the nationwide lockdown started from March 24 midnight and the Tamil Nadu police wielding sticks chased away those stranded at the station premises.

Majid and the group of migrants from Bengal were forced to take shelter in a lodge near Egmore station, paying Rs. 350 a day for a double room. Majid and others did not know how long the lockdown was going to last. The cost of a vegetarian meal consisting of only rice and daal was Rs. 60. As a result they exhausted their savings within eight to ten days. The lodge-owner said that failure to pay rent would result in their eviction. They were in a precarious situation. Fortunately, a local human rights organisation came to their aid. They sent Rs. 45,000 in two instalments to Majid's bank account to cover room rent and food for the group.

The workers used to gather in front of the Chennai Corporation building and demonstrate. According to Majid,

> One day I saw a notice (advertisement) for a bus service in the building. I took a picture of the advertisement and talked to everyone. The owner of the bus came and in the presence of the owner of the lodge, demanded Rs 10,000 for each passenger. At last all of us returned home travelling in the bus following the health protocols. The journey was not without problems – the bus was not allowed to stop anywhere in Orissa, we found it difficult to find food and had to go hungry for a day and a night. Even the bus driver survived only on tea. After three days and nights of travelling by bus, we finally reached home.

Samar Roy (26)

Purba Gurguria, Kultali, South 24 Parganas.

Work and wages

Samar was working in "Glaze Trading India Private Limited" in Bolangir town in Orissa. He worked in "Direct selling and marketing". There were no TA and DA allowances, salary was paid on a commission basis on total sales. His monthly income ranged between Rs. 10,000 and 12,000. Sometimes, however, it fell to as low as Rs. 5000.

Samar lived in a rented house in Bolangir. At times, seven people shared a single room. The shared rent varied between Rs. 600 and 700 per month per head depending on occupancy. With the announcement of the lockdown from March 24, the company was closed. Neither Samar nor any of his team members got paid for March. Everyone was stuck till June 22. Samar said,

> The municipality gave us rice, pulses, potatoes, oil and biscuits twice a month. I used to buy vegetables and other necessities when the market was open for a short window in the mornings. Later on, I had to seek financial help from home.

Returning home

When he enquired about returning home, Samar said, "The local doctors and even police suggested walking or cycling back. The risk of infection from the virus will be less, they said". Samar and some others started looking for bicycles. They noticed an advertisement on the wall of Balangir Municipality, and seven bicycles were purchased for Rs. 2300 each. They had to ask for money from home. Finally, on June 22, "seven people – four from Kakdwip, one from Maipith, one from Raidighi and I left for home". All seven of them had left Orissa for home on that day at five in the evening. For food, they packed bread, flattened rice, bananas, and water. The distance from Bolangir to Kolkata by road is 720 km. From Kolkata, Kultali is another 64 km, Maipith 96 km, Kakdwip 90 km, and Raidighi about 60 km. They reached home after midnight on June 26.

Ziarul Sheikh (26)

Ashina, Falta, South 24 Parganas.

Work and wages

When asked which company he works for in Hyderabad, Ziarul replied "Vaishali". Later, I learned that he actually worked in a boutique called "Vaishali". He lived in a house shared by six other people. He was paid Rs. 500 for eight hours of work. He had to pay Rs. 2000 per month as rent. After curfew was imposed by the state government to keep people indoors, his work in the boutique came to a standstill. And then the national lockdown was announced, and there was no question of any work.

Although Ziarul had bought a train ticket home for March 23, train services were stopped before that and he could not use it. Although his wages for the month of March were paid in full, he soon he ran out of money paying for food and rent. His wife who was back home in West Bengal had to borrow money and send him Rs. 10,000 to meet his expenses. He was literally under "house arrest" till May 18. During this period, the local residents had helped him with food and vegetables for only two days. He visited the local police station to plead for arrangements to be made for him to return back home. He was told, if there was any news about trains or buses running, they would inform him accordingly. The police station wrote down his name and address. He used to call the police station almost every day.

Returning home

Finally, the good news for Ziarul came on May 16. He received a call from the police station and they helped him board a "special train" home. Ziarul said, "The train journey did not cost me anything". The train dropped him and several others off at Malda station in West Bengal. Although there he faced no problem while on the train, after getting down at Malda early in the morning, he had to wait till the evening to get a bus. Zairul said "At Malda we had to organise a protest rally and make its video public, only then the bus was arranged. The video of returning migrant workers demonstrating for a bus had set the local administration into action". Ziarul reached Baruipur by bus and from there he reached home on his own.

Migration and hygiene

All the 26 migrant workers, who were surveyed for this article, said that they had complied with the government's epidemic-related health rules. Of the total, 24 underwent a mandatory 14-day home quarantine; one was in the government quarantine centre, while another was quarantined at a local madrasa. The government directives were implemented through police and panchayats, and there also was surveillance by the villagers. However, everyone said that their neighbours did not panic and were not hostile. The workers said that Accredited Social Health Activist (ASHA) workers visited them to monitor their health. However, it was not possible for many to maintain physical distancing at home. For example, Ziarul Sheikh of Ashina was in the same room with his wife and two young children.

Shramik Specials: West Bengal government's initial reluctance

Within eight days of the lockdown, wbtrackmigrants.com listed the names of 50,162 migrant workers from West Bengal. *Bangla Sanskriti Mancha*, a socio-cultural organisation, registered the names of 20,000 workers during this period. On April 18, Bangla Sanskriti Mancha sent details of 34,000 migrant workers stuck in different states to the Chief Minister's Office and on April 25 and May 6, two more lists of 45,000 and 60,000 workers, respectively, were sent to the Union Home Secretary Ajay Bhalla.[5]

The first Shramik Special train to reach the state came from Ajmer in Rajasthan. On May 5, it reached Dankuni Junction. The second train left Ernakulam, Kerala, and reached Behrampore on May 7. In both cases, the state government granted permission for the special trains at the request of the Rajasthan and Kerala governments. There was no initiative from the West Bengal government itself.[6] On March 4, *The Hindustan Times* wrote that West Bengal had not applied for any special trains. Only two trains were granted permission to enter the state. On May 4, the Karnataka government complained that West Bengal was refusing permission to send stranded workers in special trains. In response to the allegations, the state government said, "We have asked Karnataka to suspend the journey of migrant workers to Bengal. The infrastructure needs to be set up first to receive the workers". Similar allegations have been heard from the governments of Maharashtra and Gujarat, with no response nor permission from the West Bengal government.[7]

The trains started running from May 1, but the reason why no initiative was taken by the state government in this regard remains unexplained. One speculation is that since states like Gujarat, Maharashtra, Karnataka, Delhi, and Tamil Nadu had relatively high rates of virus infection, the West Bengal government was reluctant to bring back workers from these hotspots for fear of spreading the disease to the rural areas of the state. This finds support from the statement of the Chief Secretary of the state on May 4.[8]

On May 14, the chief minister announced that the government had arranged for an "additional 105 special trains" for migrant workers returning to the state. On May 18, it was announced that the fares of these trains would be borne by the state government. According to various media reports, till May 14, the state had allowed only ten trains to come in.

State to prepare database of migrants

In general, the migrant workers want to go back again to their places of work. The primary reason for this is the prospect of higher wages in other states. Whether it is construction workers or zari workers, wages are at least double in other states. Besides, the artisans are reluctant to work in the 100 days MGNREGA scheme, especially in public works like repairing roads or digging ponds and canals. But due to the continued recession in the construction, manufacturing, and hotel industries, a large number of migrant workers are still unable to return to their earlier jobs.

The migrant workers have no serious complaints about access to food. Government schemes ensure at least free food to them. However, the amount of rice and flour given free are not adequate, they complained. Financial constraints meant a shortage of food. Also, the costs of educating their children and medical expenses have resulted in bringing down the overall living standard of the migrant workers.

It would seem that the fear of the state government in bringing back millions of workers without adequate infrastructure in place was also not unfounded. However, invaluable time was lost in readying the infrastructure and overall planning. There was also a human cost to this lack of preparedness. For example, a young man from Murshidabad, who was working in Kerala, committed suicide when his train was cancelled. Three workers from Bankura lost their lives in an accident while returning home in a lorry. In addition, most of the workers had to return home after enduring endless hardships and paying exorbitant fares.

The chief minister claimed that 10.5 lakh workers had returned to the state by the first week of June.[9] But this number does not include all the workers who returned using makeshift modes of transport and through their own initiatives. Therefore, the total number of migrant workers who returned home is likely to exceed the official figure.

On June 4, the chief minister directed the district magistrates in the state to prepare a database of the returning workers. The officials were also asked to skill-map the migrants. This process has now started in all districts.

Notes

1 This is a shortened version of a report based on research conducted under the MCRG Media Fellowship 2020.

2 Giving work to migrants is a big thought, Chandraprabh Bhattacharya, Anandabazar Patrika, June 25, 2020.

3 (a) https://www.groundxero.in/2020/04/10/corona-taught-us-who-are-the-migrants/
  (b) https://en.wikipedia.org/wiki/Indian_state_government_responses_to_the_COVID-19_pandemic
  (c) *The Hindu*, March 21 and 22, 2020. *The Times of India* and *Economic Times*, March 23, 2020.

4 Coronavirus Fallout: From Maharashtra, an Exodus of Migrant Worker with No Work, Sukanya Shantha, *The Wire*, March 22, 2020.

5 Covid-19 Lockdown: Data show Bengali migrant workers stranded, Center, State turn a blind eye, *Newsclick*, Artitra Bhattacharya, May 11, 2020.

6 (a) Bengal allows 2 trains to carry back stranded people; opposition targets it for going slow, *Hindustan Times*, Snigdhendu Bhattacharya and Joydeep Thakur, May 4, 2020.
  (b) Fearing spread of infection, Bengal pays only lip service to idea of getting back its migrants, *Scroll.in*, Shoaib Daniel, May 8, 2020.

7 The West Bengal government refuses to accept migrants from Maharashtra, but UP climbs down. Priyanka Kokodkar, TNN, May 6, 2020.

8 "It won't be proper to allow lakhs of stranded migrants labourers all in one go. They need to be brought back in phases because detailed planning has to be made. Else every effort made till date will go down the drain". Rajiv Sinha, Chief Secretary, West Bengal.

9 Over a million migrant workers have returned to Bengal, says Mamata, Shiv Sahay Singh, *The Hindu*, June 4, 2020.

Part 5

Pandemic as an opportunity

Changing labour laws

5.1 May Day

Twelve-hour working day notifications[1]

Jane Cox

What an irony. Just as trade unions prepare to (virtually) celebrate the May Day this year, a number of State Governments have passed amendments to the Factories Act, 1948, reversing the very origins of May Day – the right to an eight-hour working day. The question is, are the amendments lawful?

The history of May Day has huge significance for Indian workers during the COVID-19 pandemic. It commemorates the struggle of 19th-century workers in the United States for an eight-hour working day. But not only this – it was a struggle waged by lakhs of largely migrant workers who had migrated to the US from around the globe searching for work during the Industrial Revolution. Living in grim hovels and ghettos, malnourished and exhausted, a common working day was 10 to 16 hours. Thousands died each year of poor working conditions and long hours.

In the mid-1800s workers started demanding a shorter working day, without pay cuts. In 1884 at its national convention in Chicago, the Federation of Organised Trades and Labour Unions (the latter-day American Federation of Labour) unilaterally declared that on and from May 1, 1886, "eight hours shall constitute a legal day's labour". An estimated 3 lakh workers in 13,000 businesses across the US downed tools on May 1, 1886, in support of the call. Chicago was the epicentre of the struggle, and by May 3 the number of striking workers had swelled to around 1 lakh. The protests were overall peaceful, but on May 3 several workers of McCormick Reapers Works were killed and wounded in a police firing.

A protest meeting at Haymarket Square was held the next day. Just as the meeting was winding down, the police moved in and an unidentified person threw a bomb, leading to the police opening fire. At least eight protesters and eight police officers were killed. The bomber was never identified, and the unions maintained it was an agent provocateur working for the police. What did follow was the unleashing of a national wave of repression. Eight of the leaders were convicted, in spite of there being no reliable evidence against them (five of them were not even present at the meeting).

DOI: 10.4324/9781003291527-34

Ultimately four were hanged and one committed suicide. The other three received a pardon six years later from the new Governor of Illinois, on the ground that much of the evidence given at the trial was pure fabrication and that not only forced confessions had been extracted from workers by the police but inducements of employment and money had also been used for the same. It is this struggle which May Day commemorates and has been celebrated as International Workers' Day by trade unions and workers throughout the world for more than a century.

History of eight-hour day legislation

In most countries, it wasn't until after the First World War that legislation was passed restricting the working day to eight hours (though where trade unions were strong enough some companies introduced it on an individual level). Uruguay was the first country to adopt it in 1915 – but only for certain work. Spain was the first (1919) to lay down a universal eight-hour working day.

In setting up the International Labour Office (now known as the International Labour Organization – ILO) the Treaty of Versailles specifically declared the eight-hour working day to be an international goal. It was then the very first issue discussed by the ILO, leading to the Hours of Work (Industry) Convention, 1919.

Most interestingly, the First World War proved to industrialists what labour researchers and trade unionists had been claiming for years – that longer working hours do not lead to increased productivity. Great Britain and the United States especially, desperate to maximise production of munitions for the war, commissioned a number of scientific studies on the correlation between hours of work and productivity. The results confirmed what similar studies in France and Germany had found – that returns from overtaxed and tired workers rapidly diminished.

The Ford Motor Company famously acted on these findings in 1918, reducing the working day to eight hours and reportedly doubling the wages of the workers. To the shock of many, production increased, with fewer hours worked, and Ford's profits doubled within two years. India's legalised eight-hour working day came with the 1946 Amendment to the Factories Act of 1934 – a result of the Bill introduced by Dr Babasaheb Ambedkar as Labour Member in the Viceroy's Executive Council.

The present ordinances

On April 7, 2020, the Gujarat State Government issued a Notification under the Factories Act, 1948, amending sections 51, 54, and 55 of the Act to provide that for the period April 29 to July 19, 2020, workers in Gujarat can be made to work 12 hours in a day, 72 hours in a week with a 30-minute break after 6 hours. The Factories Act, 1948, otherwise provides that workers can only be made to work 9 hours in a day – but 48 hours in a week, with one day off in the week – thus coming to 8 hours in a day (sections 51, 52, and 54), with a 30-minute break after 5 hours (section 55).

Most alarmingly the Gujarat Notification also enacts that no overtime will be paid for the extra four hours – these will be paid at the usual hourly rate. The Notification expressly states that wages for the extra hours will be paid "in proportion to the existing wages (e.g., if wages for eight hours are 80 Rupees, then proportionate wages for twelve hours will be 120 Rupees)". This is directly against section 59 of the (unamended) Act which provides that wages must be paid at double the ordinary rate for hours worked in excess of 48 in a week.

The Rajasthan Government followed with a Notification on April 11, allowing a 12-hour working day for 3 months, but providing for overtime pay for the extra hours worked – "up to a limit of 24 hours a week" – i.e., 12 hours a day for a straight 6 days. The rationale given is to reduce the manpower requirement for manufacturing in those factories exempted from the lockdown.

The Notification actually states that this will allow for "full capacity with around 60–65% of normal manpower". Punjab vide Notification dated April 20 has permitted a 12-hour working day for 3 months, with payment of overtime for the additional 4 hours. Himachal Pradesh has gone on similar lines allowing a 12-hour working day for the period April 21 to July 20, 2020, up to 72 hours in a week, but with overtime payment. However, this has been allowed for "all factories in the State" and not just essential services or those exempted under the lockdown.

The first question that arises is the source of the power for the passing of such Amendments. Labour being on the Concurrent List under the Constitution of India (List III, Seventh Schedule), both the Centre and State Governments can enact labour legislation, and a Central Act can be amended by a State vis-à-vis that particular State.

Ordinarily, a State Government amendment of a Central Act, if it is in contradiction to (repugnant to) the latter, will only come into effect if given the assent of the President of India (Article 254(2) of the Constitution). However the present amendments have been passed under section 65(2) of the Factories Act, 1948, itself (see below). This section empowers State Governments to grant exemption from any or all of the provisions of sections 51, 52, 54, and 56 (48 hours a week, weekly holiday, daily hours, and spread-over) "to enable the factory or factories to deal with an exceptional press of work".

Even presuming that catching up with production lost during the pandemic lockdown could be classified as "dealing with an exceptional press of work", all of the present Notifications issued by the State Governments have gone beyond the powers conferred under this section. Section 65(3) lays down a number of conditions for the granting of an exemption. Section 65(3) (iii) prohibits the total number of hours of work in any week, including overtime, from exceeding 60. Thus a 12-hour day can only be done thrice in a week. All of the State Notifications provide for up to 72 working hours in a week – i.e. 12 hours a day, 6 days a week. The Gujarat Notification is further in blatant violation of section 65(2) as this section doesn't provide for an exemption from section 59 of the Act – which provides for double pay for overtime worked.

Convention No 29 of the International Labour Organisation enjoins every member nation which ratifies the Convention to suppress the use of forced or compulsory labour in all its forms within the shortest possible period. India ratified this Convention on November 30, 1954. The Convention no doubt excludes from the definition of forced or compulsory labour

> any work or service exacted in cases of emergency, that is to say, in the event of war or of a calamity or threatened calamity, such as fire, flood, famine, earthquake, violent epidemic or epizootic diseases, invasion by an animal, insect or vegetable pests, and in general any circumstance that would endanger the existence or the well-being of the whole or part of the population.

However, Article 13 of the Convention directs that even in such a case, the hours worked in excess of the normal working hours "shall be remunerated at the rates prevailing in the case of overtime for voluntary labour". The Gujarat Notification providing for no overtime rate thus falls foul of this Convention as well, and in law amounts to mandating forced labour.

The notifications of the four State Governments are thus absolutely illegal, being in breach of the very section they are purported to be passed under, as well in the case of the Gujarat Notification, of the strictly binding Convention of the International Labour Organisation. Moreover, they provide for workers working a 12-hour day, for at least the next three months, at a time when the most basic medical and scientific advice to avoid contracting the deadly COVID-19 is to take rest and stay as healthy as possible. This new regime ensures the complete opposite. That too as we move into the monsoon season when disease and viruses are notoriously rampant, and most alarmingly for COVID-19, bronchial and lung issues abound.

Note

1 Reproduced with permission from *The Leaflet* where this article first appeared on April 30, 2020. https://theleaflet.in/may-day-12-hour-working-day-notifications/

5.2 Changes in labour laws will turn the clock back by over a century[1]

Ramapriya Gopalakrishnan

Under the cover of the economic impact of the COVID-19 lockdown, labour rights cannot be done away with.

Ten central trade union organisations have called for a nationwide strike on May 22[2] to protest against the "anti-worker and anti-people autocratic measures of the centre" and "the draconian changes in labour laws by state governments to facilitate more brutal and cruel exploitation of workers". Since 2014, the Central government has been taking a slew of measures aimed at making far-reaching changes to India's labour laws premised on the grounds that they are antiquated, complicated, and an impediment to economic growth. These measures euphemistically referred to as the "labour law reforms" include amendments to the existing laws, the enactment of new laws, codification of the laws, and the issuing of advisories, model bills, and business reform action plans.

It has been touted that the reforms are necessary to afford more flexibility to employers, facilitate the ease of business, and attract greater foreign investment. It has also been claimed that changes to the labour law inspection regime are necessary to free employers from "the tyranny of the inspection raj".[3] Making use of their concurrent powers, several state governments have taken a similar path and introduced changes to the labour laws. The government of Rajasthan had been a forerunner in this regard and had increased the thresholds for the application of the Factories Act, 1948, and the Contract Labour (Regulation and Abolition) Act, 1970, in 2014, pushing a large number of workers out of the coverage of those laws.

Trade unions have stridently opposed the "labour law reforms" on the grounds that they undermine the hard-won rights of workers and will lead to greater exploitation of workers. Trade unions have repeatedly charged that the government has been acting unilaterally, without holding tripartite consultations. On account of the stiff resistance of the trade unions, the Central government has been unable to effect the changes at the pace that it would have liked.

DOI: 10.4324/9781003291527-35

Using the health crisis as a pretext

It now appears that the COVID-19 crisis is being used as a pretext to push through the unfinished "reforms agenda" of increasing the hours of work, restricting wages to the bare minimum, reducing social security benefits, permitting the engagement of contract labour for any kind of work, easing norms for firing workers, clamping down on trade union rights, and whittling down labour inspection. For close to six years now, the Central government has been attempting to increase the hours of work of factory workers.

Citing a public emergency, the labour departments of Gujarat, Madhya Pradesh, and Himachal Pradesh last month simultaneously issued notifications extending the hours of work[4] of factory workers to a maximum of 12 hours a day and 72 hours a week. The notifications have been issued invoking section 5 of the Factories Act and are valid for a period of three months. Around the same time, the labour department of Punjab too issued a similar order under section 65 of the Factories Act as per which factories may be exempted from the stipulation regarding the daily and weekly hours of work under the Act to cope with an exceptional pressure of work. Last week, the governments of Odisha, Maharashtra, and Goa also similarly increased the daily hours of work. The fact that increasing the length of the workday may endanger the health and safety of workers seems to have been entirely overlooked.

The government of Uttar Pradesh has gone much further. The government is in the process of promulgating the Uttar Pradesh Temporary Exemption from Certain Labour Laws Ordinance, 2020, that suspends the operation of all labour laws[5] applicable to factories and manufacturing establishments in the state for a period of three years, with the exception of the Bonded Labour System (Abolition) Act, 1976, the Employees' Compensation Act, 1923, the Building and Other Construction Workers (Regulation of Employment and Conditions of Service) Act, 1996, and provisions in the labour laws relating to women and children. The draft ordinance, however, requires employers to pay the minimum wages notified by the state government and also requires compliance with the provisions of the Factories Act relating to safety. It extends the hours of work to 11 hours a day and the extension of the workday to 12 hours.

The implication of this is that employers in the state would have no obligation to pay workers anything more than the prescribed minimum wage. They need not adhere to their wage-related obligations under existing collective bargaining agreements. In addition, they would stand divested of their social security obligations. Employers will have total flexibility in the matter of firing workers and can do so without paying them any compensation. They can engage contract workers for any kind of work and run their establishments with an entirely precarious workforce. They need not provide even basic amenities to their workers. They need not have any kind of engagement with trade unions, thus depriving workers of any say in their wages and working conditions.

New trade unions cannot be registered in the state for the next three years. Furthermore, workers will not have access to any redressal mechanisms to address their grievances. Such unrestrained flexibility coupled with a total clamp down on the possibility of any kind of resistance from the workers is what employers' associations across the country are now demanding.

Two weeks ago, the government of Madhya Pradesh exempted all factories in the state from the application of all the provisions of the Factories Act except those relating to approval, licensing and registration, safety, hazardous processes, overtime wages, earned leave, and the obligation of the employer to notify the authorities about accidents that result in death or serious bodily injury. It has permitted third party certification for non-hazardous factories employing less than 50 workers, for a period of 3 months from the date of publication of the notification.

The implication of this is that the provisions of the Factories Act relating to the maintenance of health and hygiene, provision of basic amenities, and labour inspection will not be applicable to factories for a period of three months. The government of Madhya Pradesh has also issued a notification exempting new factories from the provisions of the Industrial Disputes Act except those relating to lay off, retrenchment, and closure for a period of 1000 days from the date of publication of the notification. This would mean that workers in newly established factories will not be able to exercise their freedom of association and collective bargaining rights for a period of 1000 days.

It has also exempted 11 types of industries from the application of the Madhya Pradesh Industrial Relations Act that contains provisions relating to the recognition of trade unions by employers, and this again is a move to curtail trade union rights. The suppression of trade union rights that are democratic rights does not augur well for a democracy.

Following the Uttar Pradesh model, the government of Gujarat is in the process of promulgating an ordinance exempting new units that are set up within a year of its coming into force from the application of all labour laws with the exception of the Minimum Wages Act, the Employees' Compensation Act, and the safety-related provisions of the Factories Act for a period of three years. If the ordinance is promulgated, workers in new units in the manufacturing, as well as service sectors, would be deprived of their rights to fair wages, decent working conditions and social security, and their freedom of association and collective bargaining rights as well.

Joining the list of states that are in the process of amending labour laws, the government of Karnataka has proposed to increase the threshold numbers[6] for the application of the Factories Act, the Contract Labour (Regulation and Abolition) Act, and Chapter V-B of the Industrial Disputes Act that requires prior government approval for effecting lay off, retrenchment, and closure. Increasing the number thresholds under those laws would have the effect of restricting the coverage of those laws which in turn amounts to reducing the protection available to workers under the laws.

Harbinger of things to come

Although it may appear that such measures will be in place only for a limited period of time, they may be a harbinger of things to come and may well become a permanent feature once the waters are tested. While the government may justify such retrograde measures that turn the clock back by over a hundred years claiming that they are necessary to kickstart the economy, attract investment, and create employment, the fact is that such measures infringe on the fundamental rights and human rights of workers and cannot be countenanced on any count. Indeed, there is little evidence[7] that such changes to the labour laws result in attracting big investments and boost industrialisation or job creation. Labour rights are human rights and the Indian state cannot abdicate its constitutional obligations and the commitments that it has made by reason of ratifying the International Covenant on Civil and Political Rights, the International Covenant on Economic, Social and Cultural Rights, and various conventions of the ILO as a result of which it is bound to promote decent work in conditions of freedom, equity, security, and dignity.

Notes

1 Reproduced with permission from *The Wire* where it first appeared on May 20, 2020. https://thewire.in/labour/labour-laws-changes-turning-clock-back
2 "The Much-Vilified Labour Inspector Raj". *The Hindu: Business Line*. August 9, 2015. Retrieved from https://www.thehindubusinessline.com/opinion/the-much-vilified-labour-inspector-raj/article7519064.ece. Last accessed on December 10, 2021.
3 Shikha Mukerjee. "Here's Why Trade Unions Have Called for a Nationwide Protest on May 22". *The Wire*. May 19, 2020. Retrieved from https://thewire.in/labour/trade-union-protest-labour-laws. Last accessed on December 10, 2021.
4 Vinay Umarji. "After UP, Gujarat Offers 1,200-Day Labour Law Exemptions for New Industrial Investments". *The Wire*. May 9, 2020. Retrieved from https://thewire.in/economy/gujarat-labour-law-exemption-new-industries-covid-19. Last accessed on December 10, 2021.
5 Somesh Jha. "Adityanath Govt in UP to Suspend Key Labour Laws, Workers' Rights for Three Years". *The Wire*. May 7, 2020. Retrieved from https://thewire.in/labour/adityanath-govt-in-up-to-suspend-key-labour-laws-workers-rights-for-three-years. Last accessed on December 10, 2021.
6 K. R. Balasubramanyam. "Karnataka to Join New Labour League, to Amend Labour Laws to Bail out Industrial Sector". *The Economic Times*. May 12, 2020. Retrieved from https://economictimes.indiatimes.com/news/economy/policy/ktaka-to-join-new-labour-league/articleshow/75683950.cms. Last accessed on December 10, 2021.
7 Dr Sanjay Upadhyaya and Pankaj Kumar. *Amendments in Labour Laws and Other Labour Reform Initiatives Undertaken by State Governments of Rajasthan, Andhra Pradesh, Haryana and U.P.* V.V. Giri National Labour Institute. NLI Research Studies Series No. 122/2017: Noida. 2017.

5.3 Labour law changes

Innocuous mistakes, sleight of hand, or taking sides[1]

Atul Sood and Paaritosh Nath

The changes in labour laws announced during the lockdown period in several states reflect a lack of concern for the highest levels of unemployment seen in the past 45 years and the large number of workers leaving industrial pockets and returning back to an economy ravaged by agrarian distress. The events of the last few months suggest that distinctions amongst the working class in terms of organised/unorganised, formal/ informal, and migrant/ local are being narrowed. Labour must consolidate across the board taking anchorage in the commonalities of experience that various divisions face today.

India, like the rest of the world today, is going through a pandemic. But the discussion in India, especially surrounding policy, seems to suggest it is business as usual. The government is busy pitching whatever measures it wanted to introduce before the COVID pandemic, as sure shot ways of recovering from the impact this pandemic has had on the economy. This packaging of the old in a new bottle has been suggested in various ways to the nation – be it the opening up India's defence sector,[2] disinvestment of the public sector,[3] proposing growth by supporting financial markets, or changes in the labour laws. This note specifically deals with the changes suggested in existing labour laws. For those of us who question this stance of the government, it is not enough to only look at the inadequacies of the rationale provided while introducing these reforms. These inadequacies were there before COVID as well. It is equally important to raise if not answer the question as to what is motivating the government to initiate these changes at the time of a global pandemic. What is the larger plan behind the move? An attempt will be made to discuss this at the end of this note.

Fiction or facts: Reasoning or the lack of it

As of now, the argument being made is that the labour welfare legislations embed in them aspirations of labour backed by legal coercion that are too stringent in favour of workers, which has paradoxically resulted in the

DOI: 10.4324/9781003291527-36

worsening conditions of workers.[4] This is not a new argument. The suggestion is that the laws that seek to regulate minimum wages, payment of wages, occupational safety, industrial disputes, contract labour, employment and service conditions of inter-state migrants, etc., are not only onerous, they make the cost of hiring the workforce under a formal set up too high. To compensate for this disincentive, the employers either do not employ enough workers or employ workers through mechanisms which ensure that the bulk of the workers do not fall within the ambit of law. For those supporting the current labour law changes this explains the poor working conditions, the rise of informality, and the precarious earnings of the workers.

One may ask that if the majority of workers today, for whatever reasons, already do not fall within the ambit of labour laws and the rules are easily circumvented then how will the suspension of these laws incentivise the industrialists to invest in the welfare of workers? Even within the organised manufacturing sector, where some compliance is maintained, we see that the share of wages in gross value added is not only low but has been declining over the years. As per the ASI data, this share was 28.5% in 1980–1, 21.4% in 1990–1, 15.5% in 2000–01, 10.3% in 2010–11, and 12.3% in 2015–16. Labour costs, where the law still is applicable, are low and steadily falling, and yet the solution seems to be to remove these laws as well. Furthermore, it is interesting and revealing to see what major investment consultancies advise potential investors in India and China. For instance, the consultancy firm Genimex[5] suggests

> India's manufacturing labor is more competitive when compared to China. In 2014, the average cost of manufacturing labor per hour was $.92 in India and $3.52 in China. While labor costs are much lower, one must also consider the extra costs that will accrue due to India's expensive transportation, power, and water costs. Low power availability can be a major drawback manufacturing in India.

Another investor site suggests that hourly minimum wage in China is three times more than in India ($1.73 compared to $0.61).[6] The underlying point is that labour is already very cheap in India and other factors that reduce India's competitiveness are not being addressed.

Another rationale given by those who want the suspension of labour rights is that labour-welfare legislation never considered issues like compliance costs, government capacity for enforcement, and more importantly their counter-productive consequences. The COVID crisis provides the country an opportunity to rectify these historical mistakes (see for this view Shekhar Gupta, *Yogi Adityanath Brings Massive Labour Law Reforms, Doesn't Waste Corona Crisis*, The Print, May 9, 2020). By compliance costs very often what is implied is the corruption that employers face from regulators ("inspector raj"). We are told that since there is a lot of corruption in the labour department, industrialists get blackmailed, disincentivising investment, so as a solution we need to do away with the laws themselves. One needs to pause for a moment here. Have we applied this rationale to any other situation? Have we ever said that in spite of traffic norms we have far too many accidents in this country, so let's get rid of transport regulations? Have we ever suggested that since there is a fair bit of corruption within the law-and-order machinery, so let's get rid of regulating law and order? The failure to check corruption in government departments is essentially the responsibility of governments, so it should be logical to think of it as a failure of the government. But in the case of labour that connection is seldom made.

Moreover, Figure 5.3.1 puts into perspective the factual basis of this argument – showing clearly the low percentage of factories, within the ambit of the Factories Act, that were being inspected over the last several years in India. The reality on the ground is that the factories inspectorate staff is highly understaffed to begin with. For example, in Bihar in 2013, there was one officer in charge for more than 1060 factories.[7] A similar situation exists in many more states. The solution to this overall rent seeking problem lies in checking corruption in government departments and increasing the inspectorate staff rather than doing away with inspections altogether.

Recent changes in labour laws: The myth of simplification

Public discourse is inundated with many additional arguments supporting the dilution or removal of all labour-related regulation. We are told that there is a multiplicity of laws and we need simplification, over regulation is inefficient; we should make pragmatic laws such that they can benefit the maximum number of workers rather than benefit a small section of privileged workers; and stringent regulation disincentives investment.

Table 5.3.1 provides us with the changes proposed recently by the governments of Uttar Pradesh, Madhya Pradesh, and Gujarat. As mentioned earlier,

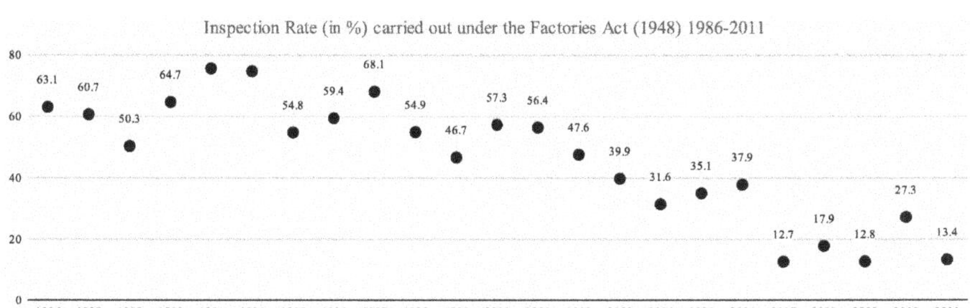

Figure 5.3.1 Inspection Rate(in%) Carried out Under the Factrories Act (1948), 1986-2011. Source: Indian Labour Year Book, Labour Bureau, Many Issues.

Table 5.3.1 Changes Proposed by States

State	*Date of Notification*	*Amendment Made*	*Points to Note*
Uttar Pradesh	6-May-2020 "Uttar pradesh katipay shram vidhiyon se asthyai chhoot"	• 35 out of 38 labour laws withdrawn[1] • Bonded labour system (Abolition) Act 1976, the Employees Compensation Act, 1923 and Building and Other Construction Workers (Regulation of employment and conditions of services) Act, 1996 remain operational • Provisions relating to the employment of women and children as well as Section 5 of the Payment of Wages Act,1936 have also been retained	Major acts done away with: Factories Act, 1948, Industrial Disputes Act, 1947, Industrial Employment (Standing Orders) Act, 1946, Contact Labour Act ,1970, Trade Unions Act, 1926 and Minimum Wages Act, 1948
Madhya Pradesh	5-May-2020	The Madhya Pradesh Industrial Relations Act, 1960 no longer applicable to 11 major industries	Industries, including textiles, iron and steel, automobiles, cement and electrical goods, exempted from the provisions that recognise trade unions as bargaining agents
		Save for Sections 6, 7, 8, Sections 21 to 41-H under Chapter 4 about safety, Sections 59, 65, 67, 79, 88 and 112, the Factories Act,1948 and the Madhya Pradesh Factories Rules, 1962 have been done away with	The retained sections deal with (a) approval, licensing and registration of firms, (b) notices provided before occupation or in the case of accidents, (c) inspection procedures, (d) safety of workers, (e) prohibition of child labour, (f) wages for overtime and (g) annual leave with wages, (h) capacity of state government to issue exemption orders and the (i) general power to make rules
		Upcoming factories are to be exempted from the Industrial Disputes Act, 1947 for the next 1,000 days save for: Chapters VA and sections 25-N, 25-O, 25-P, 25-Q, 25-R of Chapter VB of the Industrial Disputes Act [2]	• Upcoming factories—Those that register themselves and start production for the first time within the next 1,000 days after the publication of this notification. • Firms dont need permission to lay off, but still need permission to retrench

		• Third-party certification for non-hazardous category factories that employ up to 50 workers to be recognised • This is as per Business Reform Action Plan, 2016	Such firms exempted from routine inspections
		Amendment brought to Contract Labour (Regulation and Abolition) (Madhya Pradesh) Rules, 1973	Licence issued for a specified period of time. Presently, firms need to reapply/modify their licences each time new contract labour joins or leaves the firms
	6-May-2020	Amends Madhya Pradesh Industrial Employment (Standing Orders) Act, 1961	Threshold for the standing orders act (define the conditions of work) raised to 100 workers
	Madhya Pradesh Labour Laws (Amendment) Ordinance,2020	Madhya Pradesh Shram Kalyan Nidhi Adhiniyam, 1982 amended	State government can exempt any firm(s) from this law– concerned with the constitution of a welfare fund for workers
Gujarat	Announced by chief minister on 9 May 2020	New firms to be exempted from all labour laws, except the Minimum Wages, Act, the Employees' Compensation Act and safety-related rules in factories for 1,200 days	New firms—firms set up within a year of this order coming into effect

[1] See the complete list here http://uplabour.gov.in/lc/DynamicPages/ActRule.aspx

one of the key axes around which the entire debate on reforms has revolved is simplicity – the need to do away with the complexities surrounding labour laws and making them more accessible to all stakeholders including workers. However, as we note from the above discussion, the specific nature of changes sought to be implemented betrays this very call for simplicity; if anything, they make the process far more convoluted. Take, for example, the bizarre decision taken to remove entire Acts, save for a couple of sections. The Factories Act in its second section defines who according to the purview of this Act is a worker, who is the occupier, and what is to be understood when one talks about the manufacturing process itself. Having done away with this section, the enforcement of the retained sections, unless otherwise specified, stands on dubious grounds because they have no anchorage in well-defined, mutually agreed upon definitions. A factory owner could deny a worker any compensation arising out of injury by stating that the said individual does not constitute a worker in the first place or the process involved was a peripheral activity not related to the core production process. Similarly, it is rather futile to retain the section on overtime if one has already removed chapter six of the Act that deals with the length of the working day in the first place. How does one even come to an understanding of what constitutes overtime when regular time itself is up in the air? Or even annual paid leave that as per the existing regulations requires a worker to be working regularly for 240 days. A lack of clarity on whose muster rolls are to be maintained, or for that matter whether rolls are to be maintained at all renders this act of benevolence meaningless.

One obvious question that springs to mind is whether these are innocuous mistakes made as a result of an oversight. It is our opinion, in fact, that these are well thought out loopholes, a sleight of hand of sorts, that seek to absolve firm owners of any liability whatsoever. So Uttar Pradesh retains the Act that deals with compensation in case of an accident but decides to remove the very Act that defines the safety measures to be followed on the factory floor in the first place. Or the fact that all three states do away (or reform in the case of Madhya Pradesh) with the Industrial Standing Orders Act that require firm owners to define and submit to the certifying officer the terms and conditions of employment. How these changes result in a simplification of the legal redressal process is anyone's guess. Mind you, we have not even mentioned the legal hassles involved with having the presence of two simultaneously applicable and valid interpretations of the same law determined on the basis of when a factory was opened. The message is rather straightforward; simplification here is just a ruse to shift the burden of responsibility entirely onto the workers' shoulders.

Bringing everyone to the lowest common denominator

Two major takeaways are evident for all to see. Firstly, all of these states have done away with the hire and fire "restrictions" imposed upon them.

Gujarat and Uttar Pradesh (UP) have gone to the extent of removing even the option of any form of severance pay that could be given to the worker. Madhya Pradesh (MP), for its upcoming industries, removes the provisions for layoff though retains the ones for retrenchment, i.e. firms will no longer require the government' permission before laying off workers. In a post-COVID scenario, where savings would have been reduced to a minimum and debt would be high, this provision of laying off would result in workers moving away in search of other employment opportunities soon after they are laid off. Secondly, the offensive against trade unions is clear. UP and Gujarat have done away with the Trade Unions Act while MP has exempted major industries from the Industrial Relations Act. These states want to do away with any provision that spoke in favour of workers organising and collectively bargaining for their rights. This, coupled with a free hand to industries, seems to be quite ominous for an already precarious workforce.

We can already see what the new work ethos would look like. All three states, in the name of fighting the ill effects of corona, intend to increase the length of the working day from the nine hours currently specified in the Factories Act. Interestingly, while the Factories (Amendment Bill) 2016 sought to extend the number of overtime hours[8] the new regulations seem to have abandoned the overtime question. They seek to directly increase the number of daily hours to 12 and the weekly hours to 72. This shift from overtime to an increased work day is very significant and has very serious implications. Those familiar with the realities of the work-floor know that the actual number of hours worked by factory workers during a week often exceeds the existing 48-hour norm as stipulated by law. The PLFS 2017–18 data too informs us that wage workers on the shop floor work for an average of 60 hours a week, with only 7% working for 55 hours or less. These extra hours are legally considered overtime work and their rate of payment per hour varies from 1.5 to 2 times that of the regular hourly pay. What these new regulations in fact seek to do is to bring these extra hours within the purview of a regular day and thus the workers are deprived of the extra earnings that they would have received if they were counted as overtime hours. Amidst this entire brouhaha surrounding production and the need to increase the working hours these two points are simply missed. Instead of checking the increasing hours of back-breaking work that is becoming the norm in the factory, the state is not only making it official (in fact with an extended cap), but also depriving the workforce of overtime incentive they would have ordinarily received. It needs to be noted that these hours are increasing in workplaces that are no longer mandated to provide restrooms, washroom, drinking water facilities, etc., for the workforce. With ease of hire and fire and minimal union intrusion, these changes lower the minimum benchmark for the workers.

Withdrawal of labour regulation: New futuristic development or adding insult to injury to lockdown indignity

If, as suggested by supporters of these labour law changes, the cause of the underdevelopment of regions within India is the stringency of labour laws, what explains the experience and condition of labour in the more developed regions?

The question we should be asking is: Has the suffering of labour reduced in the developed states, where investment has reached? Is the experience of labour within these developed regions under COVID-19 in any way different for the labour that is from within the state and that from outside?

Between 2014 and 2016 changes in labour laws were introduced by some states, both "developed" and "underdeveloped" – namely, Rajasthan, Gujarat, MP, and Maharashtra. At that time, proposals were made to dilute the laws, but not to fully suspend them. It is interesting to note that even then all the states that went ahead with the labour reforms were marked by high levels of contractual density[9] (see Figure 5.3.2).[10] The situation with respect to employment conditions in the states that initiated labour reforms in 2015–16 also did not support the rationale that was given then to make the regulatory changes. We note that the states of Gujarat, Rajasthan, and Madhya Pradesh perform either at a par with or even worse than the national average which in itself is abysmal (see Figure 5.3.3).

Sometimes "concern" for the vast majority of labour is also used to make a case to dilute labour regulation. It is argued that labour laws tend to benefit a handful of workers as a finite set of benefits are concentrated in the

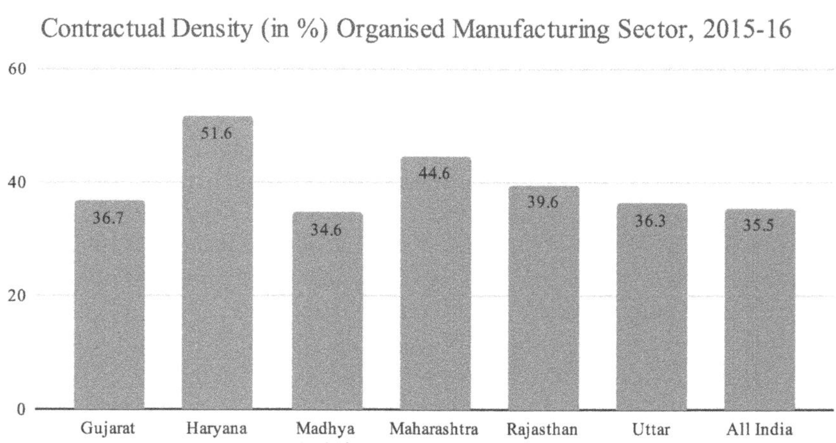

Figure 5.3.2 Contractual Density Organised Manufacturing Sector, 2015–16 (%). Source: Annual Survey of Industries 2015-16.

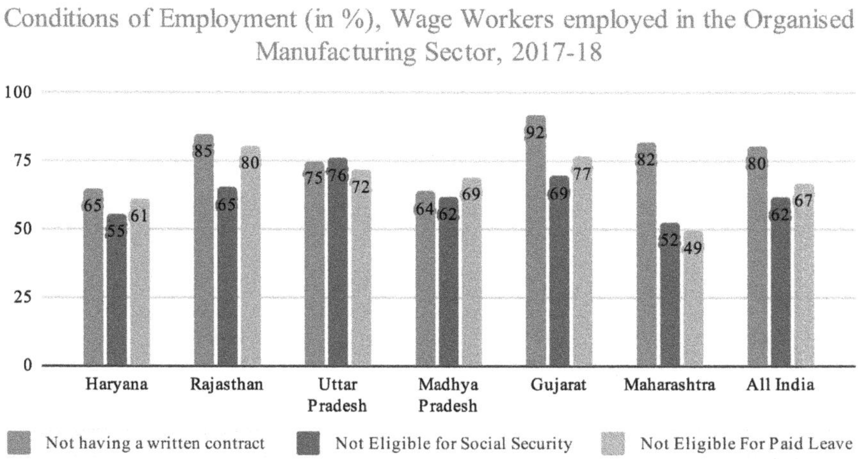

Figure 5.3.3 Conditions of Employment, Wage Workers Employed in the Organised Manufacturing Sector, 2017–18 (%). Source: Unit level PLFS Data.

hands of a few. The rest are deprived because they face barriers to access these benefits. Rather than deliberate on overcoming the barrier, the proposal is made to dilute the standards for all. Perhaps the assumption is that the share of labour is limited and it better be spread thinly amongst all. That is the only way one can comprehend the idea of pitting one set of workers against the other, rather than extending protection to all. The declining share of wages, increasing contractualisation, and poor working conditions within the organised manufacturing sector, where supposedly this "labour aristocracy" resides, clearly show that the issue of maintaining or diluting labour standards is hardly a question of economic facts, rather it is more about reducing the power of labour in general. So rather than seeking a larger share for labour in general, merely pitting one set of workers against the other has greater currency. To pin the guilt on one set of workers for the precarious conditions of the majority of the working force is unfair and unethical.

Overall, the larger context of the labour market in India in which labour laws are being suspended is worth summarising here. As per the PLFS 2017–18, 45% of regular workers earned less than Rs. 10,000 per month, and about 12% earned less than Rs. 5,000 per month. The average daily wage in rural areas for casual workers in April–June 2018 was Rs. 282 for men and Rs. 179 for women, and in urban areas, it was Rs. 335 and Rs. 201, respectively. Average gross earnings from self-employment are also low on average (for all categories barring rural males) when compared to the minimum wage of Rs. 9,750 per month arrived at by the Expert Committee. Given such low levels of earnings, it is difficult to comprehend how India's workforce sustains itself. Clearly their capacity to survive even for a few days on their savings is negligible. This labour market reality should explain to India's rich, the disturbing images of those who labour that the whole nation witnessed in the last nearly two months. It is disconcerting that workers in India struggle to make a decent living, even though they work for considerably long hours. And now they are being told that the regulatory framework to safeguard them is responsible for their plight and the hope of overcoming hunger is presented as giving up these safeguards.

How does all this add up: What is new?

What do these changes in labour laws mean for the working class? We feel that we are experiencing a new framing of the development agenda in India. The COVID crisis is being seriously used as an opportunity to strengthen the control of Capital over Labour. We have covered this deregulation of Capital and re-regulation of Labour in detail elsewhere.[11] In the past too – policies were made in the name of the poor but they benefitted the rich mostly. While the previous ruling regimes diluted labour laws and promoted voluntary regulation, this regime believes that it has the mandate to do it upfront. The nation and the national aspirations are being redefined. Those who oppose it are "outdated", not worthy of consideration, and even "anti-national". Pushing this agenda, at this time of the COVID crisis, serves another useful purpose. It helps put the onus for the current precarious condition of workers not on the government but on a regulatory framework which is a hangover of the past. It helps to cover up the fact that the state has abdicated all its responsibility towards the majority of its working people. Workers, the suggestion is, have been let down by archaic laws and not by governments.

This fits in with the current scheme of things in other ways too. The nation is now used to seeing victims as perpetrators. Victims are nowadays projected as themselves being responsible for their suffering. We saw that in cases of lynching, in the case of violence that ensued in 2018 on the day of the bicentenary celebrations of the *Bhima Koregaon* battle, and in the case of teachers/students who were injured in the attack in Jawharlal Nehru University. Those protesting against the Citizenship Amendment Act are responsible for bringing suffering to their community as a result of riots that ensued in North East Delhi during the protests. Now the same principle is being applied to the vast majority of the labouring population in this country. Those who experienced hunger, starvation, unemployment, humiliation, indignity, and death during the lockdown are now being held responsible for their precarious existence. They are being told that the attempt by the state to "over protect" them in the past has made them more vulnerable. The implication of this rationality is grotesque. Since the workers are responsible for their condition, they will have to pay the cost not only of the lockdown but also of rebuilding – the economy, as well as their livelihood and lives in post-COVID India.

As argued above, the suspension of labour laws does not make sense either in terms of benefitting labour or of attracting investment. In fact, it does not make sense even to promote growth. Remember this comes at a moment when a large section of the workforce has already lost out on their earnings because of the lockdown and is resorting to borrowing money to sustain itself. A recent study by the Centre for Sustainable Employment, Azim Premji University, found that two-thirds of their survey respondents reported a loss of employment during the lockdown.[12] There is going to be a severe demand shortage in an already stumbling economy, and to take away whatever feeble benefits or safety precautions/liability that the owners had, essentially means the workers need to finance every component of their living expenses including healthcare. The squeeze on demand will be very harmful to growth not to talk about its adverse implications for the distribution of income and its impact on increasing the precarity of the vast majority of India's labour force. How can we possibly explain why this is happening? How can we possibly explain the government's preoccupation with changing laws when millions of migrants are walking back home on foot under adverse circumstances?

Admittedly there are more questions than answers here. Is it because of apathy, incompetence, or lack of information? Any one of these suggestions would be preferable to a realisation that this hostile attitude is very much intentional and has a cold, calculated logic behind it. The latter raises serious questions regarding the manner in which the ruling class envisions its logic of accumulation and the role of labour.

Are these changes the desired ends in themselves or are they just a footnote that flags something much larger in the offing, viz. the re-invention and re-imagination of the labour market itself? A project which seems to be unconcerned that we have the highest levels of unemployment seen in the past 45 years, that is fairly content with large swathes of workers leaving industrial pockets and returning back to an economy ravaged by agrarian distress. The events of the last few months seem to suggest, more than ever, that distinctions amongst the working class in terms of organised/unorganised, formal/informal, migrant/local are being narrowed. It is also obvious from the hunger and hardships that workers across the board are experiencing with each passing day of the lockdown that the earnings of most workers do not leave them with any savings to survive for more than a few days (Jan Sahas Survey on March 27 found close to 42% of the workers in their sample without food rations[13]). At the same time, this shared experience of the working class creates opportunities for a new logic of differentiation to emerge, based entirely on the terms and conditions set by the ruling powers. The means to achieve this differentiation can be manifold – selective induction into the core labour force accompanied by technological shift, patronage via schemes and transfers for a section of the working class, exclusion from the core labour force, building relations of neo-bondage with segments of the working class by regulating the mobility of the workers and controlling the avenues for sale of labour power on the whims of Capital, taking away all rights of labour to organise and bargain with Capital, etc. Each of these, in part or full, will have far-reaching consequences not only with respect to the condition of workers but for the larger Capital-Labour dynamic in the country.

One thing is clear though. The shift in the overall attitude of the state necessitates a drastic shift in terms of how Labour pitches its future agenda. The rights-based approach seems to be inadequate, with both the state and Capital displaying utter disinterest in any appeals made within this discourse. As a logical extension to this argument, it is time for labour to consolidate across the board taking anchorage in the commonalities of experience that various divisions face today.

Notes

1 Reproduced with permission from the authors. An earlier version of this paper appeared in *Economic and Political Weekly* (Volume 55, Issue Number 22) on May 30, 2020. https://www.epw.in/journal/2020/22/insight/labour-law-changes.html
2 See https://timesofindia.indiatimes.com/india/govt-opens-doors-to-greater-private-role-in-defence-power-space/articleshow/75783007.cms
3 See https://www.outlookindia.com/newsscroll/all-sectors-open-for-pvt-cos-non-strategic-psus-to-be-privatised/1837131
4 See https://indianexpress.com/article/opinion/columns/india-lockdown-inter-state-migrant-workmen-act-6400710/
5 See https://www.genimexgroup.com/blog-manufacturing-in-china-manufacturing-consumer-goods-india-vs-china/ accessed on May 10, 2020.
6 See www.nationmaster.com/country-info/compare/China/India
7 See Nath, P., Siddiqi, U., and Sood, A. (2019) *Thinking Growth or Thinking Employment. India Exclusion Report 2018–19*. (5th ed.) (New Delhi: Yoda Press).
8 The Factories (amendment bill) 2016 sought to extend the number of overtime hours that were allowed in a quarter from 50 to 100 and in case of higher workload to 115 and further to 125 if it was deemed to be in the public interest.
9 Only Madhya Pradesh had a contractual density lower than the all-India average.
10 Admittedly, there is an argument stating that higher rates of contractual density are, in fact, a result of inflexible labour laws such as the Industrial Disputes Act, 1947, because of which plant owners are forced to hire contract workers in the place of permanent workers. However, from Table 5.3.1 we note that it is the "0–19" bin that has the highest contract intensity at 61% with the "50–99", "100–299", and "300–499" size classes having roughly the same contract intensity somewhere in the mid-30s.
11 Sood, A., Nath, P., and Ghosh, S. (2014). Deregulating Capital, Regulating Labour: The Dynamics in the Manufacturing Sector in India. *Economic and Political Weekly*, LXIX (26 and 27), 58–68 ISSN (Print) - 0012-9976.
12 See https://cse.azimpremjiuniversity.edu.in/covid19-analysis-of-impact-and-relief-measures/
13 Voices of the Invisible Citizens, A Rapid Assessment on the Impact of COVID-19 Lockdown on Internal Migrant Workers: Recommendations for the State, Industry & Philanthropies, April, 2020.

5.4 Why Adityanath's simplistic Migration Commission is a non-starter[1]

Juhie Singh

The commission, set up as a knee-jerk step to quell public anger, is unlikely to have the authority, depth, or time to develop an understanding of workers' predicaments.

In the past few months, we have borne witness to disturbing stories and images of people, struggling to find their way back home.

The tragedy that migrant workers have been subjected to is further compounded by the fact that they continue to face challenges in almost every sphere of life. They are forced to return to their native villages as they have no source of employment, no social security net, and have been abandoned by callous governments, which have opted to preoccupy themselves with publicity campaigns to build legitimacy during a time of crisis rather than dealing with the immediate problem at hand.

While the efforts to bring back such workers through railways and other means of transportation are commendable, it must be noted that the central government's ill-planned response to the outbreak of the coronavirus led to the largest mass migration in recent Indian history.

Uttar Pradesh is the recipient of the largest number of migrants coming into the state via Shramik trains. These migrant workers are returning to a state which is laden with debt – with the Adityanath government's failure to push for more funds for the state as a special relief package in view of the crisis – with no major sources of employment – most of the MoUs signed during flashy UP investment summits have not materialised in any investment – with depressed demand and a huge unskilled labour force.

Uttar Pradesh chief minister Adityanath has directed the setting up of a Migration Commission for the employment of labourers returning to the state. Since the government has failed to provide information on the constitution, powers, and role of the commission so far, we can surmise the terms of reference of the commission from newspaper reports. These include:

1. Mapping the skills of workers
2. The authority to grant "permission" to other states seeking to re-employ migrant workers from Uttar Pradesh

DOI: 10.4324/9781003291527-37

3. Providing social security to workers
4. The general welfare of migrant workers

The UP government may add additional terms, as it is quite evident that this commission does not have a great deal of planning behind it – details are not one of the chief minister's strong suits.

This measure, however, does reveal certain flaws in the state government's planning and approach itself. Unfortunately, it also suggests that the commission will not have an impact on the migrant crisis or bring about a systemic change.

First, the decision reflects a failure to recognise the push and pull factors that led to such migration in the first place. The government's lack of empathy for the migrants shows that it has failed to understand that migration for most is a compulsion and empty assurances do little to change the circumstances which compelled them to migrate in the first place.

While the decision to declare that all migrants will be provided with employment within the state may grab headlines, it is still not clear how the commission is going to accomplish this, when several government departments, investor summits, schemes (such as One District One Product[2]), and the chief minister himself have failed to do so. Limited non-agricultural employment options, coupled with depressed agricultural wages and incomes, close to no social security, and a general lack of life opportunities have come together to create a complicated problem, which cannot be addressed by government bodies working in silos.

Second, Yogi Adityanath's government has adopted a bureaucratic style of functioning by conflating the constitution of commissions, schemes, and funds (much like the central government) with a solution to the problem. The chief minister is being led to believe by his counsellors that appointing a group of bureaucrats or pro-government experts guarantees outcomes. Indian government and bureaucracy have unfortunately proven this to be incorrect.

A commission may prove to be the source for innovative solutions and a deeper understanding of the problem when it is manned by independent experts. However, with the current regime's fear of criticism, this is unlikely to happen. There is no evidence to suggest that such commissions have played a constructive role, when it comes to the implementation of solutions. They become an additional layer of bureaucratic oversight, at best, and an obstacle to field-level functionaries at worst.

Third, the government has also exhibited shocking ignorance to the extent of wilfully disregarding the details in this plan.

How will the commission work with other implementation agencies already working in the areas within its ambit? How will it coordinate with other states for the so-called "permissions"? Will the "permissions" close off the only source of employment that our migrant labourers have currently? Who will be responsible for skill up-gradation when the much-touted "skill mapping" is completed? Who will be part of the commission? How will the influx of migrant workers impact the agricultural labour market and what steps are to be taken to address this issue?

These are just a few amongst several details the government has failed to share and quite possibly not worked out yet. One of the reasons for this omission may be that it is difficult to hold something or someone accountable if their roles are not spelt out clearly. This commission is likely to be another example of this misstep.

Fourth, there is a complete lack of engagement with underlying factors that led to the problem. For example, while the commission's mandate includes a "social security net" for migrants, the state government is silent on why the plethora of social security schemes did nothing to quell the plight of our workers. Nor has the government indicated what level of social security should be assured to such workers and whether the question of a universal basic income should be taken up now. Anybody who refuses to develop an in-depth understanding of the problem and alternative solutions is unlikely to have any structural impact.

Finally, by opting for the beaten path of commissions and "new government schemes", rather than the rationalising of existing structures and designing policies based on hard data, the government has proved that it has run out of ideas. This becomes particularly serious when we consider the post-COVID-19 world. The chief minister has no answers to the problems of employment, skill up-gradation, and investment in the face of depressed demand other than "setting up a commission".

In the face of no clear policy directions, we risk losing a whole generation. During such a critical time, we are left with helmsmen (both at the state and the centre) who do not know which route to take and are dismissive of any inputs. Falling short of criticising the chief minister's competence to lead our state, we may safely assume that with the misguided advice he is currently receiving, he cannot lead us out of this crisis. While he may be able to posture and position himself as a "decisive" leader, he must take time to evaluate his own decisions, as they are likely to have an irreversible impact on our future.

All the factors above suggest the chief minister has again fallen prey to making announcements without substance. But policy decisions must be based on facts and data rather than pompous gestures. Yogi Adityanath has been vulnerable to rash decisions based on shallow advice before, such as the ordinance suspending labour laws for three years.

The state government was led to believe that labour laws were the only obstacle to investment in Uttar Pradesh. Labour laws were suspended, without taking the time to understand the protections they afford and the other, much more acute, barriers to investment the state faces today.

Yogi Adityanath has attempted to cultivate the image of a "bold leader". This has been amplified by the complete lack of leadership shown by the rest of the party in the state. However, he must recognise that when it comes to government policy a "bold" decision is not always the right one. The migrant commission has been set up as a knee jerk step to quell public anger and pacify the media, and is unlikely to have the authority, depth, or time to develop an understanding of the problems that face our brothers and sisters when they are forced to leave their homes in search of better lives in other states.

Notes

1 Reproduced with permission from *The Wire* where this article first appeared on May 29, 2020. https://thewire.in/labour/uttar-pradesh-migration-commission

2 Khabar Lahariya. "A UP Govt Scheme to Aid Stone Artisans Has Left Them Worse-off". *The Indian Express*. 19 July 2019. Retrieved from https://thewire.in/government/a-up-govt-scheme-to-aid-stone-artisans-has-left-them-worse-off. Last accessed on December 10, 2021.

5.5 Can labour reforms help women migrant workers during COVID-19?[1]

Ellina Samantroy

The COVID-19 has led to a disproportionate impact on women workers, particularly women migrant workers.

Over the last few years, India has witnessed a decline in its female labour force participation. From 31.2 per cent in 2011–12, the number stood at 23.3 per cent in 2017–18, according to the National Sample Survey Office. Besides, 90 per cent women are engaged in low-paying jobs[2] in the country's huge informal sector, without adequate coverage through labour legislations and access to social protection.

The ongoing pandemic has made things worse as it has disproportionately affected women workers,[3] depriving them of access to social protection and decent work.

Recently, the Ministry of Labour and Employment carried out labour reforms for simplifying the provisions of 44 labour legislations into four codes.

A question which arises here is how are these reforms going to help India's migrant workers – and women migrant workers particularly?

Women migrants: An integral part of urban cities?

The migrant workers have been the backbone of the urban economy working as domestic helps, home-based workers, self-employed workers, etc.

The recent Periodic Labour Force Survey (PLFS) 2017–18 estimated that 51.9 per cent women were engaged as self-employed workers, 31.7 per cent were helpers in households, and 27.9 per cent were engaged in casual labour. In urban areas, 34.7 per cent women were self-employed, 23.7 per cent engaged in own account work, and 13.1 per cent working as casual labour.

A closer look at the migrant women in the urban economy based on estimates derived from the PLFS reflects that women in urban areas are mostly engaged in community, social, and personal services, manufacturing and

DOI: 10.4324/9781003291527-38

trade, hotels, and transport and communication which are worst hit due to the pandemic.

According to the 2011 Census, out of around 45 million migrant workers, seven million women migrant workers have migrated for work, employment, or business.

The lockdown had a disproportionate impact on these women workers who were working as domestic helps, home-based workers, care workers, etc., with no secure contracts, regular paid work, or social protection.

Since most of these workers are generally excluded from the contributory social insurance schemes, the loss of livelihood during the lockdown has further pushed them to poverty and misery.[4]

Violations of the human rights of women migrant workers, including fear of xenophobia as they receive negative reactions from the local community, are further exacerbated during the pandemic.

Revisiting international labour standards for response to crisis

The International Labour Organization (ILO) from time to time has maintained and developed a system of international labour standards for the promotion of decent work and workers' well-being.

"The ILO Monitor: COVID-19 and the World of Work" on 7 April 2020 estimated that in India, 400 million workers in the informal economy are at the risk of falling deeper into poverty during the crisis.

In 2017, the ILO emphasised the need to respect human rights as a response to crisis and outlined a strategic approach, including ensuring basic income security for those losing jobs during this period, along with enhanced social protection coverage.

Also, the Migrant Workers (Supplementary Provisions) Convention, 1975, states that migrant workers who have resided legally in the territory for the purpose of employment shall not be regarded as being in an irregular situation for the mere fact that they have lost their employment (for instance as a result of the economic impact of COVID-19).

However, a question which arises is how far these standards can be adopted by nations in the changing employment scenario caused by the pandemic?

Can labour reforms help?

The Occupational Safety, Health and Working Conditions Code, 2019, seeks to regulate health and safety conditions of workers in establishments with ten or more workers. And so, it leaves behind many migrant workers, particularly domestic helps, home-based workers, and self-employed women workers, whose employment does not fall within an establishment.

And although the code has immense potential for protecting the rights of migrant workers, there are significant gaps that need to be addressed.

For example, the chapter on migrant workers has been merged with that of contract workers.

Presenting its report on 11 February 2020, the Standing Committee on Labour informed the government about the gaps in the code, including the need for a separate chapter on migrant workers.

With regard to women workers, the code does not have any special provisions. For instance, there's a lot of ambiguity with regard to the provision of crèche facilities. It is considered to be the liability of the employer, despite the Maternity Benefit Amendment Act, 2017, which mandates the establishment of crèches for organisations with 50 employees. The Standing Committee had pointed out that in the case of small-scale industries, providing crèches for them is expensive, and so the government needs to step in.

Despite all these gaps, the biggest challenge in the implementation of the code is the lack of adequate data on migrant workers. There has been no national data after the 2011 Census.

It's time that the code is revisited, particularly in the context of the pandemic and its impact on women migrant workers. There is ample scope for expanding the definition of occupational disease, and including biological hazards caused by viruses and other harmful bacteria that affect people while they are at work as proposed by international labour standards.

The code needs to be more gender sensitive – it needs to protect the rights of women migrant workers who are facing loss of income, loss of residence, psychological distress, and are deeply affected by the crisis.

Notes

1 Reproduced with permission from *The Quint* where the article first appeared on June 5, 2020. https://www.thequint.com/voices/women/labour-reforms-help-women-migrant-workers-during-covid-19

2 Mythreyee Ramesh. "Collateral Damage: Why Coronavirus Might Widen the Gender Pay Gap". *The Quint*. 13 April 2020. Retrieved from https://www.thequint.com/voices/women/coronavirus-affects-women-gender-pay-gap-jobs. Last accessed on 10 December 2021.

3 Jagan Shah. "What if Our Migrant Workers Had Safe Homes in Cities? Just Imagine". *The Quint*. 16 May 2020. Retrieved from https://www.thequint.com/voices/opinion/covid-urban-affordable-housing-govt-migrant-workers-welfare-research-development. Last accessed on 10 December 2021.

4 Arun Dev. "How 2 Tribal Women Fled Debt Bondage, Rape Amid Lockdown in B'luru". *The Quint*. 27 May 2020. Retrieved from https://www.thequint.com/news/india/bengaluru-lockdown-bonded-labour-how-2-tribal-women-fled-debt-bondage-rape-amid-lockdown-in-bluru. Last accessed on 10 December 2021.

Part 6

Media and migrant workers

Invisible become visible

6.1 Media in the time of COVID-19[1]

Bhupen Singh

These are testing times for the government and the media as COVID-19 continues to spread. The government seems rather unwilling to let critical voices have their say about the way in which the crisis is being dealt with. There is an explicit expectation that the media's coverage should be "positive" and follow the official line. While much of the media, corporate-owned as it is, has surrendered, a small section is courageously following journalistic ethics. This article examines authoritarian tendencies that undermine the autonomy of journalism as an important platform of the public sphere.

The spread of COVID-19 has proved deadly, and this is a challenging time for the union as well as state governments as they work to address this health emergency. However, in times of crisis, democratic governments may take a dangerous autocratic turn. In such a situation, journalism has a great role to play in a democracy, as it has been ideally visualised as a platform for objective information and critical-rational discourse. Thus, the health of journalism in a country can be examined in the times of a crisis.

However, corporate control over most media bodies also means that they become an instrument of the ideological apparatus of the state. There are many concerns associated with the COVID-19 crisis: ill-equipped public health systems, policies to combat the pandemic, and the lack of planning and support for the vulnerable sections. These issues demand serious examination, but the mainstream media, barring some courageous exceptions, seems to be forgetting its democratic role. The vilification of migrant labourers and a minority community whilst failing to critique the lack of measures to help these sections deal with the crisis is an important such indicator.

Manipulation of discourse

Just before the announcement of the nationwide lockdown till 14 April 2020, Prime Minister Narendra Modi reportedly called upon print and electronic media owners and editors of the country and asked them to support government efforts to combat the pandemic and also advised them to

DOI: 10.4324/9781003291527-40

present "positive news" related to COVID-19 (Sagar 2020). Plainly put, these were the owners and editors who control most of the Indian media at the national and regional levels who were advised to abide by the official narrative and present information as provided to them by the government about COVID-19.

Why would media houses follow government diktat rather than investigating the real state of affairs, unless they have associated business interests? Journalism is considered to be an ethical communicative practice in a democracy, but corporate ownership subverts the autonomy of journalism and the freedom of the press. Unfortunately, this conflict of interest has become a common feature of Indian journalism.

However, even though a majority of Indian media is under corporate control, there are many counter-voices both within and outside this grouping. Thus, the Indian mediascape has become a battleground of ideologies. Many of these alternate counter-voices have raised genuine issues of social concern during the pandemic outbreak. The prevalence of international media on the internet and small media organisations in the country has played an important role in disseminating factual and more nuanced information, but unfortunately, these platforms do not have the vast access that big corporate media platforms do. Most of the non-English mainstream media—both print and electronic—was seen to be playing a role that was far from responsible during the outbreak. A small section of the English print media has raised some pertinent questions, but they also have a select readership. The government, however, is not ready to listen to any rational criticism. The centre sought a direction from the Supreme Court on 31 March that "No electronic/print media/web portal or social media shall print/publish or telecast anything without first ascertaining the true factual position from the separate mechanism provided by the central government" (Livelaw News Network 2020).

The sudden announcement of the lockdown which gave people barely four hours of advance notice created a nationwide panic and the migrant labourers were the worst affected. In the absence of work and other support in the cities, thousands of labourers and their families desperately wanted to go back to their homes. With no transportation available, many began the arduous journey on foot, and many were subjected to police brutality along the way, and some have died on the road back home. The lockdown, thus, was worse than COVID-19 for the homeless and the poor. While a few in the media made visible their plight, a particular kind of media coverage and projection also led to the middle class blaming migrants for their "irresponsible behaviour" during the pandemic (Abi-Habib and Yasir 2020; Ellis-Petersen and Chaurasia 2020).

It seems most media organisations were compelled to cover the labourers' plight because of its sensational value, but this coverage was inadequate. However, journalism still survives because of a few courageous journalists in mainstream media and alternative media platforms. Two English dailies with their ground-level investigative reporting (one of which is known for its investigative news stories) covered the disaster with more empathy. Many others in their attempts to show the reality faced the wrath of the government (Scroll 2020). Further, even on social media platforms, doctors and nurses were heavily trolled when they voiced grievances about the lack of personal protective equipment (Bengali et al 2020).

Media shows its Islamophobic side

The media's ugliest moment, however, was its coverage of the news surrounding Delhi's Tablighi Jamaat Markaz (meeting). Many participants had left after the markaz, but many were stranded in the mosque due to the lockdown and were later found infected. However, the media outrage that followed was clearly an extension of the already prejudiced and polarised coverage, as the Tablighi Jamaat was blamed for violating lockdown rules and for "corona jihad", "Islamic insurrection", and "corona terrorism". This is clearly an example of fake news propagated by the mainstream media to further the predominant agenda (BBC 2020; News Laundry 2020). Muslims were also attacked in various parts of the country.

News presented on the markaz immediately found space in social networking sites and public opinion was quickly constructed around the premise that Muslims were responsible for the pandemic. Never mind that even though the markaz incident triggered a spread, it is not as if it was planned. The first case of the virus was identified in India in January. The abject lack of planning by the government was not adequately questioned by the mainstream media. Nor was it questioned as to why such a gathering was permitted in the first place.

People of other religious groups also gathered at religious places in large numbers even after the lockdown, but they were not criticised in a similar manner. However, when some journalists did raise questions, they were threatened with legal action (Scroll 2020).

The need for greater accountability

Since most of the people are at home during the lockdown, it is natural to see a growth in media consumption. People are using various media platforms for COVID-19-related information, but what is provided is far from factual and does not further a critical-rational discourse. Rather, the media has become a tool of propaganda and sensationalism. Some television news channels see a Chinese conspiracy in the spread of COVID-19. In such a "positive" atmosphere, the news related to labourers' mass exodus and the markaz was mostly presented due to its sensational value. The true situation would not have gained attention in the first place, if not for the ground-level reports by the committed journalists and social media coverage. The Janata curfew announced on 22 March before the lockdown failed as people came out on the streets in the evening, clapping, banging utensils, shouting religious slogans, and blowing conch shells, as if they could defeat COVID-19 with a show of such masculinity. Social distancing was forgotten. Later, people were again asked to switch off residential lights for nine minutes and light a candle or diya in their balconies. Can the virus really be eradicated by chants of "go corona?" Yet, the media became a part of this "festivity". These exercises were lapped up by a majority of the news media, as it sells the big spectacle—a hyper real experience—and accepts the obeisance to a "supreme authority" along with a large number of citizens. The trivialisation of the crisis and a toxic "positivity" are ruling the media.

COVID-19 is a serious threat to the nation and therefore many rational measures and "honest conversations" must be expected from the government, which cannot be beyond the critical radar of journalism. The government has created a Prime Minister's Citizen Assistance and Relief in Emergency Situations (PM-CARES) Fund to combat the pandemic, and many business corporations and common people have contributed to this fund. But many questions have also been raised about the need for this fund, as the Prime Minister Relief Fund had already been working from 1948 onwards for such situations (Hindu 2020; Mody 2020). All these issues demand serious journalistic investigation in the public interest.

The pandemic is also threatening an already-deteriorating economy, which also demands a thorough investigation beyond the official narratives. The media, however, has worries related to its own economic situation. Print media, especially, is dealing with a resource crunch, dwindling advertisements, and worries of reduction in circulation and readership. With concerns of job security, inadequate resource support, and abuses faced by the police, many journalists are putting their health at stake to cover the COVID-19 situation. This scenario does little to add to the morale of honest and responsible journalists. Some media houses have already begun cutting wages; an extension in the lockdown may create a new crisis in Indian journalism.

The role of larger media as observed during the pandemic, however, is not an overnight shift. It has been visible for some time now. The media has seen phenomenal growth during the last three decades, and India has become one of the biggest media markets in the world. The alliance between predominant religious fundamentalism and neo-liberalism has also shaped it. Profit, the promotion of majoritarian views, and the exclusion of marginalised voices have become its main features.

What should the role of governments be in such a situation, and what is it that journalism is meant to do? This is the time to introspect and examine the role of capitalism, the state, and the media to avoid creating a future that threatens to destabilise democracy. Will this pandemic radically change society and governance models? Will the increased surveillance and policing become the new normal, or will we see increased efforts at building solidarity and cooperation? Our media needs to introspect and pose these questions.

(The author is thankful to the anonymous reviewer for suggestions that brought more clarity to the article.)

Note

1 Reproduced with permission from *Economic and Political Weekly* (Volume 55, Issue number 16) where this article first appeared on April 18, 2020. https://www.epw.in/engage/article/media-time-covid-19

References

Abi-Habib, Maria and Sameer Yasir (2020): "For India's Laborers, Coronavirus Lockdown Is an Order to Starve," *New York Times*, 30 March, https://www.nytimes.com/2020/03/30/world/asia/coronavirus-india-lockdown.html.

BBC (2020): "Coronavirus: Islamophobia Concerns after India Mosque Outbreak," 3 April, https://www.bbc.com/news/world-asia-india-52147260.

Bengali, Shashank, Vidya Krishnan and M N Parth (2020): "Doctors Battling The Coronavirus in India Are Being Infected, Trolled and Evicted," *Los Angeles Times*, 30 March, https://www.latimes.com/world-nation/story/2020-03-30/indian-doctors-are-being-infected-trolled-and-evicted-as-they-battle-covid-19.

Ellis-Petersen, Hanna and Manoj Chaurasia (2020): "India Racked by Greatest Exodus since Partition due to Coronavirus," *Guardian*, 30 March, https://www.theguardian.com/world/2020/mar/30/india-wracked-by-greatest-exodus-since-partition-due-to-coronavirus.

Hindu (2020): "Congress Questions Setting Up of PM CARES Fund to Deal with Coronavirus," 30 March, https://www.thehindu.com/news/national/congress-questions-setting-up-of-pm-cares-fund-to-deal-with-coronavirus/article31210904.ece.

Livelaw News Network (2020): "Centre Seeks SC Direction that No Media Should Publish COVID-19 News without First Ascertaining Facts with Govt," *Livelaw*, 31 March, https://www.livelaw.in/top-stories/centre-seeks-sc-direction-that-no-media-should-publish-covid-19-news-without-first-ascertaining-facts-with-govt-154601.

Mody, Anjali (2020): "As Covid-19 Crisis Unfolds, Modi Should Dispel Negativity by Starting an Honest National Conversation," *Scroll*, 3 April, https://scroll.in/article/958065/as-covid-19-crisis-unfolds-modi-could-dispel-negativity-by-starting-an-honest-national-conversation?fbclid=IwAR1dHKPBaemYWEbYt7Sd4SG6nGIfwGed3nHdR_ad_2S16QJTEHOhVq1NkRY.

News Laundry (2020): "Coronavirus: Delhi Lawyers Denounce TV News Channels for Demonising Muslims," 3 April, https://www.newslaundry.com/2020/04/03/coronavirus-delhi-lawyers-denounce-tv-news-channels-for-demonising-muslims?fbclid=IwAR2B2hR1bWkv4CBev4bxCaPicpFUdEM7fLK83MG4iPeqYHMtzmaiQ6-U3Os.

Sagar (2020): "Speaking Positivity to Power: Hours before Lockdown, Modi Asked Print-Media Owners, Editors to Refrain from Negative COVID Coverage,"

Caravan, 31 March, https://caravanmagazine.in/media/hours-before-lockdown-modi-asked-print-media-owners-editors-refrain-negative-covid-coverage.

Scroll (2020): "FIR Filed against 'The Wire' Editor for Allegedly Making 'Objectionable Comment' about Adityanath," 2 April, https://scroll.in/latest/957945/fir-filed-against-the-wire-editor-for-allegedly-spreading-fake-news-against-adityanath.

6.2 How the Modi government manufactured public opinion during the migrant crisis[1]

Aman Abhishek

The government managed the media successfully during the pandemic so that its apathy towards the migrant workers did not result in countrywide protests. The prime minister's approval ratings in fact are believed to have increased during the crisis. Unsurprisingly, the mainstream media played a central role in this.

It is no secret that India has crores of daily-wage migrant workers who live extraordinarily precarious lives.[2] By extension, it should surprise no one – especially not the government – that a complete nationwide lockdown announced with merely four hours' notice led to the largest migrant crisis since India's Partition.[3]

Countless heart-wrenching images and accounts of hunger, homelessness, suffering, and death of migrants have been circulated on social media for months, and the crisis continues.[4] And yet, surprisingly, the government's apathy towards migrants has not resulted in countrywide protests. In fact, Prime Minister Narendra Modi's approval ratings are said to have increased amidst the migrant crisis.[5]

How could this be possible? The answer is a successful public opinion management effort by the Modi government, in which the mainstream media played a central role.

A tragedy that absolves the state

Suffering due to the COVID-19 pandemic is, unfortunately, inevitable. But government policies sharply determine the magnitude of this tragedy, and the mainstream media has dangerously blurred the distinction between what is and isn't in the government's control. Whenever the migrant crisis has been covered, it is portrayed either as a tragedy or natural calamity. It is not reported as a result of disastrous state policies – which it is[6] – nor as an opportunity to demand urgent action from the state.

Examples below from leading Hindi newspapers show that while reporting on the most horrifying moments of the migrant crisis, such as major

DOI: 10.4324/9781003291527-41

accidents on May 8 in Aurangabad[7] and May 16 in Auraiya[8] which killed dozens of migrants, newspapers at best expressed sadness and at worst blamed careless driving – and did not question the government's pandemic policies. This style of coverage was the general trend, extending beyond the coverage of these accidents. Often, as the examples show, this crisis was depicted as a tale of bravery and optimism.

"Speed and carelessness takes 26 lives". Hindustan (Patna), May 17.

"Death before life could get back on track: the journey of survival ends here. Migrants tired from walking slept on the train track, freight train crushed 16 of them". Dainik Bhaskar (Bhopal), May 9.

"Innocent childhood in an arduous journey back home". Dainik Bhaskar (Bhopal), May 9.

"A courageous journey". This man's decision to travel hundreds of kilometres despite his disability is praised as "determination". Dainik Jagran (National Edition), May 17.

At best, this type of coverage allows collective sympathy and mourning, and perhaps encourages relief work undertaken by civilians, but it completely absolves the state. It makes it possible for people to not be enraged[9] at Modi for eventually easing the lockdown, allowing migrants to make journeys that they could have made two months ago, when the cases were fewer and so much suffering could have been avoided.

Creating distractions and controlling the narrative

Scholars studying the media have noted that news media does not tell people what to think, but what to think about. After the lockdown was announced on March 24, the chaos at Anand Vihar Bus Terminal around March 28 marked the beginning of the migrant crisis. But for weeks after March 30, public discourse was relentlessly focused on Tablighi Jamaat[10] and "corona jihad".

There were other distractions too. Modi asking people to light diyas,[11] Modi asking that they bang utensils,[12] army helicopters flying over hospitals and showering petals – these were media spectacles designed to generate coverage that drowned out everything else. What did these celebrations do for the migrants who died of hunger?

The valorisation of the police as "corona warriors" severely obfuscated high levels of police brutality[13] against migrants and the poor. In enforcing the lockdown, the police[14] beat people to death; the police attacked migrants whose crime was walking hundreds of kilometres with barely any food and water, and dying during their journeys. The police are a key organ of the state's power, and the state will do its best to protect it – the US prison-industrial complex[15] is a prime example. Therefore it should not come as a surprise that the Modi government carried out a concerted and successful effort to control the narrative around the police.

Each of Modi's addresses to the nation was heavily covered in the media, which mainly focused on unity, patriotism, rhetoric of war, sacrifice, and optimism. Rather than a substantive account of government policy, it will be more appropriate to see these addresses as public relations stunts.[16] Modi's rhetoric tightly controlled the public discourse because critiquing government policy became unpatriotic.

Controlling the media

India's press freedom rankings have deteriorated[17] consistently in recent years, but one can still wonder – how exactly does the state control media coverage of such a major migrant crisis?

The mechanisms of controlling the media are numerous. Hours before the lockdown, Modi reportedly asked print-media owners and editors in a meeting to refrain from negative coverage.[18] This was not a conspiracy; it was a public and even publicised[19] event. Instead of being outraged, journalists gleefully talked about this event on social media, and agreed to comply. The patriotic image of Modi and the "war"-like situation, as well as the cosy state-press relationship result in feel-good and optimistic news coverage of the pandemic.

It is difficult for a state, especially a democratic one, to censor information that has already been published. A more sophisticated method of censorship is controlling availability and access to information. In the case of the migrant crisis, press conferences are where journalists can question government officials on its policies. Yet, it has been widely noted[20] how the Modi government put restrictions on who can attend these conferences and what questions are asked. In these conferences, government officials focused strongly on the Tablighi Jamaat, leaving little room for anything else, which shapes the news coverage. Moreover, it is easier for the media to publish official statements as is,[21] rather than invest resources or take the legal risk to challenge them – after all, commercial news media is a money-making business.

And in cases where the news coverage is critical of government policies, journalists are prosecuted.[22] Last month, the Editors Guild of India expressed[23] concern over "a growing pattern of misuse of criminal laws to intimate journalists" and the International Press Institute released a similar statement.[24] It is not necessary to prosecute each instance of critical reporting – legal harassment and action against a few serve as a deterrent for others.

No matter how successful the state is in skewing reality according to its whims, the voices of the oppressed cannot be erased. Eventually, our society will have to face the migrant, who while walking for six days with his children and wife and still far from home, said,[25] crying:

> Modi ji did a great thing by doing what he did, it's great for us. He is comfortable and in one place, isn't he? Should he not have thought about us, the poor? I guess it's fine, my kids and I will die.

Notes

1 Edited version of an article reproduced with permission from *The Wire* where this article first appeared on June 25, 2020. https://thewire.in/media/covid-19-migrant-crisis-public-opinion-modi
2 Sushant Singh and Aanchal Magazine. "Explained: Indian Migrants, across India". *The Indian Express*. April 6, 2020. Retrieved from https://indianexpress.com/article/explained/coronavirus-india-lockdown-migran-workers-mass-exodus-6348834/. Last accessed on December 10, 2021.
3 Hannah Ellis-Petersen and Manoj Chaurasia. "India Racked by Greatest Exodus Since Partition Due to Coronavirus". *The Guardian*. March 30, 2020. Retrieved from https://www.theguardian.com/world/2020/mar/30/india-wracked-by-greatest-exodus-since-partition-due-to-coronavirus. Last accessed on December 10, 2021.
4 "Government Has Created an Archive of Distress, a Museum of Misery For Migrant Workers". *The Wire*. March 30, 2020. Retrieved from https://thewire.in/rights/migrant-workers-covid-19-lockdown-crisis-swan-report. Last accessed on December 10, 2021.
5 "Modi's Popularity Soars". *The New York Times*. Retrieved from https://www.nytimes.com/2020/05/16/world/asia/coronavirus-modi-india.html. Last accessed on December 10, 2021.
6 "How Modi Failed the Pandemic Test". *The New York Times*. May 27, 2020. Retrieved from https://www.nytimes.com/2020/05/27/opinion/india-modi-coronavirus.html. Last accessed on December 10, 2021.
7 "Aurangabad: 16 Migrant Workers Killed by Goods Train, 5 Injured". *The Wire*. May 8, 2020. Retrieved from https://thewire.in/rights/aurangabad-migrant-workers-goods-train-killed. Last accessed on December 10, 2021.
8 "Aurangabad: 16 Migrant Workers Killed by Goods Train, 5 Injured". *The Wire*. May 16, 2020. Retrieved from https://thewire.in/rights/up-auraiya-migrants-workers-killed-truck-accident. Last accessed on December 10, 2021.
9 "Government Has Created an Archive of Distress, a Museum of Misery for Migrant Workers". *The Wire*. June 14, 2020. Retrieved from https://thewire.in/rights/migrant-workers-covid-19-lockdown-crisis-swan-report. Last accessed on December 10, 2021.
10 See https://www.ou.edu/deptcomm/dodjcc/groups/02B2/Literature_Review.html
11 "When Even a Pandemic Is Communalised". *The Wire*. April 1, 2020. Retrieved from https://thewire.in/communalism/covid-19-tablighi-jamaat-hindu-muslim. Last accessed on December 10, 2021.
12 K. Ashok Rao. "When Even a Pandemic Is Communalised". *The Wire*. April 6, 2020. Retrieved from https://thewire.in/energy/india-power-grid-diya-jalai-narendra-modi-revenue-loss. Last accessed on December 10, 2021.

13 "Social Distancing Forgotten, Country Raises a Racket at 5 pm". *The Wire*. March 22, 2020. Retrieved from https://thewire.in/society/coronavirus-janata-curfew-racket. Last accessed on December 10, 2021.
14 Ameya Bokil and Nikita Sonavane. "Why Relying on Criminal Law Should Not Be the Answer to a Pandemic". *The Wire*. April 11, 2020. Retrieved from https://thewire.in/law/criminal-law-coronavirus-pandemic. Last accessed on December 10, 2021.
15 See https://www.feministes-radicales.org/wp-content/uploads/2010/11/Angela-Davis-Are_Prisons_Obsolete.pdf
16 Sidharth Bhatia. "The Simple, and Simplistic, Messaging of Modi's Lectures Is a Big Hit with His Audience". *The Wire*. May 30, 2020. Retrieved from https://thewire.in/politics/narendra-modi-speech-simplistic-message. Last accessed on December 10, 2021.
17 Sangeeta Barooah Pisharoty. "As Press Freedom Rank Falls, Govt's New 'Index Monitoring Cell' to Meet on Thursday". *The Wire*. May 13, 2020. Retrieved from https://thewire.in/media/as-press-freedom-rank-falls-govts-new-index-monitoring-cell-to-meet-on-thursday. Last accessed on December 10, 2021.
18 Sagar. "Speaking Positivity to Power". *The Caravan*. March 31, 2020. Retrieved from https://caravanmagazine.in/media/hours-before-lockdown-modi-asked-print-media-owners-editors-refrain-negative-covid-coverage. Last accessed on December 10, 2021.
19 See https://www.narendramodi.in/prime-minister-narendra-modi-interacts-with-print-media-journalists-and-stakeholders-548937
20 Vidya Krishnan. "Centre Places Restrictions on Media in COVID Press Briefings; Shifts Focus to Tablighi Jamaat". *The Caravan*. April 6, 2020. Retrieved from https://caravanmagazine.in/media/hours-before-lockdown-modi-asked-print-media-owners-editors-refrain-negative-covid-coverage. Last accessed on December 10, 2021.
21 See https://chomsky.info/consent01/
22 "UP: FIR Against Journalist for Report on Mismanagement at Quarantine Centre". *The Wire*. May 18, 2020. Retrieved from https://caravanmagazine.in/health/centre-places-restrictions-media-covid-press-briefings-shifts-focus-to-tablighi-jamaat. Last accessed on December 10, 2021.
23 See https://twitter.com/IndEditorsGuild/status/1260501321695854593
24 "India Increasing Abuse of Laws to Harass Journalists". *International Press Institute*. May 15, 2020. Retrieved from https://ipi.media/india-increasing-abuse-of-laws-to-harass-journalists/. Last accessed on December 10, 2021.
25 See https://twitter.com/BBCHindi/status/1260508869849231361

6.3 Not just the media, organised politics too failed India's migrant workers[1]

Ranabir Samaddar

While political parties took time to make sense of what was happening, the neoliberal system lost no time to forge its own response.

Aman Abhishek's piece on the media during the migrant crisis in the wake of the pandemic of COVID-19 (*The Wire*, 25 June, "How the Modi Government Manufactured Public Opinion during the Migrant Crisis"[2]) is timely. Many good-hearted journalists indeed thought that notwithstanding a definite pattern in the media coverage, the media by and large played a commendable role in bringing the "migrant question" to the public eye. In the background of such innocence bordering on glib acceptance of the media's virtues, Abhishek's commentary underlines the need for a larger discussion on the idea of the public, and by extension mainstream politics, by which I mean, mainly formal, organised politics.

The media may have set the tone, as Abhishek's piece shows, but this was facilitated by the strange silence of mainstream political parties who perhaps owing to lockdown restrictions hardly raised any voice in the immediate aftermath of the breakout of the migrant crisis. By the last days of March and the first fortnight of April, the severity of the crisis was evident. Reports were coming out by mid-April that migrant workers had not been paid their dues for March and were being evicted from their shelters, and they had been frantically searching for modes of transport to go back home.

Another fact of severe consternation was the staggering, immeasurable dimension of the crisis. Central trade unions and mainstream liberal and left parties took time to understand even the surface of what was happening. There was no united statement, no attempt to build a platform of solidarity, no attempt to convene an opposition chief ministers' conclave to forge a policy on issues of the health and work of the migrant workers, no concerted effort to move the judiciary, and no minimum agenda on the issue of the pandemic and migrant workers.

Solidarity initiatives were local, and mostly spontaneous. The much-reviled NGOs, independent groups and associations, and localised political forces fared better. What we may call a spirit of militant philanthropy as

DOI: 10.4324/9781003291527-42

a form of solidarity emerged all over the country, and while we may say that thanks to the media we have now a rough picture of what happened in these two months (April–May), we have very little idea of the way solidarity emerged as a principle of social response to the epidemiological crisis – by itself a combination of three crises: A public health crisis, an economic-financial crisis, and a labour crisis.

We can only say that while acts of solidarity indicated a faint sketch of the values of a post-coronavirus society the nation desired, solidarity was not enough as a critical force in building militant opposition to the neoliberal management of the pandemic. In the wake of this new crisis, institutionalised politics was a helpless spectator. We saw its stupefied state as the repeated repression of workers, for instance in Surat,[3] went almost unchallenged.

The media not only facilitated the incorporation of the issue of migrant workers into the agenda of neoliberal reforms, the orientation of media response was also instrumental in "awakening" institutionalised politics in a particular way to the presence of the migrant workers. The migrant appeared as a fault line in the country's access system to essential conditions of life, such as health, food, and shelter.

No wonder, in the repeated statements of Rahul Gandhi, that the issue of migrant workers did not feature centrally, notwithstanding his meeting with migrant labourers[4] in the national capital near the Sukh Dev Vihar flyover on May 15. The whole month of April had passed. Likewise, the Inter-State Migrant Workmen Act of 1979 was resurrected by only do-gooder scholars and lawyers. The All India Trade Union Congress (AITUC) born in 1920 passed its centenary year amidst the silent defeat of organised working class politics in the time of the pandemic.

The question should be raised, therefore, what is the nature of this "public" that constitutes the mainframe of institutional politics, the "public" that is supposedly the stuff of public politics, public health, and public claims? More fundamentally, we must inquire, how was politics demobilised in the wake of the pandemic?

The question cannot be glossed over once we notice that the same media which, till this February, was full of politics, covering riots, killings, arrests, civil disobedience, rallies for constitutional justice, demand for citizenship, suddenly went silent and transferred attention to not only the pandemic, but to the scenes of homeward migrant workers travelling hundreds of kilometres, many of them dying and disappearing from the public scene.

What happened to the millions of migrant workers who returned "home"? Or, what happened to the earlier crisis? Did it also vanish or melt into the succeeding crisis?

We do not know if the mainstream opposition parties realised that a crisis, that much abused word, was indeed overwhelming the country. But it's important to note that while they took time to make sense of what was happening and formulate a response, the neoliberal system lost no time in forging its own response.

One of its first acts was to subsume the issue of migrant labour under an agenda of reforms. COVID-19, as Prime Minister Narendra Modi repeatedly said, called for drastic reforms. The country couldn't go back to pre-corona days. In contrast, there was the mainstream opposition's deafening silence. Its imagination of politics was limited to the old, routine parliamentary confabulations and the prescribed mode of union movement of labour protest. This imagination had no space in it for a new vision in the wake of the COVID-19 crisis. And no place for migrant workers and public health as two central elements of a society that cares for life.

Recall, in contrast, the Union government's policy reform announcements and the prime minister's addresses to the public. On May 30, as the main phase of the nationwide lockdown was ending, the prime minister in a letter to the nation[5] on completing one year of his second term, said that the nation had taken historic decisions and progressed rapidly in the last year. However he conceded that migrant workers, labourers, and others had undergone tremendous suffering during the coronavirus crisis. He assured the people that India, by addressing the plight of "our labourers, migrant workers, artisans and craftsmen in small scale industries, hawkers and such fellow countrymen (who) have undergone tremendous suffering", would set an example of post-coronavirus economic revival.

This could be achieved through policies specifically designed for migrant workers. Therefore, on June 20, Modi launched an employment scheme[6] with an outlay of Rs 50,000 crore for migrant workers who returned home during the lockdown. Modi further said during the nationwide lockdown that talent (as a national asset) returning from cities to villages would boost rural development. The Garib Kalyan Rozgar Abhiyaan was to be implemented on a mission mode in 125 days in 116 districts in 6 states of the country. On June 26, a web portal for registration was launched. Public works were now to be part of creating[7] an atmanirbhar Bharat – a self-reliant India. Make no mistake: The migrant labour issue was subsumed in this neoliberal structuring.

While the mainstream opposition rightly focused on labour[8] deregulation mooted as part of the restructuring of the economy, it did not present an alternative broader vision of a post-corona society, which would put emphasis on policies and principles of care, protection of life, and security of migrant workers and caregivers. Such a vision called for imagining a new organisation, devolving public power to the lower levels.

A critique of the two instruments on which the government's administrative-police response to the crisis rested – the Plague Act (Epidemic Diseases Act, 1897) and the National Disaster Management Act (2005) – was absent in the mainstream political discourse. The mainstream political critique turned out to be fragmentary, superficial, and haphazard.

On May 14, 2020, Finance Minister Nirmala Sitharaman said the government had initiated a move to bring all 44 labour-related laws under 4 labour codes,[9] of which parliament was aware. The proposed laws, as indicated in the respective Bills tabled in parliament, would significantly dilute the Factory Act, 1948, and reduce the role and power of factory inspectors to mere facilitators. Instead of acting as a watchdog to ensure factories are run in conformity with labour laws, the inspectors would enable the employers to run their plants. Little attention would be paid to ensuring minimum wages and stipulated working hours.

Sitharaman also announced free rations[10] for two more months for eight crore migrant workers. She confessed that the government of India had not collated any data about the workers and had arrived at this figure by adding up all the reports given by the state governments about migrant workers in various states who had been sheltered and fed at various government-run or NGO-run centres. It seemed that the old adage was coming to haunt the country once again: Never let a crisis go waste.

The crisis, using public health concerns, led to a restructuring of the economy. The emphasis was on "productive labour" and "productive economy" instead of saving lives by expanding public health systems and social security, including access to food. While money supply was further squeezed by refusing to directly transfer cash to millions of poor people, credit and loans were given a fillip. A contract farming-driven food grains market was opened up. The public health crisis became the occasion for counting only "productive labour" and letting the "unproductive" die.

That the mainstream political opposition failed to make any worthwhile intervention was not because it was ignorant of the existence of migrant workers. But the opposition could not think beyond conventional trade unionism and institutionalised routine politics. Failing to notice the impending crisis, the opposition forgot that the migrant question was a "social" question. In the absence of a new social vision, the neoliberal regime was able to co-opt the migrant question in the economic recovery agenda. All that was required was an apology from the ruler for the distress of the migrants. The prime minister tendered that apology[11] on March 29.

Notes

1 Reproduced with permission from *The Wire* where this article first appeared on July 1, 2020. https://thewire.in/politics/migrant-workers-political-parties-failure

2 Aman Abhishek. "How the Modi Government Manufactured Public Opinion During the Migrant Crisis". *The Wire*. June 25, 2020. Retrieved from https://thewire.in/media/covid-19-migrant-crisis-public-opinion-modi. Last accessed on December 10, 2021.

3 "Surat: Migrant Workers Defy Lockdown, Demand Wages and Return to Home State". *The Wire*. April 11, 2020. Retrieved from https://thewire.in/rights/surat-migrant-workers-covid-19-lockdown-wages. Last accessed on December 10, 2021.

4 "Rahul Gandhi Interacts with Migrant Workers amid Lockdown". *The Wire*. May 16, 2020. Retrieved from https://thewire.in/politics/rahul-gandhi-migrant-workers. Last accessed on December 10, 2021.

5 See https://www.livemint.com/news/india/pm-modi-s-letter-to-the-nation-read-full-text-here-11590808857664.html

6 "PM Modi Launches Scheme to Boost Livelihood in Rural India: Highlights". *NDTV*. June 20, 2020. Retrieved from https://www.ndtv.com/india-news/pm-modi-launches-garib-kalyan-rojgar-yojana-scheme-to-boost-livelihood-in-rural-india-highlights-2249346. Last accessed on December 10, 2021.

7 Pranav Mukul, Aanchal Magazine, and Anil Sasi. "For Atmanirbhar Bharat: Govt Agencies across Sectors Tweak Rules, Form Policies to Push Local". *The Indian Express*. June 15, 2020. Retrieved from https://indianexpress.com/article/business/economy/for-atmanirbhar-bharat-govt-agencies-across-sectors-tweak-rules-form-policies-to-push-local-6458993/. Last accessed on December 10, 2021.

8 "Changes in Labour Laws Will Turn the Clock Back by over a Century". *The Wire*. May 20, 2020. Retrieved from https://thewire.in/labour/labour-laws-changes-turning-clock-back. Last accessed on December 10, 2021.

9 "Craftily Written Labour Codes Exclude Millions, Pay Little Heed to Equality". *The Wire*. July 26, 2019. Retrieved from https://thewire.in/labour/cabinet-passes-labour-codes-wages-occupational-safety. Last accessed on December 10, 2021.

10 "FM Announces Free Foodgrains for 8 Crore Migrant Workers for 2 Months". *The Economic Times*. May 14, 2020. Retrieved from https://economictimes.indiatimes.com/news/economy/policy/fm-announces-free-foodgrains-for-8-crore-migrant-workers-for-2-months/articleshow/75738241.cms?from=mdr. Last accessed on December 10, 2021.

11 "Coronavirus: India's PM Modi Seeks 'Forgiveness' over Lockdown". *The Economic Times*. March 29, 2020. Retrieved from https://www.bbc.com/news/world-asia-india-52081396. Last accessed on December 10, 2021.

6.4 Migrant crisis amid COVID is why we need "journalism of misery"[1]

Smruti Koppikar

When journalism records misery, it's only doing its job, fulfilling its purpose.

Among the many changes that Prime Minister Narendra Modi's ecosystem has brought about in the last few years, is the change in large swathes of India's journalism. The very nature and purpose of journalism have shifted from being the society's watchdog to being the public relations arm of the government, from holding those in power accountable to holding citizens or the Opposition accountable.

To a large extent, journalism in the Modi-era has come to mean comfort in being close to power, preening as the government's cheerleader, skipping over inconvenient stories and questions, praising almost every move of the prime minister as a masterstroke, creating false equivalences, and shying away from the truth of the moment. This is reflected in Modi's men who preside over information management. It's no wonder then that Shashi Shekhar Vempati, CEO of Prasar Bharati, chided the media – sections that focused on millions of migrants walking home in pain and misery – for doing its job.

Journalism of misery

"Unfortunately in the last few weeks", Vempati told the anchor of Doordarshan's DD Dialogue,

> the mass media has tended to focus a lot more on journalism of misery while there's a lot more potential for journalism of hope and journalism of resilience ... (and) with that message lift the entire masses of India to the normal, the new normal.

This DD Dialogue, telecast on the night of 19 May, was titled "Containing COVID Crisis – Communication Shift and New Normal".

DOI: 10.4324/9781003291527-43

Vempati, who's also in a sense the channel's boss, shared his thoughts at the end of a panel discussion that had two joint secretaries and representatives of the UNDP and UNICEF on it.

What is the "journalism of misery" that Vempati has a beef with? It is, simply, the biggest story now, perhaps in decades. The story of millions of Indians drawn from the lower-middle and lower classes, the marginalised, indigenous people and their families, all walking hundreds of thousands of kilometres from cities back to their homes across state borders, after Modi announced the first nation-wide lockdown on 24–25 March to control the spread of COVID-19. Commentators have called it the largest migration since the Partition of India.

As Modi shut down a nation of 1.3 billion citizens with only 4 hours' notice and then extended this lockdown three times (we are in the midst of Lockdown 4 now), millions of migrant workers in Indian cities faced an uncertain future. The days wore on. With no work or wages, thrown out of their dwellings, and with no roof over their head, they began the long and arduous walk home. A government that organised flights to bring back Indians from other countries did not immediately organise buses or trains within its borders.

Millions of migrant workers had no option but to hit the highways on foot.

The story of COVID-19 in India turned into a humanitarian crisis; stories of unspeakable misery have unfolded every day over the last two months.

> *The story of Jamalo Madkam, the 12-year-old girl, who died just short of her home in Bijapur, Chhattisgarh, after walking nearly 150 kilometres from Telangana, as per this report.*[2]
>
> *The story of Priya and her three young daughters walking with tears in their eyes from Delhi to Kanpur, 475 kilometres away, as this video story in* The Quint *showed.*[3]
>
> *The story of Virendra Singh Gond, the only survivor from a group of 17 men – 16 of whom were run over by a freight train in Aurangabad, as they slept on unused tracks, exhausted after walking for days from Jalna in Maharashtra towards Madhya Pradesh.*[4]
>
> *The story of Seema, her husband, and three children walking from their workplace in Haryana all the way to Bareilly in Uttar Pradesh, their form of transport coming to naught and being turned away three times from the state borders, as this story*[5] *reveals.*
>
> *The story of Gurang Sah at Bandra station in Mumbai, struggling to board one of the Shramik trains that the government finally started for migrant workers, whose mobile fell in the melee of a lathi-charge and dashed his hopes of boarding another train, as this story details.*[6]

The Covid-19 crisis encompasses the thousands who battle it in hospitals, health workers and frontline workers who have been at their tasks at great personal risk, often without PPE, hundreds of thousands out of jobs and livelihoods, rural Indians in deeper distress, and millions of migrant workers virtually forgotten by the government.

Most walked and suffered; the few who could access trains weeks into the lockdown were squeezed for money by middlemen. It is nothing if not a story of misery, unimaginable wretchedness, heart-breaking despair. If India woke up to this, if the government was nudged into action, it's because some journalists relentlessly focused on these stories.

Misery is the story

Mr Vempati, this is "journalism of misery" because misery IS the story here. The pain, despair, and uncertainty of millions of Indians greatly overwhelm all else; this is who we are as a nation right now. You cannot control-alt-delete it or over-write it with "journalism of hope". Even if you did, it cannot simply "lift the entire masses of India to a normal".

If journalism did not tell this story, it would be less than journalism. We need this journalism of misery so we can do something – even if it means donating money for a ration kit that NGOs are distributing across the nation.

When journalism records misery, it's only doing its job, fulfilling its purpose, a few news organisations even redeeming some of their lost ground. At its barest minimum, journalism is a record of society at a given time, a mirror to society as it were. When millions of Indians face pain and despair, to deliberately focus on stories of hope would mean an abdication of the core purpose of journalism. It isn't that journalism has not captured stories of hope and resilience, but the focus has been on stories of misery, much to Vempati's discomfort.

In his earlier avatar, Vempati was CEO of Niti Digital, an online venture set up in 2012 by businessman Rajesh Jain. It brought out Niti Central, an online right-wing news and commentary website, where Vempati also wrote blogs. Niti Central, which promised to be "the voice of India's neo-middle class", was "retired" in January 2016.

Along with India Votes and India 272+, Niti Central was part of the right-wing ecosystem to push PM Modi to the national scene and build his pan-India acceptability. By its own admission then, Vempati's organisation had played a critical role in shaping the political narrative of the time. As CEO of Prasar Bharati, he wants to play a critical role in shaping the narrative during India's tryst with COVID-19 and its humanitarian crisis – by downplaying misery and pain, and focusing on hope.

What Vempati misses is that there's a limit to such manipulated shaping of narratives by vested interests and governments, that narratives cannot always be engineered to suit an agenda when the wretchedness of the human condition overwhelms all else.

When journalism sticks to its basic purpose – telling genuine stories of people with honesty, sensitivity, and comprehensiveness – it afflicts the comfortable. And the comfortable whine – not about the society's condition, but its story-tellers.

Notes

1 Reproduced with permission from *The Quint* where this article first appeared on May 23, 2020. https://www.thequint.com/voices/opinion/coronavirus-india-migrant-worker-crisis-journalism-of-misery-modi-govt-prasar-bharati-ceo-comments
2 https://www.thequint.com/news/india/covid-19-lockdown-12-year-old-chhattisgarh-girl-dies-while-walking-home-from-telangana
3 https://youtu.be/a0zyFyPsu08
4 https://www.thequint.com/videos/news-videos/aurangabad-train-tragedy-victims-families-mourn-their-loss
5 https://www.youtube.com/watch?v=cb1cEK12MnM
6 https://scroll.in/article/962451/a-day-after-a-lathicharge-at-mumbai-railway-station-shattered-phones-and-broken-dreams-of-home

6.5 Lawyer Apar Gupta on what the Indian Supreme Court's order on COVID-19 coverage means for journalists[1]

Kunal Majumder

Apar Gupta, Executive Director, Internet Freedom Foundation, is a lawyer who is an expert on digital rights and online freedom. In this interview he argues that the Supreme Court direction that media should report the government's version on the pandemic is of grave concern for press freedom. In doing so, he says, the apex court has also supported the government's request for greater censorship powers to prevent rumour mongering and further social cohesion during the pandemic.

On March 31, the Indian Supreme Court passed a directive[2] making it compulsory for news outlets to carry the government's official version on any news related to the COVID-19 pandemic.

The court ruled that media organisations are required to defer to the government version on the pandemic, and blamed "fake news" for recent migration from the country's cities, according to reports.

CPJ spoke with Apar Gupta, a lawyer who has argued before the Supreme Court and who is the executive director of the Internet Freedom Foundation, a local digital rights group, about the ruling in a phone interview on April 4. This interview has been edited for length and clarity.

How concerned should Indian journalists be about the Supreme Court order on coronavirus coverage?

The Supreme Court order is of grave concern to press freedom, which has already come under increased challenges during the time of the coronavirus pandemic. There are directions contained within the order that require the press in India—which may be print, electronic, and even social media—to refer to the official government version [of events]. The order further references provisions of law under criminal prosecutions that can be launched against them [the journalists].

This brings a worrying level of oversight and power toward the government version, which can lead to instances of censorship when the reporting

DOI: 10.4324/9781003291527-44

may not be favourable and may be in contrast to the "official government version" of events.

It is also important to examine this in the context of how the Indian government has been criticised by health reporters for not putting out timely reports of data concerning the coronavirus pandemic, especially in terms of numbers of people who have been administered tests, as well as those who have been placed under quarantine. It is worrying that in the absence of proactive transparency, which would assist fact-based reporting, quite often, there will be a desire by the government to contour and shape the messaging of journalists towards its own version of events.

What do you think about the government's explanation that "fake news" made this decision necessary?

The fundamental premise of this direction arises from a submission by the government that it was fake news that led a large number of migrant labourers who wanted to return to their homes in far and distant villages [to move throughout the country].

Given that there was a pre-existing prohibition [on travel] and shortage of private as well as public modes of transport, many of them embarked on long and perilous journeys over hundreds of miles by foot. This was widely carried in the press and social media, which provides a background to this litigation.

In the order, the court notes that this migrant exodus from metropolitan cities occurred due to "fake news" reports that suggested that the lockdown, which is imposed across the entire country, would stretch beyond the intended timeline announced by the prime minister to a period up to three months.

The basis of this determination by the court was that fake news was responsible for the migrant exodus, rather than migrant labourers' inability to meet their daily needs due to the lockdown. [The fact] that a lot of the migrant labourers don't have savings and rely on daily wages for their sustenance was not examined by the court.

The court has not taken into account the government's lack of preparation and inadequacy in addressing this humanitarian crisis. This would have been in the court's knowledge, given that it was covered widely in mainstream newspapers and respectable publications.

The order says the court does "not intend to interfere with the free discussion about the pandemic, but direct the media [to] refer to and publish the official version about the developments". How should this be interpreted?

While the court does note that they [the judges] do not intend to interfere with press reporting, there is an operative word, "but", which it uses before it directs all the media to carry the government's official version. It does not further contain much guidance, which makes this direction vague and thereby susceptible to arbitrary application.

The order also makes references to two underlying legal frameworks: firstly, under the National Disaster Management Act, and secondly under the Indian Penal Code, which would draw reference from the Epidemic Diseases Act. Both permit criminal prosecution; hence it seems that the court has also sought to criminalise what could be characterised as inaccurate reporting by repeated use of the words "fake news".

What punishments could journalists face under those laws?

Under Section 54 of the Disaster Management Act, the punishment is only [decided] post-conviction. Given the long length of trials, it is not the extent of the punishment which will matter, it is the prosecution itself.

This is the same position with regards to Section 188 [of the Indian Penal Code]. And there will be terms of imprisonment which will be prescribed post-sentencing, which may stretch for Section 188 up to six months, and up to one year for Section 54 [of the Disaster Management Act].

The other thing that is also of concern here is that if one looks at it, the Epidemic Diseases Act under Section 2 permits the state government to formulate emergency orders and rules. The court has stated that [this includes] even advisories, which in the past take on the character of an order.

The issue is, an "advisory" is often extra-legal advice which does not follow from a clear statutory authority in favour of a public authority.

For instance, under the Epidemic Diseases Act, the [central] government doesn't have the power to issue orders or formulate rules, the state governments do. However, in the Supreme Court order, there is a repeated reference to an advisory issued by the central government itself.

Such an advisory by the central government wouldn't ordinarily lead to a prosecution under Section 188 [of the penal code] for defiance of a public order; however, the court has again not examined this issue.

So it needs to be considered that this order has been passed without a careful degree of appreciation of the contours of free expression, and what value it serves during the times of a pandemic. And, the court has in fact accepted the government [request] for greater censorship powers as a need to contain rumour mongering and further social cohesion.

This is a clear choice that has been made by the court in favour of the government.

Notes

1 Reproduced with permission from the Committee to Protect Journalists from *cpj.org* where this article first appeared on April 9, 2020. https://cpj.org/2020/04/lawyer-apar-gupta-on-what-the-indian-supreme-court/

2 See https://cpj.org/2020/03/indian-supreme-court-denies-government-request-for/

6.6 Audit of bigotry

How Indian media vilified Tablighi Jamaat over the coronavirus outbreak[1]

Ayan Sharma and Chahak Gupta

Communal hatred, fake news, conspiracy theories, misinformation, misreporting. The coverage of the congregation of the Tablighi Jamaat at its headquarters in Delhi's Nizamuddin area had it all.

Having recovered from COVID-19, more than 200 followers of the Tablighi Jamaat are donating[2] plasma to Delhi's hospitals. Blood plasma containing antibodies against coronavirus from recovered patients is given to severely ill people to help them fight off the infection. It's an experimental treatment known as convalescent plasma therapy. The donation by the Tablighis suffices for the current need of the capital's plasma bank, as per the Institute of Liver and Biliary Sciences, which handles the collection.

You may have stumbled upon this news in a newspaper or on the internet. It hasn't generated the endless primetime coverage, opinion pieces, and social chatter that has become associated with the Tablighis lately. But go back to the beginning of April and a section of the media only talked about the Tablighis, holding them almost solely responsible for the coronavirus outbreak in India.

> In today's Bindaas Bol,[3] I bring you a very serious issue and appeal to the Narendra Modi government that the Tablighi Jamaat be banned. If India's mosques are posing a threat to Indians, and human bombs carrying coronavirus are roaming around freely, wouldn't you call it "corona jihad"? We should keenly monitor these jihadis and the jihadis should be strictly punished under law.

This is how Suresh Chavhanke, the head of Sudarshan News, opened his show *Bindaas Bol* on March 31. Chavhanke did not feel the need to offer evidence for his incendiary accusations. His bigotry was "news" enough.

He wasn't alone. After six people who had attended a Tablighi Jamaat congregation in Delhi died of COVID-19 in Telangana on March 31, there was an outpouring of bigotry against Muslims in much of the Indian media, TV news in particular. Over the following days, as more cases of coronavirus

DOI: 10.4324/9781003291527-45

infection across states were traced to the Tablighi function, held between March 13 and 15 at its markaz, or headquarters, in Delhi's Nizamuddin, the media ramped up its demonisation of the minority community.

To this end, they peddled fake news and made-up conspiracy theories. Maulana Muhammad Saad, head of the Tablighi Jamaat, was called a "terrorist" and "the maulana of death", the attendees were described as "human bombs" and linked to terror groups, and, of course, Pakistan. All without a shred of evidence.

The media's tirade against the Tablighi Jamaat and the Muslim community generally wasn't limited to Big Media. Some regional media outlets joined in too, like in Karnataka.[4]

"Corona spreaders"

Some media outlets claimed that members of the Tablighi congregation had conspired to spread coronavirus in India. They also carried reports and circulated videos claiming to "expose misbehaviour of the Jamaatis".

Amar Ujala, a prominent Hindi daily, alleged[5] that quarantined Tablighis in Uttar Pradesh's Saharanpur defecated in the open at the facility after their demand for meat was rejected. The claim was repeated in a report by[6] another leading Hindi daily *Rajasthan Patrika*.

It was all a lie, as the Saharanpur police confirmed on April 5.

In a tweet from the Saharanpur Police twitter account, the following statement was released:

<u>खबर बनाम सच</u>

अवगत कराना हैं, कि विभिन्न समाचर पत्रो, न्यूज चैनलो एवं सोक्ष्ल मीड़ीया प्लेटफार्म पर प्रकाशित की जा रही खबर "क़्वारंटाइन किये गये जमातियों ने खाने में नॉनवेज न मिलने पर जमकर हंगामा, जमातियों ने खुले में नॉनवेज न मिलने पर किया जमकर हंगामा, जमातियों ने खुले में ही कर डाली शौच" की सत्यता की जांच व आवश्यक कार्यवाही करने हेतु थाना प्रभारी रामपुर मनिहारान को निर्देश दिए गए थे, जिनके द्वारा जांच जी गयी तो जांच में विभिन्न समाचार पत्रों, न्यूज चैनलों एवं सोशल मीड़ीया प्लेटफार्म पर प्रकाशित को जा रही उक्त खबर पूर्ण रूप से गलत एवं असत्य पायी गयी हैं. अतः सहारनपुर पुलिस उक्त प्रकाशित खबर का पूर्णतः खण्डन करती है.

सोशल मीड़ीया सेल
सहारनपुर

After the police debunked their false claims, both newspapers withdrew their reports from their websites.

Several outlets alleged that the Tablighis were spitting on people to infect them with the coronavirus.

India TV, while praising the Modi government for its "efforts to contain the coronavirus outbreak", claimed that they were being undermined by the "spitting habit" of the Tablighis. The TV channel played[7] footage claiming that it showed a maulana advocating spitting as an antidote to "evil thoughts". A ticker running alongside the video asked, "Which maulana is behind Jamaat's corona symptoms?" The video was played and replayed, accompanied by ominously suspenseful music.

However, Alt News did a fact check[8] of the report and found the video was old, posted on the YouTube channel IRC TV in 2017. Faiz Syed, the person in the video, is an Islamic preacher and the founder of the Islamic Research Centre.

Alt News spoke[9] with an Islamic scholar who explained that the "spitting" referred to by Faiz is a gesture and not the ejection of saliva.

> When evil thoughts come to one's mind during prayer or meditation, they recite Surah al Ikhlas and make a gesture of spitting on the left side, either say thoo thrice or spit out air. This is a psychological way of believing that after taking Allah's name, the act of spitting ejects the Shaitan out of the body.

TV9 Bharatvarsh broadcast a viral video of a Muslim vendor licking his thumb while selling fruits. The channel called[10] the vendor a "corona criminal", implying that he was intentionally spreading the virus. Several versions[11] of the video were uploaded[12] on YouTube[13] as well, repeating the allegation.

As a result, the Madhya Pradesh police filed an FIR against the vendor, Sheru Khan. But *Newslaundry* investigated[14] the claim and found the video was shot in February, long before India was making any serious effort to tackle the pandemic.

"Deliberate conspiracy"

The same evening that Chavhanke's Sudarshan News discovered "corona jihad", several other TV channels raised the anti-India bogey while going after the Tablighi Jamaat.

On its show *Taal Thok Ke*,[15] Zee News featured Waseem Rizvi, chairman of the Uttar Pradesh Shia Waqf Board who is known for toeing the line[16] of the Bharatiya Janata Party. Rizvi claimed that COVID-19 had been "developed" among the Tablighis and they had been sent out across India "so that maximum deaths could be executed in the country".

As he spoke, conspiratorial tickers flashed on the TV screen, "Was it a conspiracy to turn Delhi into Italy?", "Conspiracy to set off community transmission in the country?"

What appeared to be a loaded question was soon turned into a declaration by the show's anchor, Aman Chopra. "It is being said it was a conspiracy to turn Delhi into Italy", he thundered, referring to the congregation. "You know what happened in Italy, right!"

Italy is one of the countries worst affected by the pandemic.

Chopra's boss, Zee News editor Sudhir Chaudhary, went even further on his show, *DNA*,[17] that night. He accused the Tablighi Jamaat of "betraying and lying to the entire nation". The show, as *Newslaundry*[18] documented, was full of communal jibes.

Arnab Goswami of Republic TV too sniffed a plot behind the Tablighi function to turn India into Italy. On Republic Bharat, he asked, "Is this being done deliberately? Is this a conspiracy to turn Delhi to Italy?" He kept shouting at a couple of Tablighi Jamaat members as they tried to make their arguments. At one point, questioning their loyalty to India, he scolded and repeatedly asked them if they were with India or a separate nation.

Zee News, which is known for its hysteric and outrageous theories on jihad earlier[19] too, brought it back again. On April 2, Chopra in his show[20] crafted a new form – "spitting jihad" – to target the Jamaat attendees.

Then came a "sting" by *India Today*[21] on April 10 accusing two madrassas in Delhi and one in Greater Noida of hiding their children in violation of the lockdown and linking their teachers to the Tablighi congregation. Called "Madrasa Hotspots", the "special investigation" led by the channel's news director, Rahul Kanwal, also accused the residential schools of not observing social distancing norms. *Newslaundry* decoded the sting and exposed glaring gaps in it.

Not just TV channels, the print media also indulged in this hatefest. In a piece titled "Tablighi Jamaat – Its Other, Evil Side", the *New Indian Express*[22] sought to explain that the seemingly innocuous Tablighi Jamaat had a "deceptive" exterior to invite "innocent and idealistic young Muslims into an ideological line that ultimately turns them as terrorists". It goes on to conclude,

> No government has the guts to enter any mosque, thanks to the way secularism is understood in our politics. Unless this limit is breached and the menace is outlawed, innocent Muslims attracted by its cosmetic exterior of Koran cannot be saved from becoming carriers of Kalashnikovs and makers and throwers of lethal bombs.

Dainik Jagran straightaway proclaimed[23] that Islam's "peaceful propagation and jihad are two sides of the same coin". The report, headlined "The Country Is Unaware of Tablighi Jamaat's Agenda", argued that the movement manipulated Muslims into giving up their "Hindu ways" and made them more invested in Islam. The mission of the Tablighi Jamaat, the report claimed, was to "separate Hindus and Muslims" living in harmony. It further accused the Tablighi Jamaat, without evidence, of being involved in attacks on various temples in 1992–93.

The Hindu nationalist blog OpIndia published an article[24] claiming that coronavirus patients in Chennai linked to the Tablighi Jamaat made an

"Islamic gesture popularised by ISIS". By way of proof, it showed a picture of a few individuals raising their forefingers. So, OpIndia used a common hand gesture to link ordinary Tablighis with a dreaded terrorist group.

Pakistan connection

On April 7, Amish Devgan, the managing editor of News18 India, claimed on his show[25] *Aar Paar* to have "concrete information" that Pakistan was directly responsible for the coronavirus pandemic in India. The "concrete information", supplied by "intelligence sources", was that a conspiracy was hatched to spread coronavirus in India at a Tablighi Jamaat congregation in a mosque in Kuala Lumpur's Petaling at the end of February. It was done at Pakistan's behest, he added.

The "evidence" of Pakistan's involvement was the presence of Tablighis from that country at the Petaling event, some social media misinformation regarding coronavirus in that country, and two pictures of a Muslim cleric with Pakistan's prime minister, Imran Khan, and the Indian preacher Zakir Naik. Ironically, the channel noted that the cleric's picture with Khan was from March 14 this year, when the Nizamuddin event had already begun.

Sequence of events

This demonisation of the Tablighi Jamaat didn't care for even basic facts. Given that congregants were expected to come from nations already grappling with coronavirus, the event was ill-timed. Still, it began the same day the Indian health ministry insisted that the coronavirus outbreak was not a health emergency.[26] Moreover, the Tablighi Jamaat was not sufficiently warned of the dangers of organising the function. The Aam Aadmi Party government in Delhi issued an order on March 13 and another on March 16 related to the coronavirus outbreak. The first order, vaguely worded, prohibited "sports gatherings/conferences/seminars" with over 200 people. The second, which banned all social, political, religious, and academic gatherings with more than 50 people, came a day after the function was over.

It wasn't until March 24, the day Modi declared the lockdown, that the Delhi police directed the evacuation of the Tablighis staying in the markaz and the closure of its mosque.

In its defence, the Tablighi Jamaat has said[27] that many of the congregants were stranded in the markaz due to the sudden suspension of railway services on March 21. Further, they observed the "janata curfew" called by Modi the next day. On March 23, Delhi Chief Minister Arvind Kejriwal declared a lockdown in the city. This, according to the Tablighis, left them with few options to move out the stranded members, most of whom were from out of the state. Still, around 1,500 people were moved out of the Nizamuddin premises.

When the evacuation order came, the markaz authorities asked the police for vehicle passes to ferry the remaining stranded congregants. "The requisite permission is still awaited", noted a press release issued by them on March 31. After a meeting with National Security Advisor Ajit Doval late on March 28, they agreed to get all the remaining occupants of the markaz tested and quarantined, and also to clear the mosque.

If anything, this sequence of events indicates that, far from hatching a conspiracy, the Tablighi Jamaat complied with government directives.

Other gatherings

That the media's coverage of the Tablighi Jamaat event was driven by malice is evident from how they glossed over even larger religious gatherings that took place around the same time. Just about a week ago, when India was well into the lockdown, hundreds of people gathered for a festival at a Hindu temple in Karnataka's Kalaburagi.[28] In the first week of April, when the media was busy stoking outrage against the Tablighi Jamaat, devotees thronged temples across Bengal[29] to observe Ram Navami. Shortly after the Nizamuddin event, thousands of Hindu devotees reportedly crowded prominent temples in Gujarat. After toppling the Congress government in Madhya Pradesh, BJP's Shivraj Singh Chouhan held[30] a public ceremony to take oath as the chief minister on March 23.

None of these events became a target of the media's outrage, let alone communal hatred.

Government's role

To a large extent, the media's vilification of the Tablighis was cued by the Modi government's handling of the situation. On April 1, the government singled out[31] the Nizamuddin event as a major cause of the spike in coronavirus cases. Five days later, it was blamed at the coronavirus press briefing for quickening the doubling rate[32] of infection. This was disingenuous, as an article in *Scroll*[33] noted. The protocol at the time was to only test people with symptoms for coronavirus. In case of the Tablighis and their contacts, however, even those without symptoms were tested. Also, several states rapidly and aggressively traced the Tablighis who had attended the congregation and their contacts, and tested them. As on April 7,[34] over 25,500 congregants and their contacts had been traced and quarantined. "The large proportion of Tablighi positives is simply due to the large number of people who were tested from the event, even as overall testing remains low", *Scroll* explained.

It took coverage in the international media and a statement from the World Health Organization criticising the religious profiling of coronavirus patients for the health ministry to stop[35] the practice. The Delhi government, which had been singling out patients linked to the Nizamuddin function as "Markaz Masjid cases", changed the labelling to cases "under special operations" on April 11.

The media's demonisation of the Tablighi Jamaat sparked a campaign of hate[36] against Muslims that has grown with each passing day. So much so that it threatens to endanger the country's diplomatic relations. On April 19, the human rights body of the Organisation of Islamic Countries tweeted[37] a statement condemning the targeting of Muslims as coronavirus spreaders. It urged the Indian government to take "urgent steps" to tackle the problem.

Considering that many of these nations are among India's key strategic and trading partners, Modi released a statement the same day.

> COVID-19 does not see race, religion, colour, caste, creed, language or borders before striking. Our response and conduct thereafter should attach primacy to unity and brotherhood. We are in this together: PM @narendramodi.

So, it took the threat of a diplomatic crisis for the prime minister to speak up against the growing hate amid the pandemic. Much damage, however, had already been done. According to the factchecking website Media Scanner,[38] at least 75 anti-Muslim fake videos were uploaded on social media from April 5 to 20, and there were 28 attacks on Muslims.

India, like much of the world, is still mired in the fight against coronavirus. And the country cannot afford to let this unprecedented fight be derailed by communal hatred.

Notes

1 Reproduced with permission from *Newslaundry* where this article first appeared on April 27, 2020. https://www.newslaundry.com/2020/04/27/audit-of-bigotry-how-indian-media-vilified-tablighi-jamaat-over-coronavirus-outbreak
2 Anonna Dutt. "200 Tablighi Jamaat Members, Who Have Recovered, Pledge to Donate Plasma". *Hindustan Times*. April 28, 2020. Retrieved from https://www.hindustantimes.com/delhi-news/200-tablighi-jamaat-members-who-have-recovered-pledge-to-donate-plasma/story-uCGTmL5MvH5uNXRkDnCDOL.html. Last accessed on December 10, 2021.
3 See https://www.youtube.com/watch?v=-k1e6ukL0uA
4 Kapil Kajal. "Kannada Media Paints the Coronavirus Crisis Communal". *Newslaundry*. April 8, 2020. Retrieved from https://www.newslaundry.com/2020/04/08/kannada-media-paints-the-coronavirus-crisis-communal. Last accessed on December 10, 2021.
5 "Peoples Throw Food after the Non-Veg Demand Was Not Met in the Quarantine Ward". *Amar Ujala*. Retrieved from https://www.amarujala.com/uttar-pradesh/meerut/lockdown-saharanpur-update-news-the-peoples-throw-food-after-the-non-veg-demand-was-not-met-in-the-quarantine-ward?__twitter_impression=true. Last accessed on December 10, 2021.
6 See https://archive.is/2okr3
7 See https://player.vimeo.com/video/408843150

8 Pooja Chaudhuri. "India TV Uses 2017 Video to Falsely Claim Islamic Preacher Provoked Jamaatis to 'Spit'". *Alt News*. April 18, 2020. Retrieved from https://www.altnews.in/india-tv-uses-2017-video-to-falsely-claim-islamic-preacher-provoked-jamaatis-to-spit/. Last accessed on December 10, 2021.

9 Pooja Chaudhuri. "India TV Uses 2017 Video to Falsely Claim Islamic Preacher Provoked Jamaatis to 'Spit'". *Alt News*. April 18, 2020. Retrieved from https://www.altnews.in/india-tv-uses-2017-video-to-falsely-claim-islamic-preacher-provoked-jamaatis-to-spit/. Last accessed on December 10, 2021.

10 See https://www.youtube.com/watch?v=1i_F3qjIYeU

11 See https://www.youtube.com/watch?v=wvxSU3F1t5Q

12 See https://www.youtube.com/watch?v=PdiOUEc-PFo

13 See https://www.youtube.com/watch?v=yPypBCAUKaQ

14 Ayush Tiwari. "TV9 Bharatvarsh Broadcasts Old Video of Fruit Seller as 'Corona Criminal' Spreading Virus'. *Newslaundry*. April 4, 2020. Retrieved from https://www.newslaundry.com/2020/04/04/tv9-bharatvarsh-broadcasts-old-video-of-fruit-seller-as-corona-criminal-spreading-virus. Last accessed on December 10, 2021.

15 See https://www.youtube.com/watch?v=YgInSiFE2Wk

16 See https://www.facebook.com/login/?next=https%3A%2F%2Fwww.facebook.com%2Fflx%2Fwarn%2F%3Fu%3Dhttps%253A%252F%252Fwww.outlookindia.com%252Fnewsscroll%252Fwhy-is-shia-board-chief-trying-to-please-bjp%252F1672574%253Futm_source%253Damp%2526utm_medium%253Dfbm%2526utm_campaign%253Damp%2526fbclid%253DIwAR3SJokWWht15o5ywCJmiIotgDFlOA99cDVd9JLXCXOiY-Zjs86yleYN1Jo%26h%3DAT0IgfEWRwIQOrgAniTI6cCEzcmF-jJHjaCnUnDgS3WvQLQ3nVEiv-VKL0_prr3td6YwAU1OehFdDAob88JwAtWW6YDdmFyoEziTSw1J2Yzt4c1tRKytYM_QARF6pm9To9WKJiw

17 See https://www.youtube.com/watch?v=VYmqyKQyKFg

18 Ayush Tiwari. "Coronavirus and Nizamuddin: TV News Returns to Bigotry with a Bang". *Newslaundry*. April 1, 2020. Retrieved from https://www.newslaundry.com/2020/04/01/coronavirus-and-nizamuddin-tv-news-returns-to-bigotry-with-a-bang. Last accessed on December 10, 2021.

19 Meghnad S. "Bloodlust TV: Sudhir Chaudhary's Campaign of Hate, Powered by Sensodyne". *Newslaundry*. March 13, 2020. Retrieved from https://www.newslaundry.com/2020/03/13/bloodlust-tv-sudhir-chaudharys-campaign-of-hate-powered-by-sensodyne. Last accessed on December 10, 2021.

20 See https://www.youtube.com/watch?v=hYcFhQUCNyY&t=134s

21 See https://www.youtube.com/watch?v=O9_iWSvq-9Q

22 S. Gurumurthy. "Tablighi Jamaat – Its Other, Evil Side". *New Indian Express*. April 2, 2020. Retrieved from https://www.newindianexpress.com/opinions/columns/s-gurumurthy/2020/apr/02/coronavirus-tablighi-jamaat---its-other-evil-side-2124563.html. Last accessed on December 10, 2021.

23 Bhupendra Singh. 'तब्लीगी जमात के एजेंडे से अनजान देश, इसका उद्देश्य है मुसलमानों को पक्का मुसलमान बनाना'. *Dainik Jagaran*. April 14, 2020. Retrieved from https://www.jagran .com /editorial /apnibaat -country -unaware -agenda -of -tablighi -jamaat -20188710.html. Last accessed on December 10, 2021.

24 "Muslims Discharged from Chennai Hospital Make Islamic Gesture Popularised by ISIS While Posing for Photos". *Op India*. April 17, 2020. Retrieved from https://www.opindia.com/2020/04/muslims-chennai-hospital-coronavirus-isis-islamic-finger-gesture-what-it-means/. Last accessed on December 10, 2021.

25 See https://www.youtube.com/watch?v=wN0Q4v52z-8

26 "COVID-19 Is Not Health Emergency, No Need to Panic". *The Hindu*. April 13, 2020. Retrieved from https://www.thehindu.com/news/national/

coronavirus-outbreak-union-health-ministry-press-conference-in-new-delhi/article31061163.ece. Last accessed on December 10, 2021.

27 See https://twitter.com/pbhushan1/status/1244877790467493889

28 Nehal Kidwai and Deepshikha Ghosh. "Over 100 Gather for Temple Chariot Event at COVID-19 Hotspot in Karnataka". *NDTV*. April 17, 2020. Retrieved from https://www.ndtv.com/india-news/coronavirus-lockdown-over-100-gather-for-temple-chariot-event-in-covid-19-hotspot-in-kalaburagi-karn-2213427. Last accessed on December 10, 2021.

29 "Defying Lockdown, Devotees in Bengal Assemble at Temples on Ram Navami". *The Hindu*. April 2, 2020. Retrieved from https://www.thehindu.com/news/cities/kolkata/defying-lockdown-devotees-in-bengal-assemble-at-temples-on-ram-navami/article31237211.ece. Last accessed on December 10, 2021.

30 Akshita Jain. "BJP Ignores PM Modi's Social Distancing Advice at Shivraj Singh Chouhan's Oath-Taking". *The Huffpost*. March 24, 2020. Retrieved from https://www.huffpost.com/archive/in/entry/bjp-madhya-pradesh-social-distancing-shivraj-singh-chouhan_in_5e79a7bbc5b62f90bc508234. Last accessed on December 10, 2021.

31 See https://www.theweek.in/news/india/2020/04/01/covid-19-centre-blames-tablighi-jamath-for-sudden-spike-in-cases.html

32 Rhythma Kaul. "Covid-19 Cases Doubling in 4.1 Days, Jamaat Incident Worsened Coronavirus Spread". *The Hindustan Times*. April 5, 2020. Retrieved from https://www.hindustantimes.com/india-news/covid-19-doubling-rate-in-india-at-4-1-days-govt/story-CcMgi8sSrZ7LnBp1oZ70OL.html. Last accessed on December 10, 2021.

33 Shoaib Daniyal. "Explained: Sampling Bias Drove Sensationalist Reporting around Tablighi Coronavirus Cases". *Scroll.in*. April 7, 2020. Retrieved from https://scroll.in/article/958392/explained-sampling-bias-drove-sensationalist-reporting-around-tablighi-coronavirus-cases. Last accessed on December 10, 2021.

34 Rahul Tripathi and ET Bureau. "Over 25,500 Tablighi Jamaat Members Quarantined in Country till Now: MHA". *The Economic Times*. April 7, 2020. Retrieved from https://economictimes.indiatimes.com/news/politics-and-nation/over-25500-tablighi-jamaat-members-quarantined-in-country-till-now-5-haryana-villages-sealed-mha/articleshow/75013518.cms. Last accessed on December 10, 2021.

35 See https://www.mohfw.gov.in/pdf/AddressingSocialStigmaAssociatedwithCOVID19.pdf

36 Mehraj D. Lone. "Killed, Vilified, Cut adrift from the National Community. What's the Indian Muslim to Do?". *Newslaundry*. April 15, 2020. Retrieved from https://www.newslaundry.com/2020/04/15/killed-vilified-cut-adrift-from-the-national-community-whats-the-indian-muslim-to-do. Last accessed on December 10, 2021.

37 See https://twitter.com/OIC_IPHRC

38 See https://mediascanner.in/

Afterword

Were any lessons learnt?

Bharat Bhushan

Labour migration from cities and towns in India back to villages happened twice – the first during the first wave of the COVID-19 pandemic in 2020 and the second in 2021 when the second wave of the pandemic hit India. The articles in this media reader deal with the media reportage of the first wave of migration in 2020.

The recurrence of both COVID-19 and migration forces one to ask whether any lessons were learnt from the tragedy of 2020. How did the experience of 2020 shape the attitude of the state, media, and citizens towards workers who were forced to abandon their jobs for the second time within a year?

The first lockdown of 68 days, from March 24, 2020, to May 1, 2020, saw an exodus of around 1.14 crore migrant workers who left jobs in cities and went back home with their families and sparse belongings. This number is acknowledged by the government although it is an underestimate that accounts only for those who left by public transport once services resumed.[1] There were 971 non-COVID deaths among them including 96 deaths on trains.[2] Five months after the lockdown, they began returning to the cities but as the economy had contracted, jobs were sparse. Pew Research estimated that the number of poor Indians (earning USD 2 or less a day) rose by 7.5 crore, accounting for a 60% rise in global poverty after the first lockdown. In April 2020 alone, 12.2 crore Indians had lost their jobs which represented a 30% fall in employment over the previous year.[3]

The Indian Council for Research on International Economic Relations (ICRIER) and the Inferential Survey Statistics and Research Foundation (ISSRF) conducted a survey of 2,917 migrants in 6 states (Uttar Pradesh, Bihar, Jharkhand, West Bengal, Odisha, and Chhattisgarh), which accounted for two-thirds of the migration in 2020, to assess their condition before, during, and after the lockdown. It found that 38.6% had found no work after returning home and there was a precipitous fall of 85% in their household income.[4]

A survey of young, semi-skilled migrant workers from Bihar and Jharkhand by the Abdul Lateef Jameel Poverty Action Lab and University of Warwick found that while the 2020 lockdown had led to an informalisation

DOI: 10.4324/9781003291527-46

of labour among men, most of the women just dropped out of the work force. Significantly, it also found that

> the number of out-of-State migrants halved between March 2020 and 2021, with no net effect of remigration post-lockdown. This meant the majority of these young workers were stuck in their home districts when the second wave of Covid-19 hit the rural areas, and have poor chances of regaining formal, salaried work unless there are policy interventions.[5]

The study found that by February 2021, on average 63.5% of the migrants from the six states surveyed had returned to their work-destination areas. This remigration was 92.5% from Bihar, 65% each from UP and Odisha, 40.3% from West Bengal, and 31.2% from Jharkhand. Despite increases in the household income after remigration to their destination work places, the study found that there was still a contraction of 7.7% in their income compared to the pre-lockdown period. It predicted that another lockdown or even the fear of one could upset the momentum of recovery.[6]

In 2021 when the second wave of COVID-19 hit India, there was no nationwide lockdown. Instead, lockdowns were partial, decentralised, and declared in telescoping stages by state governments. The scale of migration, therefore, was unlikely to be as high as during the first wave of the pandemic. While some migrant workers panicked as soon as the second wave started, others stayed back in the hope of keeping their jobs and a quick revival of the economy.

There are no precise estimates of migrants returning to villages in the second wave and evidence is episodic. In a report submitted to the parliamentary panel of home affairs, the Ministry of Labour and Employment said that nearly 517,073 migrants left for their homes from Delhi using trains during the second wave.[7] In Maharashtra, railway officials claimed that nearly 600,000 people left the state in the month of April 2021, i.e. during the peak of the state's second wave of COVID infections which forced a statewide lockdown. Of these nearly half left from Mumbai. The Central and Western Railway Divisions operated 370 special trains from Maharashtra to accommodate the increase in passenger numbers but claimed that this could include the normal summer rush since seats were booked before formal lockdowns were announced. Most of the special trains originating from Mumbai and Pune were headed to the states that witness large out-migration of workers in normal times – Uttar Pradesh, Bihar, Jharkhand, Odisha, Assam, and West Bengal.[8]

This time the crisis affected both those who were going back as well as those who stayed back with virtually no savings and no wages. What made the crisis in 2021 all the more acute was the fact that the second wave hit them when they had barely recovered from the impact of the first one – their savings had depleted and their debt burden was higher.[9]

The heart-rending sight of lakhs of workers out on the highways making their desperate journeys back home had shaken the nation's conscience momentarily. There was a consensus across the political spectrum on collecting credible data of the number of migrant workers in India, their wages and working conditions, lack of proper housing, and the need for implementing labour laws to address their problems. However, one year later, no one can say with confidence that the condition of migrant workers had improved or that the concern expressed during their first historic and tragic trudge home had been operationalised into systemic changes.

Three major issues on which there seemed to be a consensus in the wake of the first exodus of migrant workers in 2020 were the need for a national database of migrant workers; the portability of entitlements and safety nets, reflected in the proposal for implementing a "One nation, one ration card" policy; and a universal social security programme available anywhere in the country for vulnerable sections.

In February 2021, the government decided to conduct five pan-India surveys of migrant workers, employment generated by professionals, employment generated by the transport sector, domestic workers, and quarterly establishment-based employment. This data is to be released by November 2021. The first of the quarterly surveys is to be released by the Labour Bureau in July 2021.

Experts have pointed out, however, that even in the new plan for preparing a database of migrant workers, those in the service sector and the gig and platform economy are left out of consideration. This includes independent contractors, contract firm workers, on-call workers, and temporary workers, as well as those working for digital transactional platforms like Amazon, Zomato, Airbnb, Swiggy, and Uber. As the five pan-India surveys would leave them out there is no way to provide them social security cover without a database. Despite publicised drives by some state governments, like Delhi, there are no records available of even construction workers who, numbering more than 5.5 crore, account for slightly more than 12% of the total employment in India.[10]

In February 2021, at the behest of the Union Labour Ministry, the NITI Aayog constituted a sub-group to prepare a National Action Plan for Migrant Workers.[11] It prepared a policy framework for the portability of social protection, voting rights, right to the city, and health, education, and housing facilities as focus areas for improving the condition of the migrant workers. It proposed a governance structure for the plan with the Labour Ministry as the nodal point which would create a dedicated unit for inter-ministerial and Centre-state cooperation.[12]

One would think that an important lesson had been learnt. But think again. On June 7, 2021, the Central government extended the Pradhan Mantri Garib Kalyan Ann Yojana meant to provide free food grain to the needy till the festival of Diwali (November 4, 2021). However, migrant workers and those who did not possess ration cards were left out. This was despite the fact that the Supreme Court had already directed the Central and state governments on May 24, 2021, to provide dry food grains and cooked food through community kitchens without identity proof or ration cards to stranded migrants across the country. Even in 2020 during the exodus of migrant workers, the Centre had identified 8 crore poor people and provided them food without ration cards.[13]

Hunger was a major problem for migrant workers in the second wave also. A study of 5,047 workers during the second pandemic wave by Stranded Workers Action Network (SWAN) in Ahmedabad was an example of the dire straits they were in: about 58% workers were days away from going hungry, about 76% of them had less than Rs.300 left with them, about 65% had less than Rs.200, and 55% had less than Rs.100. As during the national lockdown of 2020 when lockdown wages were not paid, this time too 92% of the workers had not received any money since their employers stopped work. Where work was not stopped nearly 33% had not been paid due wages while 15% had been paid only partially.[14]

On 29 June 2021, the Supreme Court taking *suo motu* notice of the "problems and miseries of migrants" directed the Centre and the states to implement the "one nation one ration card" scheme and to announce an appropriate scheme for the distribution of free food grain to migrant workers as long as the COVID-19 pandemic lasts. It also asked them "to complete the process of (creating a) portal for registration under the National Database for Unorganised Workers, as well as implement the same" by July 31, 2021. It also directed that the registration of migrant workers, including those in the unorganised sector, must be completed by December 31, 2021.[15]

The Supreme Court pointed out that without the registration of migrant workers, none of the welfare schemes meant for them could be implemented. Therefore, it directed that migrant workers be registered under the laws meant to protect them: the Inter-state Migrant Workmen Act of 1979, the Building and Other Construction Workers Act of 1996, and the Unorganised Sector Social Security Act of 2008. Whether this will be done in the time frame suggested by the Supreme Court remains to be seen.

Thus Priya Deshingkar wrote,

> While we do have some understanding of the everyday interactions between the state and migrant subjects, we do not know enough about the inner workings of the government machinery and how this shapes outcomes for migrants. Jan Sahas, an organisation working with the most socially excluded groups across nine states, found that there are numerous barriers within the labour department, including a lack of guidelines on procedures related to registration, and delays in uploading data submitted in hard copy on the portal as it cannot be directly updated by others. Underlying these problems is the fundamental reality that labour departments are seriously short of staff and capacity to

> carry out the Supreme Court order. Various NGOs have pledged to monitor progress against the Supreme Court order. Hopefully, there will be learnings from the experience that can be applied to further such efforts.[16]

The legal lacunae and vacuum that existed for the regulation of wages and conditions of the migrant workers continued even after the experience of the first wave of migrant exodus from the cities. Rather the pandemic was seen as an opportunity to dilute existing labour laws. Many governments issued ordinances that included extending the working day and tinkering with the Factories Act and Industrial Disputes Act to give employers greater flexibility in hiring and firing employees. Ostensibly this was to attract foreign investment seeking to relocate from China. In many cases these ordinances pre-empted the provisions that the Central government wanted to bring in through its 4 labour codes consolidating 29 existing labour laws – the Code on Wages, the Industrial Relations Code, the Occupational Safety, Health and Working Conditions Code, and the Social Security Code.

While the Code on Wages had already been passed by Parliament in 2019, the remaining three labour codes on industrial relations, occupational safety, health, and working conditions, and social security were rushed through Parliament in September 2020 amidst an Opposition boycott over agricultural Bills.[17] They were, therefore, passed with minimal debate. The codes reinforced what several state governments were trying to do through ordinances, loosening regulations relating to closure, retrenchment, health and safety, and welfare of contract labour. There was a nod to workers' welfare – but the machinery to implement the welfare measures for the workers does not yet exist.[18]

The rules for the four labour codes have not yet been formulated by the government. Meanwhile, there is pressure by the employers on the government to hold back the implementation of the Code on Wages or to change its definition of wages. The new definition of wages stipulates that allowances cannot be more than 50% of the employee's salary. This would increase social security contributions by the employer such as 12% for Provident Fund. Currently employers split the salary of a worker into numerous allowances to reduce the social security contribution of the employer. Restricting allowances to 50% is also likely to increase the gratuity payment – calculated as a proportion of the average pay, which employers have to compulsorily give to workers who have completed five years of service in their firm. Employers are in no mood to increase their social security contributions to workers and want the new definition of wages deferred till the economy revives and buoyancy returns.[19]

Since the new codes cannot be implemented till new rules are framed and meanwhile the old laws are no longer valid, labour law experts point out a "legal void" has been created. This means that the "inclusive definition of migrant workers including voluntary migrant workers along with contracted migrant workers cannot be implemented".[20] The new Social Security Code does not provide for mandatory registration cards while the old Unorganised Workers Social Security Act 2008 did. As new rules for the Social Security Code have not been formulated, the old law remains in force leaving it unclear whether and under which law the unorganised sector workers are being registered, if at all. It includes unemployment assistance and insurance in the definition of social security but does not provide for any structured scheme for providing such assistance or insurance.[21] In short, the migrant workers are no better in terms of legal protection and social security than they were during the first wave of the pandemic.

Another important area of national consensus after the first lockdown was increasing the access of migrant workers to employment under the Mahatma Gandhi National Rural Employment Guarantee Act (MNREGA) and rural employment schemes such as Pradhan Mantri Garib Kalyan Rozgar Yojana. However, not many migrant workers seem to have got jobs under these schemes. Only 20% of the migrant workers surveyed by Gaon Connection had managed to finds jobs under MNREGA. While many migrant workers may have enrolled for MNREGA, that did not translate into jobs. In any case, these schemes would not offer jobs that would match their skills.[22]

An important policy measure announced by the government in the wake of the first exodus of migrant workers was the provision of cheap rental housing. On May 20, 2020, the Ministry of Housing and Urban Affairs announced the Affordable Rental Housing Complexes (ARHC) scheme for urban migrants; an initiative under the Pradhan Mantri Awas Yojana, it represented a shift in public policy from emphasising homeownership to rental housing. It sought to aggregate the demand for housing by migrants at any given site and provide them affordable rental housing alternatives.

Researchers from the Indian Institute of Technology Bombay and the University of Pennsylvania compared the ARHC with previous attempts by governments to build rental housing for migrants and found it short on several counts. They studied two previous schemes for providing rental housing: one by the Bombay Development Department (BDD) in the 1920s to build single-room tenements known as *chawls* for textile mill workers and a later one in 2008, a public-private partnership-based scheme called the Mumbai Metropolitan Regional Development Authority Rental Housing Scheme (MMRDA-RHS). Although the BDD scheme's target was to construct 50,000 single-room tenements, construction stopped at around 15,000 because of mounting construction costs and rents which ruled out most of the intended beneficiaries. The ambitious MMRDA-RHS which was to build half a million single-room tenements did not take off because of "factors such as uninhabitable density targets, lack of interest by private players, and lack of capacity of the public agency to manage rental housing stock".[23]

From the MMRDA-RHS experience where overreliance on the private market had virtually scuttled the scheme, the study apprehended that the ARHC could also suffer from this and other shortcomings of past schemes. These would include low participation by private players, inability to match the expectations of beneficiaries who might require expandable housing as their family sizes increase, lack of an explicit means test for beneficiaries which threatened to push poorer migrants out of the rental scheme, restrictions on the use of the dwelling exclusively for residential purposes which would rule out home-based work crucial for migrant families, excluding any participation from the community of migrant workers in planning, while favouring real estate developers and job contractors who already exercise disproportionate control over the lives of migrants.[24]

It would seem that even the largest migration in India since the Partition of 1947 did not spur the state to build structures and institutions to protect migrant workers. Attempts to remove domiciliary barriers through schemes like "one nation, one ration card" have been so half hearted that the Supreme Court has been forced to step in and direct the Executive to complete the process of its implementation. The progress in creating a national database of migrant workers is slow with software development issues being cited as the hurdle slowing it down. Labour laws have not been able to formalise or structure ways of implementing and ensuring the rights, health, or even access to the justice system for migrant workers. As of now they neither have safety nets in their states of origin nor in their destination states. In effect, they remain as dis-empowered as they were before the massive exodus in March 2020 which signalled their disbelief in the ability of the state to look after their interests. The same dim view of the state once again triggered another journey home when the second wave of COVID-19 hit India in 2021. Whether free doles of food grain some of them received has helped overcome their diffidence is far from clear.

In the past, a major social impact of epidemics was the creation of institutional structures to prevent their recurrence. They were mostly in the field of medical research. The malaria epidemic in India led to the creation of the Central Malaria Bureau (1909) which became the Malaria Survey of India (1927) and then the Malaria Institute of India (1938) which was renamed first the National Institute of Communicable Diseases (1963)[25] and then the National Centre for Disease Control (2009), as it is presently known.[26] The "Beri Inquiry" led to the creation of the National Institute of Nutrition. The Indian Research Fund Association (IRFA) through its experience with malaria research, kala-azar, and control of Filariasis transformed itself into the present-day Indian Council of Medical Research (ICMR). These are remarkable achievements in healthcare research in India.

However, there has been no equivalent innovation in developing institutions to prevent the social, economic, and political damage wrought by epidemics and pandemics on the lives of people either then or now. Registration lists, databases, and migrant labour-specific laws are left to be implemented by an apathetic bureaucracy. Rather than develop participatory and statutory institutions for protecting the migrant workers and address the exploitation inherent in their jobs, the government in thrall of neo-liberal economics in fact has proceeded to dilute labour laws and the social security of workers to favour capital.

How did the media cover the second wave of the COVID pandemic? The stellar coverage of the forced march of March 2020 was not repeated during the second wave. Perhaps because this time the lockdowns were localised, shorter, and telescoped. The scale of the exodus was neither as "spectacular" as the one in 2020 nor was the suffering of migrant workers perceived to be as acute.

The issues of a national register of migrants, the adoption of the labour codes by Parliament, the initial exclusion of migrant workers from the free food grain programme this time round till the Supreme Court directed the government to include them, were all reported but there was barely any indignation at the state's failure in dealing with the problems faced by the migrant workers for the second time in a year. It was as if having reported it the first time the media had done its job and the problems would be resolved. The coverage was episodic rather than sustained.

The exceptions were once again the digital media which proved itself to be far more caring and empathetic than the mainstream newspapers. The *Indian Express*, however, stood out for its eight-part "IEThinc Migration" (i.e. Indian Express Think Migration) series of webinars[27] in association with Omidyar Network India which brought together labour economists and activists to discuss a wide range of issues ranging from lack of data on migrants, their rights to health, inadequate government policies, criticism of nativist employment policies in some states, and the inadequacy of state governments in protecting migrant workers. By and large, however, having touched the issue of migrant workers once during their first wave of migration home, the media seemed to have lost interest in the issue or chose not to sustain the interest of readers/viewers and policy makers in the subsequent wave of jobless migrants returning home.

Notes

1 Keerthana Chavaly, Migrant Labour Crisis and the Imperative of a Robust National Database, Observer Research Foundation, July 17, 2021. https://www.orfonline.org/expert-speak/migrant-labour-crisis-imperative-robust-national-database/

2 A Year After Exodus, No Reliable Data or Policy on Migrant Workers, IndiaSpend, March 24, 2021 https://www.indiaspend.com/governance/migrant-workers-no-reliable-data-or-policy-737499

3 Rakesh Kochhar, In the Pandemic, India's Middle Class Shrinks and Poverty Spreads While China Sees Smaller Changes, Pew Research Centre, March 18 2021. https://www.pewresearch.org/fact-tank/2021/03/18/in-the-pandemic-indias-middle-class-shrinks-and-poverty-spreads-while-china-sees-smaller-changes/

4 Kaushik Deka, Covid-19 Second Wave: Has the Situation Improved for Migrant Workers? *India Today*, April 24, 2021. https://www.indiatoday.in/magazine/cover-story/story/20210503-covid-19-second-wave-has-the-situation-improved-for-migrant-workers-1794150-2021-04-24
5 Prescilla Jebraj, COVID Pushed Men into Informal Labour, Women out of Workforce: Study, *The Hindu*, June 15, 2021. https://www.thehindu.com/news/national/covid-pushed-men-into-informal-labour-women-out-of-workforce-study/article34816203.ece
6 Ashok Gulati, Shyama Jose, B Singh, As Covid Cases Rise, Can India Protect Its Most Vulnerable? *Indian Express*, April 12, 2021. https://indianexpress.com/article/opinion/columns/coronavirus-cases-rise-lockdown-migrants-crisis-second-wave-covid-mgnrega-demand-7269342/
7 Deeksha Bharadwaj, Over 1.3 Million Migrants Left Delhi During 2nd Wave of Covid-19, Shows Data, *Hindustan Times*, July 2, 2021. https://www.hindustantimes.com/cities/delhi-news/over-1-3-million-migrants-left-city-during-2nd-wave-shows-data-101625173931020.html
8 Ibid.
9 India Failed Its Migrant Workers Yet Again during the Second Wave of Covid-19, *Scroll.in*, June 26, 2021. https://scroll.in/article/998278/india-failed-its-migrant-workers-again-during-the-second-wave-of-covid-19
10 K R Shyam Sundar, May Day 2021: What Has (Not) Changed Since the Pandemic Ravaged Livelihoods of Workers, *The Wire*, May 1, 2021. https://thewire.in/labour/may-day-2021-india-migrant-construction-workers-covid-19-labour-codes
11 Press Statement of Ministry of Labour and Employment, Press Information Bureau, February 10, 2021. https://pib.gov.in/PressReleasePage.aspx?PRID=1696812
12 Kaushik Deka, op. cit.
13 Shagun Kapil, Free Food Grain until Diwali: What about Migrants, Those without Ration Cards? *Down to Earth*, June 8, 2021. https://www.downtoearth.org.in/news/governance/free-foodgrain-until-diwali-what-about-migrants-those-without-ration-cards--77328
14 Stranded Workers Action Network, IndiaSpend, May 24, 2021. https://www.indiaspend.com/uploads/2021/05/31/Responses-from-Labour-helplines-SWAN.pdf
15 Implement 'One Nation One Ration Card' by July 31: Supreme Court, *Down To Earth*, June 29, 2021. https://www.downtoearth.org.in/news/governance/implement-one-nation-one-ration-card-by-july-31-supreme-court-77694
16 Priya Deshingkar, Why the Supreme Court Order on Registration of Migrant Workers Is Welcome, *Indian Express*, July 22, 2021. https://indianexpress.com/article/opinion/columns/why-the-supreme-court-order-on-registration-of-migrant-workers-is-welcome-7415997/
17 Parliament Passes Labour Bills amid Boycott, *The Hindu*, September 23, 2020. https://www.thehindu.com/news/national/parliament-passes-three-key-labour-reform-bills/article32675729.ece
18 K R Shyam Sundar, op. cit.
19 Industry Bodies to Press for Holding back New Wage Definition in Meeting with Govt on Dec 24, *The Economic Times*, December 22, 2020. https://economictimes.indiatimes.com/news/economy/policy/industry-bodies-to-press-for-holding-back-new-wage-definition-in-meeting-with-govt-on-dec-24/articleshow/79865602.cms?_oref=cook&from=mdr
20 K R Shyam Sundar, op. cit.
21 Ibid.
22 Ayesha Pattanaik, Ishita Patil, The Issue Is Exploitation, Not Migration, May 18, 2021. https://idronline.org/the-issue-is-exploitation-not-migration/

23 Manav K and Indivar Jonnalgadda, Affordable Rental Housing Complexes for Urban Migrants: Problems and Prospects, March 1, 2021. Centre for Advanced Study of India, University of Pennsylvania. https://casi.sas.upenn.edu/iit/manavk-indivarjonnalagadda
24 Ibid.
25 About NCDC, https://ncdc.gov.in/index4.php?lang=1&level=0&linkid=28&lid=33
26 Citizen Charter, National Centre for Disease Control, https://ncdc.gov.in/index4.php?lang=1&level=0&linkid=102&lid=177
27 You Cannot Build a Skilled Society on Low-Cost Labour, *Indian Express*, July 23, 2021. https://indianexpress.com/article/india/you-cannot-build-a-skilled-society-on-low-cost-labour-7198855/. See the webinar series on YouTube at https://indianexpress.com/events/migration-in-india/

Index

Note: Page numbers in *italic* indicate figure and in **bold** indicate table, and page numbers followed by 'n' refer to notes.

www.ingramcontent.com/pod-product-compliance
Ingram Content Group UK Ltd.
Pitfield, Milton Keynes, MK11 3LW, UK
UKHW020150200926
475702UK00016B/2636
9781032271378